Social Work and
Social Welfare
Yearbook 3

Still available

Social Work and Social Welfare Yearbook 1
Social Work and Social Welfare Yearbook 2

Social Work and Social Welfare Yearbook 3

1991

Edited by
Pam Carter,
Tony Jeffs and
Mark K. Smith

Open University Press
Milton Keynes · Philadelphia

Open University Press
Celtic Court
22 Ballmoor
Buckingham MK18 1XW

and
1900 Frost Road, Suite 101
Bristol, PA 19007, USA

First Published 1991

British Library Cataloguing in Publication Data

Social work and social welfare yearbook
  1. Great Britain. Welfare work
  361.3'0941

  ISBN 0–335–09796–0
  ISBN 0–335–09795–2 (pbk)

Library of Congress Catalog number 89–657492

Typeset by Scarborough Typesetting Services
Printed in Great Britain by
Biddles Ltd, Guildford and Kings Lynn

Contents

Notes on editors and contributors   vii
Introduction   ix

1   Locking up our daughters   1
Pat Carlen and Julia Wardhaugh

2   Social work, justice and the common good   17
Bill Jordan

3   Clearing a path through the undergrowth: a feminist reading of
recent literature on child sexual abuse   30
Mary MacLeod and Esther Saraga

4   A new model for child care   46
Andrew Kerslake and Julia Cramp

5   Family centres   57
Hilary Walker

6   Analysing policy–practice links in preventive child care   69
Pauline Hardiker, Ken Exton and Mary Barker

7   Blinded by family feeling? Child protection, feminism and
countertransference   83
Janet Sayers

8   Race, social work and child care   95
Mark R. D. Johnson

9   Drug problems and social work   108
Geoffrey Pearson

10   The last days of 'juvenile' justice?   127
      Mike Nellis

11   Care in the community: the social security issues   141
      Geoff Fimister

12   How social fund officers make decisions   152
      Robert Walker, Gill Dix and Meg Huby

13   Social work: a force for good or a suitable case for treatment?   166
      Jeremy Walker

14   The 'new' managerialism in the social services   178
      Aidan Kelly

15   Residential care after Wagner: developments in policy and
      training   194
      Ian Sinclair and John Brown

16   A new diploma for social work or Dunkirk as total victory   205
      Noel Timms

Notes on editors
and contributors

Mary Barker · Part-time Research Associate, School of Social Work, University of Leicester (Retired Social Work Lecturer)

John Brown · Lecturer in Social Policy, Department of Social Work and Policy, University of York

Pat Carlen · Professor of Criminology, Centre for Criminology, Keele University

Pam Carter · Department of Economics and Government and Social Welfare Research Unit, Newcastle upon Tyne Polytechnic

Julia Cramp · Social Services Management Consultant, Price Waterhouse Management Consultants

Gill Dix · Research Fellow, Social Policy Research Unit, University of York

Ken Exton · Previously Research Associate, School of Social Work, University of Leicester, now Area Social Services Manager North Yorkshire Social Services Department

Geoff Fimister · Principal Welfare Rights Officer, City of Newcastle upon Tyne and Welfare Rights Adviser to Association of Metropolitan Authorities

Pauline Hardiker · Senior Lecturer, School of Social Work, University of Leicester

Meg Huby · Research Fellow, Social Policy Research Unit, University of York

Tony Jeffs · Department of Applied Social Sciences and Social Welfare Research Unit, Newcastle upon Tyne Polytechnic

Mark R. D. Johnson	Senior Research Fellow, Centre for Research in Ethnic Relations, Warwick University
Bill Jordan	Reader in Social Studies, Sociology Department, Exeter University
Aidan Kelly	Principal Lecturer in Sociology, Polytechnic of East London
Andrew Kerslake	Director of Social Services Research and Development Unit (SSRADU), Bath University
Mike Nellis	Lecturer in Probation Studies, Department of Social Policy and Social Work, University of Birmingham
Mary MacLeod	Senior Lecturer in Social Work, Child Abuse Studies Unit, Polytechnic of North London
Geoffrey Pearson	Wates Professor of Social Work, University of London Goldsmiths' College
Esther Saraga	Senior Lecturer in Psychology, Child Abuse Studies Unit, Polytechnic of North London
Janet Sayers	Psychology Lecturer and Social Work Tutor, University of Kent
Ian Sinclair	Professor of Social Work, Department of Social Policy and Social Work, University of York
Mark K. Smith	Tutor and Research Fellow, Centre for Professional Studies in Informal Education, YMCA National College, London
Noel Timms	Emeritus Professor of Social Work, University of Leicester
Hilary Walker	Lecturer in Social Care, Southwark College, London
Jeremy Walker	Social Worker, currently employed London Borough Wandsworth
Robert Walker	Director, Centre for Research in Social Policy, Loughborough University of Technology
Julia Wardhaugh	ESRC Research Fellow, Centre for Criminology and Department of Education, Keele University

The views expressed are those of the contributors and should in no way be taken to represent those of their employers or other agencies with which they are connected.

Introduction

As editors, whenever a contribution arrives our first task is to apply 'the photocopy test'. This test, not one normally popular with publishers, asks, will this piece arouse sufficient interest in the reader for them to reprint it for circulation? It may be a statement of the obvious but the *Yearbook* is intended to be read and used. We and the publisher hope that chapters will be copied and shared. That they will stimulate debates amongst colleagues in the workplace, provide material for students to analyse and a resource for managers and policy-makers. The basis on which contributors are commissioned varies. Some are asked to look back over developments in policy and practice; others to explain and account for contemporary events and changes; some are asked to predict and promote change; a few are asked to bring to the notice of the readership areas which have been ignored or overlooked. None of the contributions is the last word nor would we want any of them to be. They are, we hope, invitations to dialogue.

As always our thanks go to the contributors, who have to work to very tight deadlines and some of whom have had to make changes at a late stage due to policy developments. All have responded in a good-natured way including one who searched for material two hours before flying to Paris! Our thanks also to all those at Open University Press and at the typesetters and printers for the fast turnaround they achieve on this book.

Pam Carter
Tony Jeffs
Mark K. Smith

1
Locking up our daughters

Pat Carlen and
Julia Wardhaugh

Although the majority of young people in local authority care are there because their parents have fallen on hard times, young women tend to be disproportionately admitted to residential care on the grounds that they are in moral danger. In fact, since the nineteenth century when the state first commenced its formal regulation of young women via its industrial schools, inebriate reformatories and penitentiaries, a prime aim of women's incarceration has been the regulation of female sexuality. This concern persists to the present day and its victims are primarily working class and disproportionately black (Carlen 1988). In this chapter we shall first trace out the complex of ideological discourses and disciplinary practices within which the sexuality of certain working-class white and many black women is officially constituted as being always-already pathological and subversive of respectable womanhood (cf Worrall 1990). Then, on the basis of that analysis we shall put the case for a feminist charter for young women in care. The text is illustrated by quotations from two pieces of ESRC-funded research: one, undertaken in 1985–6 into women's criminal careers,[1] the other, an ongoing investigation (1988–91) of non-attendance at school.[2] All names used in the text are pseudonyms.

Sexuality and gender-discipline

For well over a century, the sexualization of all types of troublesome behaviour committed by young females has been a constituent of the discursive technologies whereby a gender discipline has been systematically imposed on adolescent girls. The early attempts of criminologists to explain women's lawbreaking in terms of their sexuality are well known (e.g. Thomas 1923; Pollak 1950). Yet the academics who appeared to assume that what goes on in women's reproductive or hormonal systems is more important than what goes on in their heads (or society) were not alone in their beliefs. Police, magistrates, judges, social workers, teachers and the administrators of women's prisons have also formulated policies in relation to young women which suggest that deviating females are at least doubly deviant both as citizens and as women. As citizens who break the law or violate social conventions they deviate from socially acceptable standards of behaviour. In deviating thus they also deviate from their conventional socio-sexual destinies as women – unless they can be redefined as being mentally ill, a state which though always seen as pathological in men is too often adjudged as being *normal for women* (see Allen 1987).

The sexuality/gender/sexualization axis of social control whereby deviations from *any* gender conventions are stigmatized as being evidence of a distorted sexuality (the girl is a 'slag' or a 'butch' or both!) is not merely the site of a punitive regulation. It is also an all-pervasive mode of preventive regulation which can inhibit not only women's sexuality (see A. Hudson 1985; Griffin 1985; Lees 1986) but also their use of public space (Hagan *et al.* 1979), the successful presentation of self (Worrall 1990), and the acquisition of effective self and social knowledge (Cain 1989). While young women remain within the conventions of family, home, school, workplace or a male-related domesticity they are usually seen to be gender-controlled and are accordingly treated as being invisible. Once, however, they come to the attention of the authorities as a result of, say, aggressiveness, rowdiness, truancy or 'promiscuity', they are then likely to be seen as being very gender-deviant indeed, and ripe for assessment and categorization as 'cases for care'. These assessments are constituted not only within conventional constructions of female sexuality and femininity, but also within individualized typifications drawn from class and racist stereotypes.

Sexuality and social structure

The development of the personal social services has always had the policing of working-class families as one of its primary functions (Meyer 1983, Hall *et al.* 1978; Donzelot 1979). In return for access to 'welfare', working-class women have been regularly called upon to open up their households to expert inspection and what Donzelot has called 'tutelage'. Much of that tutelage has focused on the regulation of sexuality. The deployment of sexuality as a mode of social structuration has been pinpointed and analysed by Foucault, who notes

the deployment of sexuality which first developed on the fringes of familial institutions . . . gradually became focused on the family. . . . In the family, parents and relatives became the chief agents of a deployment of sexuality which drew its outside support from doctors, educators and later psychiatrists. . . . Then these new personages made their appearance: the nervous woman, the frigid wife, the indifferent mother . . . the hysterical or neurasthenic girl, the precocious and already exhausted child. . . . And lo and behold, from the mid-nineteenth century onward, the family engaged in searching out the slightest traces of sexuality in its midst . . . opening itself unreservedly to endless examination.

(Foucault 1979: 110–1)

Today, the sexuality of young women taken into local authority care for a variety of reasons – often unconnected with any form of sexual activity – is still, as we shall illustrate in the next section, of overriding concern to their state guardians and assessors. The moral economy of welfare has, moreover, become more refined in its sifting and controlling of potentially deviant populations. Racist stereotypes relating to 'ideal' family patterns result in ethnic minority children being disproportionately represented in the care population (House of Commons 1984: CXIX). Indeed, the *Second Report from the Social Services Committee: Children in Care Volume I* concluded that 'the unnecessary removal of black children from their families (House of Commons 1984: CXX) was 'said to spring from "Eurocentric" views held by social workers about ideal family patterns and ideal family behaviour'. Idealizations of femininity are also operative in care proceedings. A number of research studies (e.g. Casburn 1979; A. Hudson 1985; Webb 1984) support the view that

the majority of girls do not get drawn into the complex web of the personal social services because they have committed offences. It is more likely to be because of concerns about their perceived sexual behaviour and/or because they are seen to be 'at risk' of 'offending' against social codes of adolescent femininity.

(A. Hudson 1985: 1)

Working-class people claiming benefits and already in touch with social workers are much more likely than are their middle-class counterparts to feel called upon to show that they are 'good' parents by being censorious of their daughters' burgeoning sexuality. Already opened up to the social work gaze by virtue of their poverty, the familial relations of poorer people are also much more likely to be pathologized and subject to official intervention (usually by the children being taken into care) than are the more privatized family relationships of the better-off. Furthermore, the 'less-than-ideal' family arrangements of black people may be translated into racist stereotyping of 'black sexuality' once the young black woman is removed from her family (cf Lewis 1981; Lees 1986: 141; Chiqwada 1989). Certainly in her 1985/86 study of women's criminal careers, Carlen found that young women who had been in care had been very conscious of the ways in which racism, class and sexualization of all aspects of their lives had structured official responses to them: yet, at the same time, they had been deprived of education about both sex and their own ethnic origins and cultures. Listen:

they were definitely a lot stricter with girls than boys, I found out *why* because I took my file out of the office. It said how I was an attractive 13 year old West Indian girl and that, if I kept on like I was, I'd soon have a couple of babies.

(Donna, in Carlen 1988: 86)

I can remember going to Marks and Spencer with a social worker to buy clothes. . . . we had a welfare grant form . . . this is when you realise that you're being given charity handouts . . . put in a low bracket . . . that is probably when I started to become aware of class barriers.

(Josie, in Carlen 1988: 87)

I thought I was white until I went to junior school, then the black children kept asking why I lived with white people . . . then the social workers kept having these meetings about me but, as I was the only black person there, I couldn't relate to any of them.

(Kim, in Carlen 1988: 88)

Donna, Josie and Kim were talking about their experiences of being in care in the early 1970s. In the next section we shall describe and discuss the gendered class discipline imposed in 1989 on young working-class women in the north Midlands who had, in the main, come to the attention of the authorities initially because of the *families'* difficulties but who, at the time of our contact, were living either in residential care or under official surveillance because of their own non-attendance at school.[3]

Technologies of gender and class discipline for the regulation of adolescent girls in care and/or out of school

Once young women are brought under the surveillance of state officials they become subject to assessment and categorization procedures which in turn usually result in their being subjected to particular types of informal and formal disciplinary programmes. Social workers, education welfare workers and teachers operate with cognitive maps which assist them first in placing young women in the relevant structural and moral categories and then in deciding on the appropriate interventionary practices. These processes of categorization and disciplinary practice together form a series of gendered class technologies which, because they provoke even more resistance to authority in their young women subjects, fail to solve the problems of either those who would control (the social workers, etc.) or those to be controlled (the young women in care). On the contrary, the coercive techniques designed to control them merely harden the troubled young women's resolve to step-up the rate of their (passive or active) resistance to discipline, and, as a result, some carers then become hardened in their oft-reiterated view that young women are 'other' – more 'difficult to understand' and less 'rational' in their delinquencies than males. Unfortunately delinquential resistance (for example truanting, absconding or drug-taking) being individualistic in its nature, and emanating from a position of utter powerlessness, more often than not lessens the youngsters' chances of keeping out of trouble in future. It is therefore in the belief that the following ideologies and practices are detrimental to the future life chances of adolescent working-class females that we shall, in the final section of this article, outline a feminist charter for young women in care. These ideologies are as follows.

1 'By their class shall ye know them': official stereotypes of the sexuality of working-class girls in trouble

2 'With her being coloured you have to be careful or people will accuse you of being discriminatory'
3 Recognizing a 'hard-faced little bitch'
4 Refusing to take girls seriously
5 Shaming the 'slags'
6 Pinning them down (physically)
7 Swamping them (psychologically)
8 The pharmaceutical fix.

'By their class shall ye know them': official stereotypes of the
sexuality of working-class girls in trouble

At the commencement of the research into school attendance we were already well-appraised of the fact that at least since the inception of state regulation of youth in the nineteenth century, sexualization of their conduct has been a constant feature of both the formal and informal control of adolescent girls. We were, none the less, surprised to find that in 1989 so many female social work clients (both young women and their mothers) were still being defined most explicitly in relation to their (actual or suspected) sexual activities.

> Stephanie, for instance, is only 13 and is known to be having sex with her boyfriend with her mother's knowledge. This means she is in moral danger and should be taken into care for her own protection.
>
> (EWO, David Brown, 1989)

> She will do all right, that one, do well on her back, because that is where she spends most of her time.
>
> (Social worker, Anne Parker,
> about a young woman in a Family Centre, 1989)

Implicitly too, the young women were being defined in terms of what was to be expected of an unregulated 'underclass'. Indeed constant criticism of their personal style from teachers had helped several of the young women decide that school wasn't for them. Susan had definitely had it drummed into her that good jobs were for a different class of person to herself.

> I just don't bother with school now. Can't be bothered doing that stuff. You know they don't like me hair, they don't like the way I dress, they don't like the earring in me nose – you know – jewellery and everything . . . when I say I'm going to do clerical work they all laugh. They say 'you won't do that, not with that hair' and all this.

Kerry also was aware of, and had become apprehensive about, class barriers which would make it impossible for her, she thought, ever to get on with certain types of foster parents:

> like these people who like going to restaurants for their tea and that. No, they got no hope of getting on with me, because I'm just not like that. I

couldn't go out to a restaurant, I'd get all the forks and that mixed up. I'd prefer to go to the chippy. Can't do with it.

That the young women's self-esteem was low was not surprising, given the views of them held by some teachers. For instance one teacher talking about a group of non-attenders explained:

They're a rat-bagging lot. The sooner they leave the better anyway. They are the sump class. They behave like the sump.

(Kevin Watson, 1989)

And, as will be apparent throughout this chapter, derogatory remarks regarding the young women's class position were as frequent as – and usually linked to – remarks about their 'pathological' sexuality.

Education welfare officers (EWOs) could, in describing their 'beats', also give detailed sociological explanations of their clients' lives and behaviour. In some areas truancy is unthinkable. As they approached the middle-class home of one non-attender, an EWO (Helen Walker) remarked to one of the authors:

I don't think it can be truancy, not in a street like this. There must be something wrong, probably somebody's ill or there is a funeral or something – there must be some explanation.

But whereas judgement is suspended for the middle-class resident, the denizens of council estates are likely to be pre-judged:

You find a lot of parents are not committed to school . . . they do not see the point of sending the kids. . . . You get that a lot on some council estates. With most truants you would be going into a working-class home and there won't be any books. Nobody in the house will read.

(EWO, Geoffrey Potter, 1989)

You find it is often a question of geography. Like in my patch . . . I would say that 70 per cent of my truants come from just five streets.

(EWO, Alan Simpson, 1989)

People in [this particular area] do not generally acknowledge non-attendance as a problem. Local police say the problems are because of a high level of inter-marriage and this causes low IQ. I'm not sure about the IQ but they are very close-knit. You get negative attitudes to education going back three or four generations.

(EWO, David Brown, 1989)

Having classified the area, EWOs find it easy to know what to expect of the parents. After interviewing a mother about her daughter's truancy one EWO ruminated darkly (and suggestively) upon the likely relationship between the mother and a male visitor present in the house at the time of the call. However, a household not based on a male-related domesticity at all came in for even more prurient comment when two women were referred to as

> a lesbian family who have had a love child, though God knows how they managed that. One of them has tattoos all over. She sits there like an Irish navvy.
>
> (EWO, David Brown, 1989)

Distaste for both manual workers and a working-class woman's robust sense of humour was apparent in the following outburst:

> The father works in the methane plant at the mine and that just about sums him up. He's got hands like shovels and a foul mouth. He'd land you one as soon as look at you. . . . I asked Mrs X why she had had nine children and she just said, 'He likes his drink and I like sex.' What can you expect of the daughter when the mother talks like that?
>
> (EWO, David Brown, 1989)

In fact, social workers too often expect 'the worst' of young working-class women whose interest in sexual pursuits is generally assumed to undermine their capacity for schooling and/or education. Talking of one young woman, a teacher explained:

> She has now been excluded from school; school won't have her back. She has been taken into care. Her problem seemed to be her early physical maturity which led her into contact with boys to the neglect of her school work. This led to truancy and to other trouble, such as housebreaking. School seemed to be irrelevant – she prefers to spend her time with a friend – an unmarried mother – and will probably enter into early motherhood herself.
>
> (Sandra Peterson, 1988)

Moreover, and as B. Hudson (1984) has argued, whereas much behaviour seen to be peculiar to teenage boys is legitimized by discourses of adolescence that allow males a developmental space for behavioural experimentation prior to their emergence into adulthood, no such leeway is allowed to girls who engage in the same behaviours. In particular, young women are often faced with a choice between sex and schooling. Regular school attendance seems to be equated with the continuation of childhood status, while sexual activity (especially if it results in motherhood) is seen as being indicative of an adult womanhood, both threatening to the school system and essentially subversive of a young woman's desire to learn. Indeed acquisition of sexual knowledge by young women is often equated with an undesirable and all-pervasive knowingness which again is seen to undermine both their respectability and their femininity.

'With her being coloured you have to be careful or people will accuse you of being discriminatory'

While children from ethnic minority groups 'are disproportionately rep-resented in the care population', the number of children of mixed parentage in care has been found to be '*alarmingly* disproportionate' (House of Commons 1984, emphasis added). In our present study we have had only one young woman of mixed parentage brought to our notice but certainly in that one case EWO Helen Walker's comments to one of the authors suggested that she saw the sexuality of both mother and daughter as being of more relevance to the girl's absence from school than Leah's own contention that she had stayed away because of being bullied and called 'nigger'.

> There are three children in the family who each have different fathers and Leah is a half caste. She has a lot of problems in the school. As for her relationships out of school, well, the rumours are that she's anybody's, though I don't know how true that is. The past few weeks she has been complaining of stomach pains and I wonder if she has got an infection – you know. But you have to be careful how you put it. It's a delicate issue and then with her being coloured you have to be careful or people will accuse you of being discriminatory. You know how it is.
>
> (EWO, Helen Walker, 1989)

Recognizing a 'hard-faced little bitch'

A constant complaint of young women in care is that, despite the state's supposed concern for their moral 'safety', they are seldom given informed and sensitive information or counselling about sexual matters or even the care and development of their own bodies. One reason for this may be that social workers and EWOs implicitly invoke the old Adam and Eve myth to conflate sexual activity with sexual and social knowledge. For in our project we had innumerable references to 'hard-faced little bitches' whose sexual activity (or even experience of sexual abuse) was seen to be the source of all their delinquency. Indeed even being a victim of sexual abuse was frequently taken as evidence that a young girl had been the sexually precocious instigator of the abuse in the first place! EWO David Brown's references to Tracy and Melanie illustrate this process:

> Tracy was raped by her uncle while she was still in primary school. Recently she's accused her friend's uncle of abusing her as well. She is sexually precocious, though . . . she's known as 'Miss Wet T Shirt'; I believe she won some competition.
>
> (EWO David Brown, 1989)

> Melanie was sexually abused by her father, though I'm not sure how far it went. He's of very low intelligence so I don't think he really knew what he was doing. Now if he tries to discipline her to make her attend school she will just say 'I will get the Social Services' or 'I will get the NSPCC on to you' so you see, really he is scared to do anything.
>
> (EWO, David Brown, 1989)

Refusing to take girls seriously

That young women's reports of sexual abuse are not taken seriously becomes less surprising when it is revealed how frequently the other problems of young women in care and out of school are trivialized. In fact, although the behaviour of both young men and young women can be viewed with cynicism by social workers and EWOs, it is the behaviour of young women which is more likely to be trivialized. The delinquent behaviour of adolescent girls is most frequently explained by reference either to a sexual 'maturity' which renders young women unamenable to 'reason' or to a presumption of a particular youngster's cunning which renders her own definition of the situation worthless.

> Oh yes, the girls are much more stroppy. They are more stubborn. You can talk to the boys and they will listen to you but once the girl has made up her mind there is no talking to her. They mature more quickly. They know what they want.
>
> (EWO, Walter Mitchell; the two others present agreeing, 1989)

> I told Kerry she is in danger of becoming a hypochondriac and will have to try to break the pattern. Last week she took Monday and Tuesday off, and on Wednesday she did a silly thing: she took a knife and cut her wrists. . . . she probably did that because she knew she had been off school and thought perhaps this would justify it in some way.
>
> (Mrs Roberts, social worker, 1989)

Shaming the 'slags'

> I get on with lads mainly. Like I've been called a slag and everything because I get on with the lads.
>
> (Kerry, 1989)

> They call all the girls different names, on aspects of the body.
>
> (Sarah, 1989)

It has already been well-documented by Griffin (1985) and Lees (1986) how young men control women and young women similarly control each other through a process of name-calling related to sexual reputation. The girls in our studies were well appraised of this and mention was continually made of fights being triggered off by name-calling incidents. What was more disturbing was the way in which verbal abuse and shaming was also incorporated into the discursive and disciplinary modes of EWOs and residential care staff. The following conversation between two female staff in a family centre illustrates the dubious logic which presently inseminates both the informal and formal control of adolescent female sexuality:

Social worker Anne: They don't want her back at home, not at the moment. Her mum says that if her dad sees the love-bites on her neck he will go mad, so mum is just trying to prevent that. I mean that's fair enough.

Social worker Fiona: It's keeping them apart here, that's the trouble, I saw them out the window the other day, messing about, so I just called out 'Is it your turn on top then, Glenda?' I know I oughtn't to have said that but it worked, as it embarrassed them. Sometimes I sit on the landing outside her room because I saw David trying to get in there one night. I just sit there with my knitting. That annoys them.

When shaming fails, more systematic methods of control are employed. Those that came to our attention included a programme of close physical control (known to the social services department authorizing it as 'pindown'); a programme of close psychological control (known to the social services department authorizing it as 'swamp'); and pharmaceutical control (generally referred to as 'putting her on a course of injections').

Pinning them down (physically)

'Pindown' they call it. You have to stay in your room with just your night clothes on, and you can't go out of your room. You have to be in bed at seven, all the lights out. It's dead depressing. Many people have put the windows through and all that. . . . The most I've been in there is two months. I run off once. I was on the run for a month and a half and when I came back they kept me under a pindown. That was bad, that was very bad. It doesn't really help because you just hate them, the people who've put you there. It makes you a lot worse and you're still going to school. You know they'll give up in the end.

(Susan, 1989)

During the spring and summer of 1989 several social workers contacted us to say that they were disturbed about the use of 'pindown', especially as it seemed to provoke young people to abscond. Although young men were also subjected to this mode of control, concern was particularly expressed about the irony of taking young women into care on the grounds of their being in moral danger and then subjecting them to regimes which resulted in their absconding and thereby being at even greater risk. At the time of writing the fears of these social workers had been vindicated. In October 1989 questions were raised in the Crown Court in relation to one young woman who had tried to escape from 'pindown'. The practice of 'pindown' has now been stopped. However, we know that in other areas there still exist similar disciplinary programmes and packages which, though designed to contain young people in residential care, actually result in them absconding – with particularly catastrophic effects for young women (see Christina and Carlen 1985).

Swamping them (psychologically)

The pressure put on young people in care to define and share their problems was one of the constant complaints of the young women in Carlen's 1985/86 study (Carlen 1988): 18-year-old Audrey summed up the feelings of many when she said

I always felt that, being in care, they sort of put things into your mind and make you feel as if you're all mixed up when really you haven't got a problem. It's very hard to explain, but they make you feel that you're very special because you're in Care and that you've got problems. Really, they're just messing up with your head.

(Carlen 1988: 86)

Susan (in the 1989 study) also remarked upon the fact that she had always felt different, noting, however, that she had never understood why she had been sent to a psychiatrist for misbehaviour in junior school:

I mean, when I was young, I was only about 10 and I saw a psychiatrist. I was in junior school. And I thought 'What's going on?' That was because I wasn't behaving in school. That was only junior school.

(Susan, aged 16, 1989)

Yet psychiatric and psychological controls are known to be more routinely and frequently imposed upon deviant women than upon delinquent men (Allen 1987). Moreover, although Blagg (1987) argues that amongst school phobics there are fairly even numbers of males and females, EWOs and the general literature tend to refer overwhelmingly to the 'daughter' rather than to the 'son'. The persistence of this common assumption that the school phobic is more likely to be female suggests that there is still an adherence to the belief that females are by nature passive, anxious, over-attached to parents (usually the mother) and home and with a tendency towards neurosis and/or hysteria. With this knowledge of the armoury of psychiatric and psychological ideologies already mobilized against women, we were not especially reassured by the male social worker who, in condemning 'pindown', told us that he much preferred 'swamp', the coercive technique used to contain delinquent children in care in a county adjacent to that of the 'pindowners'.

I, personally, find it much more difficult to deal with girls. I know about 'pindown' and I don't agree with it. I think 'swamp' is better. You still isolate the girl or boy but you don't just leave them alone. You have a team of social workers focusing on them and their problems. You just keep at it. That's why it's called swamp.

(Social worker, 1989)

The pharmaceutical fix

For several years there has been concern about the use of drugs to control the behaviour of children in care (see Taylor *et al.* 1979: 80; Freeman 1983: 172). In the 1985 study young women described how a range of drugs had been used either to calm or control them. Nadia saw the irony of being dosed up with largactyl while being allowed only one cigarette a day. Yasmin vividly remembered her introduction to a secure unit:

I went to this secure place. It was meant to help you sort out your life a bit better. I threw a fit the first time I went in there. Got a needle right up the bum. (Laughs) I was out flat.

(Carlen 1988: 93)

During research for the non-attendance at school project, medically prescribed drugs were mentioned to us only in the context of controlling young women's fertility. For example, at one children's home it had been decided that as 15-year-old Sarah's sexual activity could not be curtailed,

> it was best if she was put on a course of injections. We couldn't stop her sleeping with her boyfriend so we had to do something about it. She was another victim of abuse. She is very promiscuous, or at least she was. She probably still is, but does not make a lot of noise about it now. But we have put her on a course of injections anyway.
>
> (Worker in family centre, 1989)

No mention was made of any counselling concerning alternative forms of birth control: this was especially disturbing in view of the research on Depo-Provera (an injectable birth control pill) which shows not only that it is a contraceptive which has a number of serious side-effects but also that in Britain it has been routinely administered (often without their knowledge) to Asian women and to young women seen to be 'illiterate, unreliable or irresponsible' (Girotti and Hauser 1970, quoted in Rakusen 1981).

The case for a feminist charter for young women in care

In *Women, Crime and Poverty* Carlen (1988) suggested that residential care can itself have deleterious effects on women's subsequent careers, the major reasons being

1 Girls 'particularly end up being committed to care orders because there is really no adequate provision for them within the tariff system' (Gelsthorpe 1984).
2 Care's over-emphasis on 'assessment'   This results in some young people believing that they are in care as a consequence of some (unknown) individual pathology, rather than as an effect of a social situation beyond their control.
3 Care's movement of some children and young persons from placement to placement which prevents the young people from establishing long-standing friendship ties   This can precipitate them into a quest for excitement and friendship in circumstances of risk and danger which their sheltered life in care has not equipped them to cope with.
4 Care's punitive response to misbehaviour within children's homes as contrasted with the 'turning of a blind eye' to criminal behaviour outside the homes   This can result in young people being escalated through the whole gamut of secure places in the care system without anyone pointing out to them that it is their *criminal* behaviour which, if continued, will eventually land them in very serious trouble indeed. The punitive response to bad behaviour within children's homes can also result in the absconding that almost inevitably leads to lawbreaking and, especially in the case of young women, sexual exploitation.
5 The failure of some local authorities to ensure that young people in their care have adequate information about all aspects of sexual activity   This lack of sex education can obviously have disastrous effects for young women – and their ensuing offspring.

6 *The failure of the care system to prepare young people for non-institutional
   living* This can result in post-care money problems and depression of such
   magnitude that some young people see lawbreaking, and maybe a subsequent return to institutional life (but this time in a penal institution), as
   attractive alternatives to isolation and penury in an inner-city bedsit.

Additionally our most recent researches have led us to believe that there is an
especially urgent need to counter the all-pervasive sexualization of adolescent
female deviance and delinquency. A start could be made by constructing a
feminist charter for the treatment of young women in care and/or out of school
which would at least insist on the following.

1 Young women's own accounts of their difficulties should be taken seriously
   and not be 'explained away' by reference to their sexuality.
2 Sexist and sexually abusive language should be banned in children's homes
   and family centres.
3 Young women who refuse to go to school should be encouraged to continue
   their education in a variety of other settings, for example by special courses
   (on general and vocational education) being set up in further education
   colleges in conditions suitable, and at hours convenient, for pregnant,
   nursing and new mothers.
4 Physical and psychological forms of coercion like 'pindown' and 'swamp'
   should be banned on the grounds that they too often provoke young women
   in care into absconding.
5 Young women in care should receive full counselling before being given
   contraceptive injections.
6 Before compulsorily taking a girl into residential care local authorities
   should be required to show not only that she is in moral danger or not
   attending school but also that by taking her into care they will be able either
   to reduce the moral danger (a moot point in the cases of Susan and Sarah
   quoted above) or to ensure her attendance at school (an intention seldom
   achieved).
7 A number of 'safe houses' should be provided for victims of sexual and
   physical abuse where they may live voluntarily and without harassment
   from education welfare officers attempting to compel them to attend school.

Conclusion

In 1987 29,300 females were in local authority care in England and Wales (as
compared with 36,700 males). Yet although the total of 66,000 young people
in care in 1987 continued the 1980s' downward trend in the numbers of
children in care (for example in 1977 there were 96,203 and in 1984 74,845:
Department of Health 1977; 1984) there is no room for complacency about
the treatment of the thousands of young people still being taken into residential
care.
    In terms of gender, it is worth noting that while the numbers of young people
in care are declining steadily, the rate of decline is far slower for young women
than it is for young men. Between 1984 and 1987, for example, the number of

young men in care declined from 42,349 to 36,700, while the reduction in numbers of young women was far less, from 30,459 to 29,300. (Department of Health 1984; 1987). In particular the distinctly sexist treatment of young women in care and/or out of school needs to be monitored. For although the Children Act 1989 decriminalizes truancy, recent research concerning the use to which magistrates routinely put the social (inquiry) information about youngsters before the courts (Brown 1989) suggests that truancy will continue to remain an important factor in magisterial decisions on whether or not to take an offending young woman into care or custody. Likewise, the 1988 Education Act's devolution of power to local level, combined with the funding of schools according to pupil numbers, may well result on the one hand in local authorities stepping up their policing of truancy and, on the other, head-teachers turning a blind eye to the absence of pupils seen to be either intractable or giving the school bad publicity. Whatever calculations LEAs and head-teachers make to further their specific financial interests, the research which we are currently conducting (part of which is reported here) suggests that under the new legislation the pupils most likely to lose out will still be those whose social circumstances make them most vulnerable to racist, sexist and anti-working-class stereotypes.

In this chapter we have been mainly concerned with the dismissive and dis-criminatory treatment of certain young women in care and/or out of school. Yet we have not wanted to imply that *all* teachers, social workers, EWOs, and so on routinely stereotype all young people along racist, class and gender lines. (Indeed we suspect that, for most of the time and with reference to most of their charges, the majority do not.) Rather, what we have attempted to show is how when young women are seen to be especially difficult – when in fact the chips are down for professionals at their wits' end as to how best to deal with some youngsters – *then* it is that socially all-pervasive anti-working-class, racist and sexist discourses are invoked. Their invocation serves two related purposes: they demonstrate the (supposed) inevitability and intran-sigence of some young women's deviance; and they justify writing-off diffi-cult adolescent females as being essentially unfeminine, ineducable, uncontrollable and irrational. It is because we do not believe that such dis-criminatory stereotyping best informs the very complex decisions which have to be made concerning exceedingly troubled and troublesome teenage women that we have, in this chapter, argued the case for a feminist charter for young women in care and/or out of school.

Notes

1 ESRC Grant no. E06250010, grantholder, P. Carlen.
2 ESRC Grant no. R000231018, grantholders, P. Carlen and D. Gleeson.
3 At the time of writing twelve young women had been interviewed; nine education welfare officers, ten social workers, six residential care staff, and twelve teachers had been spoken to; visits had been made to four high schools and two primary schools, nine residential establishments, including three children's homes, three young persons' and three family centres, two juvenile justice (formerly Intermediate

Treatment) centres, and six other agencies in the voluntary, medical and social services sectors. In the course of the fieldwork innumerable cases of truancy were discussed.

References

Allen, H. (1987) *Justice Unbalanced*, Milton Keynes: Open University Press.
Blagg, N. (1987) *School Phobia and its Treatment*, London: Croom Helm.
Brown, S. (1989) 'Social information and its "usefulness" in the juvenile court: an analysis of magistrates' accounts in organizational context', unpublished Ph.D thesis, Teesside Polytechnic.
Cain, M. (1989) 'Feminists transgress criminology', introduction to M. Cain (ed.) *Growing Up Good*, London: Sage.
Carlen, P. (1988) *Women, Crime and Poverty*, Milton Keynes: Open University Press.
Casburn, M. (1979) *Girls will be Girls*, London: Women's Research and Resources Centre.
Chiqwada, R. (1989) 'The criminalization and imprisonment of black women' *Probation* 3, September: 100–105.
Christina, D. and Carlen, P. (1985) 'Christina in her own time', in P. Carlen, D. Christina, J. Hicks, J. O'Dwyer and C. Tchaikowsky (eds) *Criminal Women*, Cambridge: Polity Press.
Department of Health (1977) *Children in Care of Local Authorities at 31st March, 1977*, London: HMSO.
— (1984) *Children in Care of Local Authorities at 31st March, 1984*, London: HMSO.
— (1987) *Children in Care of Local Authorities at 31st March, 1987*, London: HMSO.
Donzelot, J. (1979) *The Policing of Families*, London: Hutchinson.
Foucault, M. (1979) *The History of Sexuality, Volume 1*, London: Allen Lane.
Freeman, M. (1983) *The Rights and Wrongs of Children*, London: Frances Pinter.
Gelsthorpe, L. (1984) Evidence given to House of Commons Social Services Committee Inquiry, *Children in Care*, London: HMSO.
Girotti, F. and Hauser O. (1970) *Therapeutische Umschau und medizische Bibliographie*, Band 27 p. 671, Bern.
Griffin, C. (1985) *Typical Girls*, London: Routledge & Kegan Paul.
Hagan, J., Simpson, J. and Gillis, J. R. (1979) 'The sexual stratification of social control: a gender-based perspective on crime and delinquency', *British Journal of Sociology* 30, 1: 25–38.
Hall, S., Critcher, C., Jefferson, T., Clarke, J. and Roberts, B. (1978) *Policing the Crisis*, London: Macmillan.
House of Commons (1984) *Second Report from the Social Services Committee: Children in Care*, vols I, II and III, London: HMSO.
Hudson, A. (1985) 'Troublesome girls – towards some definitions and policies', paper presented to European University Institute Conference, Florence, November.
Hudson, B. (1984) 'Femininity and adolescence', in A. McRobbie and M. Nava (eds) *Gender and Generation*, London: Macmillan.
Lees, S. (1986) *Losing Out*, London: Hutchinson.
Lewis, D. K. (1981) 'Black women offenders and criminal justice: some theoretical considerations', in M. Q. Warren (ed.) *Comparing Female and Male Offenders*, London: Sage.
Meyer, P. (1983) *The Child and the State: The Intervention of the State in Family Life*, Cambridge: Cambridge University Press/Editions de la Maison des Sciences de l'Homme.
Pollak, O. (1950) *The Criminality of Women*, Philadelphia, Pa: University of Pennsylvania Press.

Rakusen, J. (1981) 'Depo-Provera: the extent of the problem – A case study in the politics of birth control', in H. Roberts (ed.) *Women, Health and Reproduction*, London: Routledge & Kegan Paul.

Taylor, L., Lacey, R. and Braken, D. (1979) *In Whose Best Interests?*, London: Cobden Trust and National Association for Mental Health.

Thomas, W. I. (1923) *The Unadjusted Girl*, Boston, Mass: Little, Brown.

Webb, D. (1984) 'More on gender and justice: girl offenders on supervision', *Sociology* 18, 3: 367–81.

Worrall, A. (1990) *Offending Women*, London: Routledge.

2
Social work, justice and the common good

Bill Jordan

The dramatic world events of the winter of 1989/90 prompt the question: are we witnessing a sea change in social relations, and the emergence of a new kind of social order? If the apparent triumph of possessive individualism and property ownership continues, a fundamental transformation of the institutions of social welfare and social work – to make them more in line with neo-liberal values and commercial priorities – seems inevitable. Yet in this chapter I shall argue that there are enough paradoxes and contradictions in these changes, and within economic individualism itself, to suggest that principles which now are marginalized or dismissed may emerge as important in new social relations.

After all, those who seemed to gain most power and prestige from the revolutionary events were by no means unambiguous winners. Margaret Thatcher, arguably the dominant global figure of the 1980s, suddenly suffered mass revolt over the poll tax and plummeting popularity among her most reliable supporters. Mikhail Gorbachev, hailed throughout the world for his part in the liberation of eastern Europe, was reviled by many Soviet citizens, especially in those republics seeking independence. Japan's ruling elite, while enjoying the reputation of running the most successful advanced society, suffered scandals and electoral upsets, as well as stock market decline, at home. All these might be seen as examples of a theme – Trouble In My Back Yard (TIMBY) – that has afflicted a variety of regimes, not least South Africa, where Marxism, apparently decisively defeated in its European heartland, nevertheless sustains a triumphant African National Congress.

What links people-power in eastern Europe with violence and destruction in British prisons and South African townships is the lack of any coherent set of principles for resolving the claims of conflicting interests or achieving co-operation around agreed social goals. At the nub of these issues are disputes about fairness in the distribution of property, work and income, often focused on the institutions for social welfare and social control. So social work is not far from the centre of certain mega-problems in emerging social relations, and it may be that its principles and values are more relevant to their resolution than is widely recognized (Jordan 1990).

Justice and the New Right

Central to the changing institutions of social welfare in Britain is the New Right's redefinition of fairness, from social to individual justice. This shift involves an emphasis on self-ownership: people have rights to choice in how to conduct their lives, and entitlements, to what they earn, buy or inherit. Along with the strengthening of property rights goes a stress on individual responsibility: people are accountable for the consequences of their choices. Justice is defined in terms of a fair process of voluntary exchange, in which these rights and responsibilities are upheld (Hayek 1960; Friedman and Friedman 1981.)

Most social relations can therefore best be conducted through markets, which allow exactly such exchanges (Acton 1971). But certain needs, arising from dependence in childhood, illness, handicap and old age, are better met through household and kinship groupings, and involve long-term obligations, based on emotional and moral bonds. Hence society, consists of a dominant sphere of self-interested transactions (the economy) and a lesser one of altruism (the family). The New Right's ethic regards it as natural that men should be primarily concerned with the former, and women with the latter.

Charity and voluntary work can quite easily be fitted into this model of social relations, as extensions of altruistic concern to 'those less fortunate than ourselves'. But collective provision is essentially anomalous. While sophisticated libertarians like Robert Nozick (1974) can make a case for compensating the poor for lost rights to common benefits (for example hunting and gathering in woodlands), vulgarizers of the new orthodoxy can find no persuasive arguments for community support. Residual welfare provision is largely a matter of expediency: visible suffering and death is unaesthetic and a public health hazard.

This is well reflected in the current round of reforms in social services, which recasts as much as possible of the welfare state in terms of economic transactions. For example in health care, the National Health Service is redesigned as a business, purchasing the best value for money on behalf of the taxpayer, through a system of internal markets. Instead of being members of an inclusive club, with access to collective provision, patients are remodelled as consumers, contracted for by cost-conscious budget-holders (hospital managers and GPs), seeking bargain buys on national price lists (Department of Health 1989a).

In local government, the culmination of more than fifty Acts of Parliament since 1979 is a system which disguises local taxation as a price (the community charge), and tries to substitute accounting for political principles as the guiding decision procedure. Community care echoes the National Health Service

(NHS) reforms, but takes much further the maxim that commercial and voluntary organizations are preferable to public provision. Local government is left as the contractor, assessor, monitor and residual provider of services to the most demanding, deviant or dependent groups for whom the family cannot and commercial agencies will not care at any price (Department of Health 1989b).

In all these policy areas, the state acts as a kind of prudent enterprise, offering taxpayers the most cost-effective measures for tidying up regrettable failures in economic and family life. Need is portrayed as blame-free; sickness, handicap and old age are unavoidable and expensive conditions, against which not all can afford to insure themselves. Hence from the point of view of justice these issues have little significance; like waste disposal or street lighting, they just happen to require a public authority for their organization, though this authority should act as much like a business as possible.

But this logic does not apply nearly so well to able-bodied groups, especially unemployed people and single parents. By the 1980s families with children were the biggest constituent group among the poor; of these, about half had a 'head' in work, the other half a 'head' outside the labour market (DHSS 1985a). Ethnic minorities were over-represented in this total because of discrimination in employment. These were the people who, on the New Right's account, either lacked the skills to command a wage sufficient for their family's subsistence, or were unwilling to accept the work available at the going rate. Either way, important issues of fairness were at stake.

The instrument of justice for such people was the means of selecting out those in 'genuine need', that is demonstrably poor, despite strenuous efforts to maximize their earnings. While mass unemployment was at its height, poverty alone was considered sufficient evidence, but as it began to fall, the government's philosophy required a process for denying the claims for benefit of those whose efforts to earn were regarded as less than strenuous. After the introduction of various new ways of testing 'availability for work' in the period 1986–9 (which, along with statistical manipulation, were highly successful in reducing official unemployment), legislation required that from October 1989 claimants registered as unemployed should be able to demonstrate – by evidence including diaries and notebooks – that they are 'actively seeking work'. A whole new range of officials, euphemistically titled 'advisers' and 'counsellors', now police the system, checking claimants' willingness to pursue low-paid, inconvenient, distant and dirty employment, and using any signs of reluctance as a reason for refusing benefits.

Like the former levels of unemployment, these measures can best be understood as part of the government's economic restructuring. The main casualties of its policies in the 1980s have been those forms of employment which provided the steps on the ladder between low paid, casualized, short-term and part-time work on the one hand, and secure, decently paid, permanent jobs on the other. Many unskilled workers displaced from regular work now have to rejoin the labour market as irregulars. For example between December 1986 and December 1988, male unemployment fell by 750,000; yet regular employment for men grew by only 100,000 (Department of Employment 1989).

Twice as many men entered 'self-employment' – an impressive title which often conceals precarious, unprotected hand-to-mouth activities (James *et al.* 1990).

Selectivity in this situation can be self-defeating. The means-tested benefit system traps claimants in several ways. The basic benefit penalizes part-time work and makes low-paid employment unattractive. Lack of child-care allowances gives major disincentives for single parents. Withdrawal of wage supplements (Family Credit and Housing Benefit) combines with income taxation – and now the poll tax – to minimize extra earnings. Above all, complexity and delay, combined with the unreliability of earnings, make the incomes of poor people precarious and unpredictable and expose them to debt and stress. The whole system offers much stronger inducements for claimants to do undeclared cash work than to take insecure, low-paid employment.

Hence the dynamic of self-interest which drives the economy breaks down in this sector, where the lure of higher earnings is annulled by the impact of taxation and benefit withdrawal. Worse than this, the missing steps on the employment ladder deny unskilled workers the long-term prospect of access to property – pensions, owner-occupied houses, savings, shares – which gives the majority their rights and choices. Their interests within this structure of disincentives and penalties lie in maximizing their incomes from claiming, and from various forms of illegality.

Taking its lead from the USA, official British thinking now recognizes this paradox and takes the obvious step of blaming its victims. The underclass are prisoners not of the benefits system or the labour market, but of a 'culture of dependency' (Murray 1984; 1989). They are victims of a contagion of depravity, spreading outward from a core group of demoralized, pauperized, criminalized deviants – drug addicts, prostitutes, thieves, muggers, idlers and drunkards. The only way to reintegrate the redeemable fraction of the underclass is through work – the fulfilment of the duty they owe the taxpayer for the support they receive through state benefits.

Hence the New Right's theory of justice now includes an obligation on poor people to repay society for its assistance, by accepting employment or retraining on any terms offered. Although there is no such compulsory duty on people with property incomes or other means of support, this obligation is cast in terms of 'citizenship'. This term therefore refers not to the membership rights of the political community, but to the compulsory powers of the state. Justice demands that the poor should perform service on behalf of taxpayers. Where self-interest fails to motivate, coercion must apply (Mead 1986).

The paradox of this account of justice is that stronger property rights, while allowing greater market choice for some, entail harsher compulsion for others. In order that society may become a free association of self-interested individuals, the power of the state to coerce the poor must be increased. By implication, better-off people join (or remain members of) a political community which supports poor people only if the latter are forced to work for them by state officials. This entails a set of social relations which falls somewhere between early capitalist exploitation and the forced labour of recently overthrown east European regimes. It is a clear instance of a TIMBY irony that most of the violent young demonstrations against the poll tax in west

London in March 1990 were probably members of an inner-city underclass, experiencing itself as inhabiting a gulag-style existence of official surveillance and repression.

Although social workers are not directly involved in these particular processes, they are very much concerned with their consequences. The able-bodied poor are disproportionate consumers of services for children, adolescents and families, and their situation in the whole system of social relations is directly relevant to these needs. I shall return to this topic on pp. 24–5.

Care and the family

In contrast with the self-interested dynamic of wider social relations in economic individualism, the family is seen as the 'natural' sphere for morality and altruism. Ties of 'blood' kinship and affection create binding obligations that require individuals to sacrifice their short-term interests for each other's good. However it is the primary responsibility of men to provide economic support and of women to provide unpaid care within this system of relationships. This mixture of economic and moral relations within the household has all sorts of paradoxical implications.

Given the assumptions of economic individualism, why should households form at all? Why does everyone not live alone, dividing their time between paid work for others (exchanging services for cash) and unpaid work for themselves? Alan Carling has recently shown that, under conventional economic assumptions, and in the absence of all other considerations, households will form only if both parties can gain from an exchange of paid and unpaid labour between them, such that the one who commands the higher wage rate in the labour market is enabled to do more paid work, and the one with the lower wage rate to do more of the unpaid work, but at a 'wage' higher than that commanded in the labour market. In other words, the higher-earning partner subcontracts unpaid work to the other for money, but it is a necessary and sufficient condition for household formation that there should be a wage differential between them (Carling 1990).

In an economy where such a differential is structured on gender lines, women do the larger share of unpaid work and in any formable household, women do more work (if paid and unpaid work are included) than men. This can be elaborated into a demonstration that women are exploited by men, using concepts derived from Roemer's theory of class (Roemer 1982). In other words, far from requiring a quite different (moral) explanation household relationships might plausibly be analysed in terms of economic transactions between self-interested individuals, leading to systematic exploitation of women by men, deriving ultimately from the economic and political power through which men impose differential wage rates in the labour market.

Of course it is equally possible to construct an account of households as shared projects in which the moral standards of members require them to contribute according to their abilities, and to benefit according to their needs, to reciprocate services in a generalized way (not counting the immediate costs to themselves) over long periods, to have regard for the whole unit in reaching joint decisions, and so on (Curtis 1986). These standards, which contrast with the competitive, opportunistic behaviour of economic activity, can be constructed as rational if we regard the household as a sphere in which sharing common facilities, practices and purposes is positively valued, membership is lifelong and unconditional, and hence there is a high premium on actions which promote harmony and allow flexible, negotiated solutions to a wide range of everyday problems (Jordan 1987; 1990).

However, this account does not explain structural features of household roles, unless we also believe that women are 'naturally' suited to such tasks as care, housework and shopping, and men to paid activities. Indeed neither the purely economic model nor the moral model of the household predicts the actual configuration of gender roles in present British society. Since some women command higher wages than some men, and some households are formed with this combination of earning power, the economic model would predict role-reversal in all such partnerships: in fact, research shows that it occurs in only a tiny proportion of such cases (McRae 1986). A sociological account could use the economic model as a background explanation for the evolution of gender roles, showing how comparative wage rates and unpaid work requirements provide the macro-foundation for the ideology that informs gender relations, which is gradually adapted under the pressure of long-term change.

However, if we treat the New Right's account of household responsibilities as an example of such an ideology, it contains many contradictions under present conditions. For example demand for women's labour has been buoyant during the 1970s and 1980s, with female employment expanding as male employment declines. Yet women's wage rates remain stubbornly at around the same two-thirds ratio to men's and men continue to enjoy a high proportion of secure, well-paid jobs, with access to training, promotion and pensions, while women disproportionately occupy part-time, temporary posts with no such benefits. At the same time, there is clear evidence of an increased demand for women's unpaid work in the home, as demographic factors and community care policies combine to raise the quantity of care given to elderly and handicapped relatives. Under these conditions, how can the economic and the moral elements in household relations be reconciled, and what is a rational division of paid and unpaid labour?

Two contradictory processes seem to be at work. On the one hand, as good jobs become scarcer as a result of technological change and economic restructuring, men use their political and economic power to secure these for themselves, while as the amount of care to be given to older people rises, the ideology of female responsibility binds women to these unpaid tasks. However, against these pressures, the growth of low-paid, part-time and casual work, especially in services, has been facilitated by the availability of women willing to take such employment; this expansion has included a growth in paid care for the same groups and the same needs (old age, handicap) in the form of private residential homes, day care, home care, and so on.

What factors determine the proportions of paid and unpaid care given to these groups of people, and who should give them? The system of kinship obligations which operates in Britain is complex; it tends to select a woman (normally a daughter) who is 'close' (emotionally and geographically) to the person who needs care as the member of the network with the sole or main responsibility, especially if she does not have a full-time job. Hence the role of full-time unpaid carer tends to fall on certain women, while men and other women can give reasons which are accepted as legitimate for avoiding the role (Ungerson 1987; Finch 1989). Conversely many people with needs for care can find no unpaid carer, because there is no female member of their kinship network with the required relationship and characteristics.

But as the need for care rises and the supply of eligible female kin dwindles, economic factors become important. Where elderly people have access to the resources, paid care tends to grow, and unpaid care tends to decline. This is evidenced by the figures on commercial residential care in the 1980s; as entitlement to supplementary benefit (later income support) for those entering residential care became established, the number of commercial homes and places mushroomed. The fact that public expenditure under this head grew from £10 million in 1980 to £1,000 million in 1990 was repeatedly cited as one of the main factors giving impetus to the White Paper proposals (*Caring for People*) on community care (Department of Health 1989b). A primary aim of new policies is to stop 'unnecessary' admissions to care, and hence give taxpayers better 'value for money'.

This means that, under the banner of giving 'more effective support to unpaid carers', new policies and practices are designed to sustain those who take up this role. Social workers, who are likely to be the professional group chiefly involved in assessment and case management, will be required to design 'packages of (paid) care' to preserve kinship arrangements as long as possible. What this approach largely ignores are issues of justice over the selection of unpaid carers, and the differential income opportunities of individuals and households.

Economic factors skew the choices open to individuals, so that kinship obligations fall unfairly on some and not others. In high-income households, both partners may well escape the duty to care because of their paid work commitments; even if they do not, it makes good economic sense for them to employ low-paid care workers to do their caring. At the opposite end of the scale, a woman with low earning power and without full-time employment is much more likely to become an unpaid carer. New policies reinforce rather than offset these structural injustices between classes and genders over care.

These factors are systematically obscured by the rhetoric of 'freedom' and 'choice' in the White Paper. In practice, both people who need care and unpaid carers will lose access to residential care, the option chosen by a growing proportion in the 1980s. Instead it will be social workers who will assess their needs, and contract for them with commercial and voluntary agencies. The driving force behind the new system is a managerial imperative – economy and efficiency – linked with the pseudo-consumerism of the New Right's approach to social welfare. As in competitive tendering over mowing the council's grass, it is the local authority which will have the choice over placing the contracts. Old people will not be the contractors: they will be the grass.

Partnership in child care

So far I have argued that recent government social welfare reforms follow closely the logic of economic individualism and family responsibility. However, there is one area of policy where this does not seem to apply – child care. The Children Act 1989 sets out a framework for closer co-operation between parents and social workers, and better safeguards for families and children where legal interventions occur. Its spirit – elaborated in a *Review of Child Care Law* (DHSS 1985b) and a White Paper (DHSS 1987) which the Act seems to follow in essentials, if not always in detail – is captured in such words as 'partnership', 'support' and 'agreement' (Department of Health 1989c).

In one respect the Act can be seen as in line with the New Right's thinking: it places strong emphasis on parental *responsibility*, insisting that it is not extinguished by divorce, or by the child coming into care, on a voluntary or compulsory basis. But this responsibility is not the exclusive duty that characterizes so much of the ideology of economic individualism; instead it is shared within a community, whose support is expressed in local authority provision. There are children who – because of their own physical, emotional or learning difficulties, or because of their parents' economic, health or relationship situation, or in a crisis – have needs which cannot be met, temporarily or in the long term, by their families. Instead of characterizing this in terms of a failure of parental duty, the new Act requires the local authority to offer various kinds of support, on terms agreed with parents, and in partnership with them, including home care, day care and 'accommodation' (a new term, comprising foster and residential placements, replacing the notion of 'voluntary care', and with strong implications of including parents both in the arrangements themselves and in their implementation). It is only when such support cannot prevent harm to the child's proper development and a court order can be shown as necessary for that development, that compulsory measures should be used; even these should not exclude parents and other family members from positive involvement with the child.

In many ways these changes run counter to trends in child care since the Maria Colwell scandal in the mid-1970s. A succession of child abuse enquiries have recommended earlier and more decisive interventions in abusive families, the identification and exclusion of dangerous parents, and the increased use of the courts in issues of care (London Borough of Brent 1985; London Borough of Lambeth 1987; London Borough of Greenwich 1987). These recommendations have been reflected in the policies and practices of social services departments – increased legalism, a more impersonal approach, more reliance on compulsory orders and a mistrust of voluntary routes into care (Packman 1986). Yet the findings of the inquiry into events in Cleveland, following the rapid increase in care orders for sexual abuse, pointed rather in the opposite direction; there social workers had been uncritical in their use of compulsion, and uncaring in their dealings with parents and children according to the report (Butler-Sloss 1988). With the evidence of research in the early 1980s, and shepherded through Parliament by civil servants strongly influenced by these criticisms of recent practice, the new Act reflects a reversal of long-term trends, and the adoption of values which sit awkwardly with those of economic individualism.

It is true that the clauses which require local authorities to give support (including accommodation) to the children of poor, sick, baffled or conflict-ridden families are rather unspecific, and will allow social services departments to farm these out to voluntary agencies or ignore them altogether, concentrating on their responsibilities for legal interventions in cases of abuse. But it is also true that the new Act provides a framework for a positive and progressive local authority to develop services in a way which is both much more supportive of families with children and much more collectivist than is possible under other Conservative legislation. Whereas the White Paper on community care (Department of Health 1989b) clearly relegates the public sector to a role of assessor, enabler, monitor and provider of the last resort, the new legislation on children requires it to take the lead in providing a network of support whose ethos is co-operative, communal and collective, and whose methods are those of negotiation, sharing and consensus.

This optimism can be contested on at least two grounds. First, the notion of 'children in need' makes positive interpretations of the Act vulnerable, both politically (if a local authority's political control changed hands) and possibly even legally (if challenged by a community chargepayer, for example). It also provides shelter for restrictive and negative interpretations, by departments wishing to restrict services to children suffering abuse. Second, the fact that local authorities depend on parental agreement for all supportive arrangements, including accommodation, may well defeat the aim of providing these in any planned or constructive way. It is easy to see how impoverished, marginal, indebted or homeless parents, or people in marital crisis, might make repeated requests for short-term accommodation for children, and how social workers could adopt defensive policies and practices in response. This might be even more the case with teenagers, where new responsibilities for accommodating homeless young people who are estranged from their families fit rather too conveniently with restrictions in social security payments by central government.

These are specific instances of a general problem: if the great bulk of social welfare legislation tends towards restriction, surveillance, compulsion or punishment of poor people in relation to income, housing, access to public resources, health education, and so on, how can one service (child care) feasibly offer a more generous, co-operative approach? Will not the young families with children who now form the biggest constituent group in the underclass simply reframe their needs for money, houses, health care or whatever as child care needs, and press them more insistently upon social workers? And would it not be a rational strategy for a single parent living on a run-down estate to request temporary accommodation for her children, while she tries to find a decent job, better housing or a new partner?

Morality and the social order

What I have argued so far is that the social welfare reforms carried out in the name of economic individualism contain many paradoxes and contradictions. While defining justice in terms of a process of voluntary exchange between individuals bearing rights and responsibilities, they none the less embody strong powers to compel members of the underclass to work against their will, because of their lack of economic incentives. While restricting morality to the sphere of family relationships, they none the less require social workers to define the boundaries between paid and unpaid care, since kinship obligations and gender roles conflict with economic opportunities. Conversely attempts to provide poor families with children assistance and support through social work risk being overwhelmed by demands for care which stem from other unmet needs in the economic sphere.

In so far as social workers deal in complex personal needs, interpersonal conflicts and issues around the control of behaviour which threatens social order and stability, the basis of their practice is ultimately a moral one. Attempts to resolve the problems they encounter appeal to standards of fairness, between individuals, in groups, and among members of communities. Methods which rely on detailed attention, good listening and empathetic communication can achieve their aims – needs met, conflicts resolved or behaviour changed – only if people can recognize these as in some sense fair outcomes and the right things for them to do. If social workers cannot help their clients to make such decisions voluntarily in a large proportion of cases, then there seems little point in providing these services in this way; it would be quicker and more efficient to use methods of compulsory legal enforcement.

Supporters of the New Right's social philosophy would argue that it provides just such a basis for social work. In so far as it relies on clear definitions of individual rights and responsibilities, it prescribes just such a code of personal conduct, which reasonable people can recognize as fair. If social workers uphold this system of social relations, they have only to use compulsion against those deviant or disturbed individuals who are unwilling or unable to recognize what it is their duty to do. Yet I have argued that the structure of economic relations and of households is such that injustices are built into people's roles, so that clients can fairly appeal against the invisible 'rules' (governing class, gender and race relations) which hold them in exploited or subordinate positions.

This is well recognized in the anti-discriminatory principles which are an increasingly important element in social work values. This perspective draws attention to issues of power, and the structural advantages of some groups over others (Dominelli 1988). Individuals and coalitions with such assets as wealth, whiteness and maleness use these to further their interests and deny other choices (Jordon 1989). The rules of encounters between the powerful and the subordinate reflect these structural inequalities, yet the disadvantaged have no opportunities to change those rules. Asset-holders use their entitlements under neo-liberal social relations, and the procedural account of justice, to legitimize their advantages. In challenging racism and sexism, social workers can address this conflict of values, and draw attention to alternative interpretations of justice; but they can seldom change the underlying inequalities, or the basic rules which sustain them.

Yet there is another sense in which social work practice can contribute to this alternative approach to justice and morality, and one which I would argue is central to its values and methods. In spite of the emphasis on individuals' rights in books about social work ethics, its practice is more concerned with negotiating agreements and achieving co-operation. In this sense, the implicit morality of the Children Act 1989 is in tune with social work's aspirations, as is the moral, as opposed to the economic account of family relations. Ultimately social work, like other social welfare provision, appeals to a notion of membership of an interdependent community, in which the good of the individual is related to the good of all other members. Personal traumas, interpersonal conflicts and disputes about the social order are resolvable through the shared concern and co-operation of citizens for the sake of the common good (Jordan 1989; 1990).

In the ethical reasoning derived from this model of social relations, agreements are possible because, in any set of circumstances, it should be possible to consider individual actions in the light of their effects on others who are linked into a shared system of benefits and obligations. This does not mean that there are never conflicts of interests or of priority, but it does imply that what people have in common as fellow citizens and members of groups and communities, sharing certain standards, traditions and resources, is an important basis for potential agreement about the ends and means of their actions. In the last resort, this is the foundation of democracy; collective self-rule implies that people bind themselves to uphold collective decisions, because they value what they share as members of the whole community above what they could achieve by ruthless pursuit of their sectional interests (Cunningham 1987; Graham 1986).

In this sense, the moral basis of social work is not individualistic but democratic. It appeals to the possibility of co-operation around contestable notions of justice, through detailed negotiation, give and take. Indeed its informal methods, both in team organization and in practice, reflect these democratic roots. But they depend in turn on a wider system of social relations which commands a democratic consensus, and does not rely on the exclusion of minorities from benefits of membership, on unequal terms of membership, or on the coercion of some groups for the political and economic advantage of others.

I have argued that class, gender and race relations in present-day Britain involve fundamental injustices in all these respects. Hence the ethical problems faced in practice by social workers, in relation to their poor, black and women clients in particular, reflect the crisis in democratic decision-making. The New Right's economic individualism cannot provide a basis for non-exploitative, non-coercive relations in any sphere; instead injustice threatens the civil and political rights of vulnerable people in all these groups. The poll tax and prison riots of the spring of 1990 were not random outbursts of a violent streak in the British character; they were the manifestations of Mrs Thatcher's particular version of TIMBY. It is social work's misfortune that, although it has the potential to provide many elements of an ethical alternative to individualism, it is condemned to being in the front line of Britain's backyard brawls (Jordan 1990).

Yet social work itself does offer an alternative approach to these issues, and one which is of considerable relevance to the TIMBY phenomenon. If the New Right's philosophy triumphs, and economic individualism becomes the universal basis of social relations, structural injustice and conflict along class, ethnic or gender lines could become endemic. Furthermore, environmental issues will increasingly demand solutions, yet defy the principles of this regime – you cannot privatize the ozone layer. The social environment, like the physical, requires decision-making that takes account of the needs of all members of the community, and preserves a sustainable culture of co-operation, mutual respect and solidarity.

One part of the alternative approach to social relations involves a redefinition of the basis of citizenship – of the universal terms of membership – so as to provide an inclusive structure of rights and responsibilities, giving all citizens common interests in the good of the community, its cultural diversity and quality of life. But the other part is finding ways of resolving conflicts and reaching binding collective decisions which can be accepted as fair on all. Here social workers are experienced in involving disadvantaged groups, including the excluded, and negotiating contested issues. It is very important that these skills in participation, partnership and conciliation should not be allowed to decay in the face of increased demands for economic accounting, monitoring, surveillance and authoritative intervention. Social work in the 1990s should cultivate its links with democracy and mediation as its contribution to this new basis for social relations.

References

Acton, H. B. (1971) *The Morals of Markets: An Ethical Exploration*, London: Longman/Institute of Economic Affairs.
Butler-Sloss, E. (1988) *Report of the Inquiry into Child Abuse in Cleveland 1987*, Cm 412, London: HMSO.
Carling, A. (1990) *Social Division*, London: Verso.
Cunningham, F. (1987) *Democratic Theory and Socialism*, Cambridge: Cambridge University Press.
Curtis, R. F. (1986) 'Household and family in theory of inequality', *American Sociological Review* 51: 168–80.
Department of Employment (1989) *Employment Gazette* 97, 11: Table 1.1, p. S9.
Department of Health (1989a) *Working for Patients*, Cm 555, London: HMSO.
—— (1989b) *Caring for People: Community Care in the Next Decade and Beyond*, Cm 849, London: HMSO.
—— (1989c) *An Introduction to the Children Act*, London: HMSO.
DHSS (1985a) *Reform of Social Security*, vol 3, Background Papers, London: HMSO.
—— (1985b) *Review of Child Care Law: Report to Ministers of an Interdepartmental Working Party*, London: HMSO.
—— (1987) *The Law on Child Care and Family Services*, Cm 62, London: HMSO.
Dominelli, L. (1988) *Anti-Racist Social Work*, London: Macmillan.

Finch, J. (1989) *Family Obligations and Social Change*, Oxford: Polity.
Friedman, M. and Friedman, R. (1981) *Free to Choose*, Harmondsworth: Pelican.
Graham, K. (1986) *The Battle of Democracy*, Brighton: Wheatsheaf.
Hayek, F. A. (1960) *The Constitution of Liberty*, London: Routledge & Kegan Paul.
James, S., Jordan, B. and Redley, M. (1990) *Labour-Market Decisions in Low-Income Households*, University of Exeter, Department of Economics.
Jordan, B. (1987) *Rethinking Welfare*, Oxford: Basil Blackwell.
—— (1989) *The Common Good: Citizenship, Morality and Self-Interest*, Oxford: Basil Blackwell.
—— (1990) *Social Work in an Unjust Society*, Hemel Hempstead: Harvester Wheatsheaf.
London Borough of Brent (1985) *A Child in Trust: The Report of the Panel of Inquiry into the Circumstances Surrounding the Death of Jasmine Beckford*, London: Borough of Brent.
London Borough of Greenwich (1987) *A Child in Mind: Protection of Children in a Responsible Society: The Report of the Commission of Inquiry into the Circumstances Surrounding the Death of Kimberley Carlile*, London: Borough of Greenwich.
London Borough of Lambeth (1987) *Whose Child? The Report of the Panel Appointed to Inquire into the Death of Tyra Henry*, London: Borough of Lambeth.
McRae, S. (1986) *Cross-Class Families: A Study of Wives' Occupational Superiority*, Oxford: Clarendon Press.
Mead, L. (1986) *Beyond Entitlement: The Social Obligations of Citizenship*, New York: Free Press.
Murray, C. (1984) *Losing Ground: American Social Policy, 1950–80*, New York: Basic Books.
—— (1989) 'Underclass', *Sunday Times Magazine*, 26 November.
Nozick, R. (1974) *Anarchy, State and Utopia*, Oxford: Basil Blackwell.
Packman, J. (1986) *Who Needs Care: Social Work Decision about Children*, Oxford: Basil Blackwell.
Roemer, J. E. (1982) *A General Theory of Exploitation and Class*, Cambridge, Mass: Harvard University Press.
Ungerson, C. (1987) *Policy is Personal: Sex, Gender and Informal Care*, London: Tavistock.

3
Clearing a path through the undergrowth: a feminist reading of recent literature on child sexual abuse

Mary MacLeod and Esther Saraga

When children die, or are abused, at the hands of their parents, the questions often asked are: what have individual workers done wrong? What has gone wrong in the public response? But the workers in tragic cases have not been working, nor have systems developed, in a vacuum. Both policy and practice have arisen out of public and professional explanations of child abuse. Yet, it was possible, following Cleveland, to have a public inquiry looking at what went wrong which made no attempt to examine the nature of the phenomenon about which so much anxiety and outrage was voiced, nor to examine the bases of intervention.

> How could he do it? Why did it happen? . . . the same question obsesses sufferers of abuse and their relatives. . . . Alarmingly, in all the storm of words about child sexual abuse, there has been a deafening silence on why it happens. Yet doctors and social workers . . . perform their work, make their observations, their judgments on the basis of a theory.
> (MacLeod and Saraga 1988a: 15)

Reluctance to scrutinize explanation continues and has been expressed recently as an exasperation with the debate about family dysfunction ideas and a reluctance to take seriously feminist ideas. O'Hagan (1989a) has ranted against the ongoing debate between feminist and family dysfunction explanations. In more sober tone others have done likewise (Stevenson 1989; Wattam *et al.* 1989) while being careful to offer 'feminism' its due. Texts, even those from within the family dysfunction position (Bentovim *et al.* 1988), give a token recognition of the contribution that feminists made to bringing child sexual abuse (CSA) to public awareness, before manifesting their reluctance to take on board the analysis in a misinterpretation or marginalization of feminist writings. Even those writings which produce a more interesting and complex account of sexual abuse fight shy of the difficult questions which feminism poses (La Fontaine 1990: 105, 214, 218). Feminist contributions to theory and practice remain, it seems, disturbing.

> The effects of the increasingly public conflicts among the experts resonate powerfully within the multi-disciplinary network as well as in individual social workers. . . . The consequences for decision making and the performance of staff are self-evidently harmful to children, parents and workers alike.
>
> (Wattam *et al.* 1989: 66–7)

The message is clear: debating theory is dangerous. It is 'self-evidently' so. When evidence to support a contention is dispensed with, the wary reader will ask, why? Debate undermines certainty; and certainty is what is required.

Responding to the demand for certainty

Since Cleveland, the tenor of the writings, from whichever point of view, has been a response to the demand for certainty about what to do. The desire for certainty in child protection is very well put by Stevenson: 'social workers . . . understandably, crave certainty in an uncertain and stressful area of work. We are not yet at a stage when such certainties (as evidenced in Dale *et al.* 1986) are sustainable' (Stevenson 1989: 172).

But Stevenson suggests that theoretical positions, particularly when polarized or assertively pressed, are of little benefit to practitioners who may seize upon them and apply them uncritically. This argument ignores the existence of theory as a constant underpinning to action. The danger here is that actions become harder to challenge and to evaluate, surely posing a greater threat of uncritical application. For example Stevenson herself does not recognize the implicit theory in her account each time she refers to 'parents' without acknowledging the different relationships of women and men to children, to each other, and to abuse (Stevenson 1989: 155, 171).

A further example of theory masked in apparent neutrality is to be found in use of the newly invoked term 'child-centred', which has been adopted by the NSPCC and other writers to describe their approach to explanation and practice, and to differentiate it from family dysfunction ideas. Let us scrutinize the term. It is not neutral, though it is being peddled as such. When an approach to work is called by a name to which every right-minded person would agree, it claims for itself the moral and theoretical highground by a sleight of hand rather than by demonstration and argument, and suggests, by implication, that other approaches are wanting. Who would wish to argue with a child-centred approach? Well, we want to know more than that. We want to know what this means in practice and what research and theory inform it. What assumptions lie behind it about the causation of abuse, and about the nature of men's, women's and children's relationships?

One 'source' of the so-called child-centred approach is the work of Miller

(1987). 'It is worth noting, too, that the theories of sexual abuse which do exist (with the exception of Alice Miller's work) are theories written from the adult point of view, rather than based on children's own experience' (Wattam *et al.* 1989: 66). But Miller, like all theorists, invokes meaning and ascribes it to children's experience; a critique exists of her conception of childhood (see Scott 1988). It is neither neutral nor uncontentious. When children can begin theorizing their own experience we shall be happy to call such an approach child centred; in the meantime we listen to what children tell us and we try to take a critical approach to the meanings we invoke for what they say. Of course, children's needs and rights must be put first. But it is not a simple matter to know what children's needs are in the long or the short term. Even less is it easy to produce the correct strategies through which to intervene to meet their needs: if only it were.

Far from being dangerous, theoretical debate is essential if we are to be able to explore the complex areas of judgement involved when the state intervenes in children's lives. Danger arises when the theory underpinning an approach is not made explicit and thus available to criticism. Strategies then make their appearance as 'common sense', as 'procedures', as 'clinical/practice experience'.

Identifying the theoretical substructure, examining it critically, debating theoretical differences, are not the sterile blocks to progress in the development of practice O'Hagan suggests, but its very lifeblood. Consensus may be comfortable, but without criticism and debate we lose opportunities to see things differently and to work differently. There is no place for an embargo on debate within the public response to child abuse; nor need we be apologetic about disagreements: they have frequently led to new insights. In this chapter we propose to continue the process of scrutiny, and to continue the elaboration of a feminist approach to child sexual abuse because we remain convinced that addressing the question 'why?' is an imperative part of developing a public response.

The public construction of CSA and its impact on practice

The craving for certainty has had an impact on the development of policy and practice. It is felt by front-line social workers and, perhaps more so, by the public. It arises from the desire to get things right for children, and from the way child protection work has been viewed in the public domain, manifested through the press reporting on child abuse, and the inquiries into child deaths and the Cleveland affair.

The day after the Cleveland Report (Butler-Sloss 1988) was published, Phillips (1988) described the 'vacuum' at the centre of the report: that is the report did not tell us how many children were sexually abused and how many were not. In assuming that such information could be known, she was continuing a discourse long established in the reports of commissions of inquiry. For example Blom-Cooper's report on the death of Jasmine Beckford states that Jasmine's death 'was both a predictable and preventible homicide' (London Borough of Brent 1985: 287). The reports of many inquiries since suggest that sound social work practice, in a good framework of procedure, with appropriate use of legal intervention can do this. This entirely takes for granted that we have the knowledge and the art to prevent abuse of children – all that is required is to apply it properly.

The acceptance that something can be done has led to the process of medicalization, legalization and management of child protection work. This trend had developed into an avalanche of policies, procedures, instruction manuals, and guidelines in the period since Cleveland (Department of Health 1988; 1989a; 1989b; DHSS 1988a; 1988b; 1988c) which have made it much harder to be creative, to take risks of one sort (but not of another), to think of different ways of working, or to adapt to individual circumstances, encouraging the growth of a desire for rules and categories. Child sexual abuse, particularly, has become something to be diagnosed and treated, to be 'comprehensively categorised' (O'Hagan 1989a: 13).

These ideas are not theoretically neutral. They assume that abuse is produced by particular family, individual and situational factors. This leads to a belief in the existence of a definable set of circumstances which are predictive, a recognizable set of signs and symptoms which can be found, and a determined series of effects of abuse which can be treated. The worker's task then becomes to learn the signs and symptoms, the risk factors, the likely outcomes and apply the knowledge *in situ*. It is as if child sexual abuse were a disease, like cancer, where the variety of whose forms can be recorded and measured, alongside the impact upon the cancer of the medicine or surgery prescribed. But, as Glasgow says, 'child sexual abuse is not a diagnosis' (1989: 141) and sexual assault is not a syndrome requiring treatment. It is an experience which children can be helped to survive. A lexicon of child sexual assault to which social workers could run and consult in order to find the appropriate action plan for 'victim/aged 4/exhibitionism/stepfather/mother unsuspecting', would condemn children to prescription rather than assistance or therapy. Prescriptions deskill workers, turning them into technicians rather than professionals. Successful helping is as much an art, relying on imagination, skill and thought, as it is anything else.

This is not to argue against research, against outcome studies examining the impact of a variety of interventions, or against appropriate public scrutiny of child protection policy and practice. It is an argument against the production of theory, policy and practice as a defence against anxiety instead of as an analysis of what is known about abuse and its context. The outcome of this state of affairs is dismal for children and families, when discredited ideas continue to influence the ways in which help is offered to them, and increasingly children's cries for help are 'real' only if they take place in a disclosure interview which is being video-recorded.

That the picture is not more grim is due in great part to the strengths of individual children, women and men who find ways to face up to and struggle with abuse and its consequences; and to the practice of those least respected of people, the social workers, who struggle to offer help to troubled people despite the constraints of resources, policy, procedure and practice theory. One of the very depressing aspects of the training work we do is the despair of the workers faced with these constraints, yet burdened with the sense of responsibility to 'manage' the whole business, with which the crisis in child protection endows them. They describe their experience of finding issues different from what theory had led them to expect, resources inappropriate or inadequate, support absent, and urgency placed on the technicalities of managing disclosure rather than offering succour and comfort. They are overflowing with ideas for improving the work. They have little say, though, in the development of practice theory, policy or procedure. That is the sphere of the politicians and the professional lobbies.

Into any attempt to tackle such problems comes politics, at two levels (at least): one, the way the problem is described or defined; the other, the solutions which can be undertaken. This leads to obfuscation for political ends, and restriction of solutions to those which do not upend the balance of power at all levels of 'interest' in the problem. This is as true of sexual violence as it is of the hole in the ozone layer or the nation's health: ideology intrudes.

The ideological battleground

Any serious attempt to explore why children get abused in families forces attention on to the nature of family life and the nature of relationships between men, women and children inside and outside families. The grossness and extremity of the misconduct taking place when a child is sexually abused is such that it magnifies aspects of the relationship between gender, sexuality, age and power which are less overt, less noticeable, even entirely acceptable elsewhere. As we have argued elsewhere (MacLeod and Saraga 1988b), it is only because these aspects exist in completely acceptable forms that the extremities of misconduct can exist.

It is this aspect of a feminist analysis of child sexual abuse which has raised most animus in public and professional spheres. In raising questions about the adequacy of professional policy and practice, in offering a considered critique of highly influential ideas which were dominating practice, but especially in placing child sexual abuse in its context of sexual violence and posing the questions about masculinity suggested by doing so, feminists were decried for splitting the professional consensus at a time of professional difficulty and causing 'unnecessary conflict' (Bentovim 1988: 29); even causing 'Cleveland' (Anderson 1988; Ingrams 1988; O'Hagan 1989b). 'Cleveland demonstrated the disastrous and inevitable consequences of a half-baked child sexual abuse strategy clearly based on extreme feminist views' (O'Hagan 1989b: 98).

In fact the practice in Cleveland, as even the main protagonists made clear, had little to do with feminist ideas (though press reporting made this connection again and again); but a lot to do with a set of ideas which located the cause of sexual abuse in pathological family dynamics, leading to the notion that families, not abusers, abuse children. In an astounding distortion of events, the real culprits in 'Cleveland' become not the men who abuse children, not the policies which see children as unsafe with their families, but feminist ideas. A small skirmish in the ideological battle, pointing to the unacceptability of raising questions about the 'normal', the 'ordinary', and particularly about masculinity.

We continue to find in the literature that what is offered as explanation disguises, hides or exonerates. It remains problematic to identify and gender abusers. Because ideology operates at the level of the implicit, the taken for granted, discovering its influence depends on a scrutiny of language to allow us to see the theory lying behind the apparently neutral sheen of description and advice. The press on Cleveland demonstrated exactly what we mean; there were families and parents, but rarely fathers, despite the fact that only one alleged perpetrator was a woman. Clinical accounts and expert advice on policy and practice are not different. Suddenly a world that is completely unapologetic about using masculine pronouns as generic terms, studiously avoids them, showing a remarkable reluctance to attach a gender to the abuser.

A scrutiny of more recent texts, including the Department of Health's (1988) recent guidance on assessment, *Protecting Children*, demonstrates that family dysfunction ideas are alive and well, not in the gross forms we have been used to but in a more subtle variety: parents are not differentiated, abusers are not gendered, and the terms 'sexually abusive families' or 'abusing families' are in constant use to describe the families of children who have been abused, as if the family is abusive, not the abuser. A recent NSPCC occasional paper has as its title: *Breaking the Habit: The Need for a Comprehensive Long-Term Treatment for Sexually Abusing Families* (Fawcett 1989: 2).

In recent writings, new forms of disguise emerge, for example 'sexually abusive situations' (Violence Against Children Study Group 1990: 188). Here an event, the actual abuse, is transformed into a situation, an act becomes its context. When these terms are used the implications are clear: it is the family or the situation, not the abuser who abuses the child.

Why should this be a problem? First, and most importantly, because it implicitly conveys a meaning which confuses responsibility for the abuse. Berliner and Conte (1990) write of the difficulty child victims have in believing just how calculated were the actions of their abusers; the discourse of explanation must not comply with 'ideology of abuse' to which children and their mothers have been exposed. The explanation which sufferers take from the theory and the discourse of helping has a considerable influence on what they are able to do about the abuse and how they feel about themselves.

Second, rejecting the importance of gender – an aspect of abuse which raises feelings of acute discomfort among women and men – denies workers the opportunity of examining the impact of their feelings on practice. Alarmingly attention is focused only on some aspects of worker's personal 'business' with the issue. Again and again texts carefully make reference to the complications (as they see it) for worker's practice should they have been abused in childhood (Richards 1989; Wattam *et al.* 1989; O'Hagan 1989b). The likely complications occasioned should the worker have been or be an abuser are not mentioned, far less the problems caused should the worker be someone who regularly sexually harasses others or views pornography or pressures partners into unwanted sex. About these silence reigns.

Third, placing a heavy emphasis on the family/situation rather than the abuser limits the search for solutions. For example guidelines and textbooks lay great emphasis on reconstituting families; yet most workers and therapists write of their pessimism at the likelihood of this happening (Bentovim *et al.* 1988: 255, 256; Wattam *et al.* 1989: 76). Why persist? Or, at the very least, why not debate the question?

Reclaiming the story

Feminism's most important contribution to policy and practice on child abuse is its concern with ideology and its emphasis on the importance of meaning. This contribution is not mere polemic, but concrete suggestions for every level of intervention: conducting case conferences and investigations; handling what to say to whom at what point; making decisions about strategy; understanding and taking account of the impact of racism and of cultural difference in planning appropriate interventions and carrying them out; and developing an understanding of those feelings and attitudes which constitute workers' emotional business with the issue, thus enhancing 'the capacity to manage within oneself the inherent and essential ambivalence engendered by the (at times) conflicting needs' (Stevenson 1989: 171). These conflicting needs being those of what Stevenson calls 'parents and children', and we prefer to call mothers, fathers and children.

At a conference in Glasgow in 1988, a leading clinician, Kee McFarlane, was asked how she responded when children asked her, 'Why did he do it?' The reply she normally gives is 'Because you were there'. Consider the message conveyed. Perhaps there is no answer to that question: but if one is to be hazarded why not 'Because he was there'? We suggest that answer is not given because 'he' is not the subject of this story, this explanation. Whose story is told by the theory in turn defines the meaning that sufferers take for what has happened to them. As this example demonstrates, explanation influences the words that workers use, and the messages conveyed to those involved. For many people, as for the child described above, 'Why?' is an anguished cry: 'Why? Why me?' The feeling of defeat, felt in the face of the question, is very well put in the novel *The Bluest Eye*: 'There is nothing more to say – except why. But since *why* is difficult to handle, one must take refuge in *how*' (Morrison 1981: 9, emphasis in original).

If we are to take responsibility for the proper care of abused children, we cannot make do simply with 'how': the 'why' has to be tackled. Otherwise we are doomed merely to take abuse for granted. We have to start with the evidence (quite unequivocal despite the recent hunts through the clinics to 'discover' the hidden hordes of female abusers) that it is overwhelmingly men who abuse sexually.

But first, let us be clear, what a feminist perspective does not say is that only men abuse sexually, that abuse by women is less serious, or that it requires another set of explanations. Nor does it say that women are better than men; simply that they are 'bad' or 'good' in different ways. Because one group has more power they have more opportunity to be 'bad'; opportunity is a not inconsiderable part of the production of 'wrongdoing', but not all of it; the desire, motivation, means and will remain to be explained. What it does say is that gender must be taken into account in any theory which purports to explain the sexual abuse of children.

The question 'why' can be asked at several different levels and in different ways: Why did he do it? Why did he do it to me? Why does sexual abuse occur at all? Why is it overwhelmingly men who sexually abuse? Why is the abuse sexual rather than physical violence? Furthermore, why is sexual abuse of women and children commonly associated with other forms of domination and subjugation of communities and peoples in slavery, war, colonialism and racism? Why is it allowed to continue? What are the ideological and material forces that sanction, legitimize and encourage sexual abuse?

The answers to these questions are obviously related. We spell them out to show that the answers must be complex. Answers at different levels must be compatible. For example answers in terms of family dysfunction or individual pathology do not provide an explanation at the broader social or global level. Similarly answers in terms of patriarchy may provide a framework, but not an explanation at the individual level.

Dissatisfaction with explanations in terms of individual pathology or family dysfunction has led, in the literature, to either an avoidance of the question, or the substitution of description or correlation for explanation. We can see the appeal of the idea of addiction as a way of describing the compulsive nature of abusive behaviour, yet it is not an explanation, and raises as many questions as it answers. To say that 'sexual abuse is an abuse of male power' is also a description, albeit a more acceptable one, but it is not an explanation. It does not begin to look at why power was abused, and why it was abused in a particular way.

In a similar fashion, the argument that the majority of abusers were themselves abused is not an explanation. Being abused is not a *cause* of abuse. The majority of victims of sexual abuse are girls and yet little sexual abuse is perpetrated by women (La Fontaine 1990: 86, 105). Thus most women and many men who were abused do not go on to be abusers, and not all abusers were previously victims of abuse. This does not mean the experience was irrelevant – for some men it may be part of a process of surviving the abuse through acting out. We need to analyse that process, and consider why this rarely occurs for women.

Finkelhor's multi-factor theory involving motivation, overcoming internal and external inhibitions, and overcoming the child's resistance, claims to incorporate influences at several of the levels we have identified (Finkelhor 1984). But the child who did not resist, or the 'mother' who did not protect, should not be part of an explanation. This may tell you 'how'; it does not tell you 'why'. While resistance or protection may have been nonexistent or ineffective, they do not account for the abuse.

An explanation must include a number of elements: the opportunity to abuse, the motivation or desire, the objectification of the victim and a set of beliefs that make it legitimate. These are all constructed within a social structure of power inequalities, and ideologies of childhood, femininity and masculinity.

Opportunity includes the physical power to abuse that all adults have in relation to children, emotional power to entrap children, to confuse them and overcome their resistance (through enlisting their love, trust and lack of knowledge and understanding of sexuality); and the privacy which all carers, particularly parents, are likely to have. But opportunity is not enough: not all adults abuse children.

The motivation for sexual abuse has been variously described as sexual desire, domination or aggression; it may in particular cases be any or all of these. Furthermore, the abuser's conscious motivation may give few clues to its true nature. We have argued elsewhere (MacLeod and Saraga 1988b) that boys grow up learning to experience their sexuality as a driving force, powerful, capable of being used to dominate and control, and of being felt as out of their control.

These feelings are fortified by a set of beliefs about the meaning of the desires that are experienced; about the nature of sexuality; and about children. We do not think that the beliefs or the feelings are created by pornography, though they may be legitimized and sanctioned by it. Of course, the rationalizations and excuses that abusers put forward may not be what they actually believe – although it is easy to persuade oneself of the truth of one's own rationalizations. We know that abusers understand it is wrong because they persuade, coerce or threaten children into secrecy. The currently fashionable description of abusers as addicted may reinforce rather than challenge their notion of being out of control. Abusers' beliefs (like those of professionals) do not arise in a vacuum. They arise within an ideology of masculinity that relates power to sexuality, encourages young men to 'sow their wild oats', making men who feel powerless or inadequate seek to redress this through domination and abuse of women and children. In describing inadequate men as having 'no balls', a clear message is given about what male adequacy is.

In order to abuse it is necessary to objectify one's victim, to diminish her or him in every way, to ignore pain and suffering. Objectification is applauded within 'normal' male sexuality, when 'getting your rocks off' is used to describe making love. Here also a scrutiny of language reveals the assumptions about sexuality which men imbibe from the culture. Though feminists are attacked for these accounts of male sexuality, we see them all the time in judges' comments on abuse and rape cases, in press coverage, and in cultural expectations of women and men. Most people want to retain the image of masculinity as powerful, objective, and unemotional but object to the idea that the price for this may be sexual abuse. Images of femininity as peace-loving and tender, which lead some critics of Thatcher to describe her as a pseudo-man, are especially misleading. We are not arguing that all violence is masculine; we know that women can be and are cruel, physically violent and ruthless. But it remains the case that they rarely sexually abuse.

We have not provided the kind of answer (looked for by professionals and the public) that would allow one to identify actual or potential abusers. For women, the inability to identify abusers raises terrifying questions about their partners, fathers, their own sons. It is difficult to love someone and at the same time live with constant suspicion. For men a different set of questions are raised: 'Could I do this?' 'How can I prove that I'm not an abuser?' These fears cannot be allayed by providing false solutions or simplistic answers; responses that allow us to distance ourselves from the abuse, nor by attacking theory and looking for procedures or categories.

We need to develop these questions and answers further, to foster research which looks at why some men abuse and others don't, and why men and women are likely to abuse in different ways. If we argue the power of ideology in the development of personality and behaviour, then it follows that sexual violence may be the vehicle for expressing acute distress, anger or pathology. This can then be used by men and women, although the route by which they come to this particular abuse of power is likely to be different as is its meaning to them. Thus sexual abuse will happen to a child within a number of different contexts and it will always be important to establish the problems within family relationships in order to help; but it confuses everyone very seriously if we lay responsibility for the abuse on the difficulties of the family.

Theorizing which takes no account of gender is not confined to family dysfunction theorists, for example the line taken by the anti-state-intervention theorists of the left in social work, like Holman (1988) and N. Parton (1985), who wrote about the family without analysing gender and generational differences, and the impact of racism on them. Holman (1988) reviewed the history of prevention in child care without a mention of the refuge movement. Parton (1985), as he now concedes, offered no analysis of gender and throughout viewed the family as monolithic. The changes in the positions of Parton and Parton in their recent chapters (Stevenson 1989: ch. 3; Violence Against Children Study Group 1990: ch. 1) is part of a broad rethinking of theory in response to feminist and black critiques. Parton now concedes that a class analysis is insufficient to account for abuse, that gender must be included and argues that the key is adult–child power relations. But this leads to another disconcerting plunge away from analysis and into unreality, because the power differences between adults and children are of a different nature from those between men and women. There are severe limits to the possibilities of 'empowerment' of children as a tool for dealing with child sexual abuse.

Retelling the practice

Contrary to the usual critiques which assert the impracticality of feminist ideas, they are intensely practical. Even writers like C. Parton, who describe themselves as feminist, though acknowledging the development of a feminist-based practice within the statutory sector as well as outside, write of these ideas posing 'enormous problems for statutory agencies and individual workers' (Violence Against Children Study Group 1990: 56). Her subsequent description of feminist practice concentrates on support to the mother–child bond. And if feminist practice amounts only to a series of injunctions to support mother and child, it offers little indeed and can only be frustrating to workers who ask for 'a coherent position on the role and responsibility of mothers' as 'critical to effective *management* of child sexual abuse cases, especially because the mother's response is so vital to the children's subsequent recovery'

(Wattam *et al.* 1989: 67, emphasis added); and who think that 'learning to work effectively with mothers who do not, or cannot, believe that their children have been sexually abused, is the biggest and most critical challenge facing workers' (Wattam *et al.* 1989: 72).

Let us examine the practicality of current practice in its management of child sexual abuse cases. A great deal of child protection case conference time is still spent on the woman who is mother to sexually abused children: asking the question is she a 'colluding' mother? Or, perhaps less overtly: did she know what was 'going on'? An ominous echo is the preoccupation of earlier social workers with whether their clients were deserving or undeserving. A rule of thumb is evolved to distinguish those accessible to help from those who are not. As if once the question 'Did she know?' were answered then a clear light would shine through the gloom of confusion and we would know what to do.

What feminism offers here is not a clear light or a rule of thumb, but a different way of understanding what can be observed, of thinking about what to do and what to say, which will place workers in a 'dynamic' rather than a static position. Of course, as feminists have predicted and practitioners have found, if you assume that the abuse serves a function for a family, that the woman's interests are served by it, that she colluded with it or indeed aided and abetted it, you are likely to push her into an alliance with her partner against you, against the agency and against her own and her child's interests. The intervention brings about the very dynamic about which we have heard so much. Recognition of this is nicely demonstrated in O'Hagan's (1989b), coming at the question from anything but a feminist perspective.

It may be that the abuse, in the short term, made things easier for a mother (making it less likely that her partner would physically or sexually assault her or other children), and that discovery makes things worse. This does not mean that she knew about the abuse, or wanted it to be happening at any level. The proverb 'it is an ill wind that brings no one any good' sums up easily what child sexual abuse experts seem to find perplexing: even really destructive things can have, or appear to have, 'positive' outcomes. Discovering an 'outcome' does not mean you have found the 'cause'. This kind of slipshod theorizing is dangerous. Yet it continues to enjoy respectability and to have a profound impact on practice.

If it is rejected in favour of a different reading of the 'mother's' position, it becomes possible to understand that such a woman is likely to be in shock, experiencing the kinds of feelings we recognize from our knowledge of bereavement work. She is experiencing a major assault on her identity as a woman, as a partner, possibly as a member of her community, culture, religion, her extended family, and perhaps most of all as a mother. These kinds of things, after all do not happen to the children of good mothers, do they? It's a contradiction in terms (Byerly 1989).

If this leads us away from anger, suspicion and blame and towards a clear understanding that the abuse is not her fault, we will see that someone in shock is highly unlikely to be able to make decisions and assume responsibility, and will question procedures which rely on her doing so. We grasp that disbelief is an aspect of shock, and that moving from disbelief to belief is a process to which we can usefully – and sensitively – contribute. And finally, we can recognize that some carers will never be able to believe, or may take a very long time getting there, and thus workers will have to make judgements about what this means for their children's emotional recovery. The process of disbelief and denial which we describe here for 'mothers' is similar to that experienced by fathers, siblings, and other non-abusive relatives (Cochrane 1988). The practice that follows is also similar.

Our expectations of mothers are absurdly unrealistic. If we say clearly to such a woman: 'It is true; it is serious; your partner or husband was very wrong; but whatever you have done, this is not your fault and I am not holding you responsible', we demonstrate that denial is not a way through, nor is minimizing what has happened, nor is blaming her child; we also demonstrate that we do not hold her to blame for the abuse. Affording her the respect she is due as the parent of a troubled child, attempting to be alive to pressures under which she is suffering, alive to the impact on her culture, religion and family circumstances, and even explicating for her what is known about abusers and how they operate, about the impact of abuse on children, their mothers and siblings, all would be very appropriate strategies for workers to assume. Why is it never supposed that parents require training in handling child sexual abuse, when everyone else is assumed to need it? Many authorities who have set up groups for women in this position are now finding that they have an invaluable resource willing and wanting to help other women (Neate 1990).

This approach does not preclude the possibility of some women 'collaborating' in the abuse of children: it does not assume it as a starting-point. We have elsewhere outlined in detail the extent of the mother-blaming in the literature on incest (MacLeod and Saraga 1988b). From Kempe and Kempe (1978), who had never seen an innocent mother, through twenty years of the writing of clinicians, to the key practice texts by Sgroi (1982) and the British clinicians, and to Dale (1984), who states confidently that 'The couple act as one in the abuse of the child . . . the "failure to protect" behaviour of the partner with the passive role is at least as crucial and pathological as the role of the aggressor' (Dale 1984: 21). Maternal responsibility seems inescapable. Not only are these ideas to be found among those who work directly from a family dysfunction theoretical stand, but also they are in the textbooks of other approaches to work in this field, for example psychoanalysis: 'the evolution of an incest situation goes through many stages . . . very often the process begins with the wife refusing to have sex with her husband' (Weldon 1988: 134), and are enshrined in government guidelines and the Cleveland Report (Butler-Sloss 1988).

The critique outlined above emerges from a tradition which critically examines both the position of women in every aspect of their lives, and the ideology supporting it. Rejecting the mother-blaming, establishing the circumstances which do not cause abuse enables a change in practice direction of enormous importance to children. We know from research and from the testimony of adult and child sufferers of abuse, that being believed by their mother at the time (or later) is, more than anything else, important to them in finding a way through the trauma (Gelinas 1983). That is why we persist in offering the critique and in asking why abuse occurs, not because we are consumed with antagonism towards family therapy (O'Hagan 1989a). We wish to expose theories or explanations which influence intervention, or non-intervention, into the lives of vulnerable women and children, black and white, but which do not take account of their lived experience, and its meaning for them. Such explanations effectively silence them about their rights and needs. We also wish to pose questions about abuse and why it happens. There is no straightforward and immediate answer to these questions. But asking 'Why?', continuing to ask 'Why?', and rejecting the falsehoods, the hypocrisies and the bad faith associated with some explanations is essential to the practice of social work.

First, because surviving abuse involves a struggle to find meaning. That is nowhere better demonstrated than in the work of the Italian writer, survivor of the holocaust, Primo Levi (1988). How professionals render incest explicable is enormously important in constructing the meaning that survivors find for the abuse. People need to be free to explore the meaning for them safe in the boundary of their experience and memories.

Second, asking 'Why?' is important because work with abusers, if it is to be effective, demands that we try to understand why they abuse. Already work with abusers in the USA, and now in the UK at the Gracewell Clinic in Birmingham, has benefited from an approach which recognizes the place of ideology in constructing abusive acts (Morrison 1989).

Third, such questions are essential if we are to find ways of helping to prevent abuse. Children can learn to say no until the cows come home, but until men stop abusing them sexually, abuse will continue. Whether we like it or not, prevention has to mean intervening in the way that boys learn to be sexual and use their sexuality, and providing good mental health services for children. (*Childline*'s success is that it is the only mental health service open to children to use. We ought to be able to be more creative in our response to children's difficulties.)

Fourth, an emphasis on meaning and its importance allows us to explore the impact of culture, class, religion and racism on sufferers and their families, so that we can ask the questions we need to ask when offering help. The literature on child sexual abuse is chilling in its emptiness on the impact of culture and racism – though these have an influence on every aspect of the experience of sufferers. Though we cannot, indeed must not, make definite predictions about their impact on people, we need to be alive to all the possibilities without limiting the options we make available to people on the basis of our assumptions about the choices they feel are open to them. The best way we know of doing this is asking: 'I wonder whether . . .?' 'I may be quite mistaken but . . .' 'I am guessing that . . . but perhaps I've got it wrong . . .'

Fifth, such questions are important for workers. They enable us to take account of the impact of our gender, our colour, our culture, religion and class on the people we aspire to help, to discover the feelings we might engender in those we try to help and the difficulties we might represent for them. An explanation which takes account of gender enables us to acknowledge that men and women have some different relationships with this issue. This breaks a silence, enabling us to explore the feelings aroused in us, and considering the nature of our emotional business. If we are women, is our business to deny our anger or to vent it? To abuse the perpetrator or to defend him? To protect ourselves from anxiety about our children and the men we love, or to expose every abuser? For men, can we listen to anger at abusers and men, or is our business to prove that we are not abusers? Is this our vehicle, for the expression of violent feelings by proxy? Can we bear it that we cannot rescue sufferers and make it better?

Finally, asking 'Why?' enables us to question what is done in the name of welfare. Take, for example, the recommendations of the Pigot Report that parental consent to the videotaping of children's interviews should not be required (Home Office 1989). This reveals astounding blindness to the possible meanings which children might take from the experience (linking it with their experiences of pornography), disregard for the likely feelings of children, and lack of consideration of the question of access to the videotape. The rush towards the establishment of technical aids to the conviction of abusers – necessitated in part by the low value placed by courts on children's evidence – does not take account of meaning, leads to the taking of hasty decisions and, arguably, a reduction in civil liberties.

It would be dangerous to give up the debate or to lapse into a discreet and decorous silence in the belief that things have changed. Earlier we indicated how extensive is the influence of the notion that sexual abuse is a product of family problems. Indeed in our view, the increasingly coercive nature of child protection practice can be traced to the predominance of these ideas in this political climate, when the 'normal' family is romanticized, mythologized, ikonized, and the tenor of more and more press reporting is the sanctification of one form of 'family' about which no uncomfortable questions must be posed.

When we talk about family, or family rights, whose privacy and liberties are we talking about (Gordon 1989)? Gordon's historical study of child protection work in one American town, showing as it does how theory and explanation have a profound impact on welfare practice (because what we do comes from what we 'see' and what we 'see' comes from how we explain) demonstrates that 'family' is not an unproblematic concept. Family organization benefits some members to the detriment of others, and state intervention – and the theory underpinning it – privileges some forms of family organization.

Though we have acknowledged that there are no easy answers, we have argued the importance of clearing a path through the undergrowth in order to expose false answers, to suggest a different starting-point for inquiry, and to discover the remaining questions. We do this not in the hope of achieving certainty, but to establish clarity.

References

Anderson, D. (1988) 'Abusing the family', *The Times* 8 June: 13.
Bentovim, A. (1988) 'Who is to blame?', *New Statesman and Society* 5 August: 29.

Bentovim, A., Elton, A., Hildebrand, J., Tranter, M. and Vigard, E. (eds) (1988) *Child Sexual Abuse within the Family: Assessment and Treatment*, London: Wright.

Berliner, L. and Conte, J. (1990) 'The process of victimization: the victim's perspective', *Child Abuse and Neglect* 14, 1: 29–40.

Butler-Sloss, E. (1988) *Report of the Inquiry into Child Abuse in Cleveland 1987*, Cm 412, London: HMSO.

Byerly, C. M. (1989) *The Mother's Book*, Dubuque, Iowa: Kendall Hunt.

Cochrane, S. (1988) 'Torn apart at home', *New Statesman and Society* 1 July: 21–5.

Dale, P. (1984) 'The danger within ourselves', *Community Care* 1 March: 20–2.

Dale, P., Davies, M., Morrison, T. and Waters, J. (1986) *Dangerous Families*, London: Tavistock.

Department of Health (1988) *Protecting Children: A Guide to Social Workers Undertaking a Comprehensive Assessment*, London: HMSO.

—— (1989a) *Working with Child Abuse: Guidelines for Training Social Services Staff*, London: Department of Health.

—— (1989b) *The Care of Children: Principles and Practice in Regulations and Guidance*, London: HMSO.

DHSS (1988a) *Child Protection Guidance for Senior Nurses, Health Visitors and Midwives*, London: HMSO.

—— (1988b) *Diagnosis of Child Sexual Abuse: Guidance for Doctors*, London: HMSO.

—— (1988c) *Working Together: A Guide to Arrangements for Interagency Co-operation for the Protection of Children from Abuse*, London: HMSO.

Fawcett, J. (1989) *Breaking the Habit: The Need for a Comprehensive Long-Term Treatment for Sexually Abusing Families*, Occasional Papers Series 7, London: NSPCC.

Finkelhor, D. (1984) *Child Sexual Abuse: New Theory and Research*, New York: The Free Press.

Gelinas, D. J. (1983) 'The persisting negative effects of incest', *Psychiatry* 46: 312–22.

Glasgow, D. (1989) 'Play-based investigative assessment of children who have been sexually abused', in C. Wattam, J. Hughes and H. Blagg (eds) (1989) *Child Sexual Abuse*, Harlow, Longman.

Gordon, L. (1989) *Heroes of their Own Lives*, London: Virago.

Holman, B. (1988) *Putting Families First: Prevention and Child Care*, London: Macmillan.

Home Office (1989) *Report of the Advisory Group on Video Evidence*, Pigot Report, London: HMSO.

Ingrams, R. (1988) 'Richard Ingrams', *Observer* 2 July: 18.

Kempe, R. S. and Kempe, C. H. (1978) *Child Abuse*, London: Fontana/Open Books.

La Fontaine, J. (1990) *Child Sexual Abuse*, Cambridge: Polity Press.

Levi, P. (1988) *The Drowned and the Saved*, London: Sphere.

London Borough of Brent (1985) *A Child in Trust: The Report of the Panel of Inquiry into the Circumstances Surrounding the Death of Jasmine Beckford*, London: Borough of Brent.

MacLeod, M. and Saraga, E. (1988a) 'Against orthodoxy', *New Statesman and Society* 1 July: 15–18.

—— (1988b) 'Challenging the orthodoxy: towards a feminist theory and practice', *Feminist Review* 28: 16–55.

Miller, A. (1987) *For Your Own Good: The Roots of Violence in Childrearing*, London: Virago.

Morrison, T. (1981) *The Bluest Eye*, London: Triad Grafton.

—— (1989) *Treating the Untreatable: Group Work with Intra-familial Sex Offenders*, Occasional Paper Series 7, London: NSPCC.

Neate, P. (1990) 'Mother's little helper', *Community Care* 12 July: 16–18.

O'Hagan, K. (1989a) 'Split decisions prevent progress', *Community Care* 9 March: 13.
—— (1989b) *Working with Child Sexual Abuse*, Milton Keynes: Open University Press.
Parton, N. (1985) *The Politics of Child Abuse*, London: Macmillan.
Phillips, M. (1988) 'The wrong and the wronged', *Guardian* 8 July: 21.
Richards, M. (1989) *Key Issues in Child Sexual Abuse: Some Lessons from Cleveland*, London: National Institute of Social Work.
Scott, A. (1988) 'Feminism and the seductiveness of the "real event"', *Feminist Review* 28: 88–102.
Sgroi, S. (1982) *Handbook of Clinical Intervention in Child Sexual Abuse*, New York: Lexington Books.
Stevenson, O. (1989) *Child Abuse: Public Policy and Professional Practice*, London: Harvester Wheatsheaf.
Violence Against Children Study Group (1990) *Taking Child Abuse Seriously*, London: Unwin Hyman.
Wattam, C., Hughes, J. and Blagg, H. (eds) (1989) *Child Sexual Abuse*, Harlow: Longman.
Weldon, E. (1988) *Mother, Madonna, Whore*, London: Free Association Books.

4
A new model for child care

Andrew Kerslake and Julia Cramp

In 1985 the Department of Health and Social Security published a controversial report bringing together a range of research studies which criticized child care practice by local authority social services departments. The report, *Social Work Decision-Making in Child Care*, was originally intended for an internal DHSS audience, but, as it comments in the introduction, 'the contents inevitably indicated a need to make it available to a much wider audience' (DHSS 1985: 2). It went on to state that 'the accumulative evidence of these 9 reports is weighty and convincing . . . it has to be said that the scene portrayed is generally quite disturbing and depressing' (DHSS 1985: 5). Below are listed some of the main findings of the report.

1 Parents who request care for their children are 'put through hoops' in an effort to prevent admission and if admission is refused, few services are offered.
2 Social workers consider themselves primarily responsible for most decisions about admission to care but are often under strong pressure from outside agencies or from the children's families.
3 Most decisions are made rapidly and often in crisis. As a result admissions are not well planned.
4 Far less attention is given to what is to happen after admission than to whether or not to admit and if children stay long in care, social work attention fades.
5 Discharge or remaining in care is not usually the result of social work planning.

Given these results it was with some interest that we accepted a commission from a voluntary organization to complete a new study of admission to care in one area of a local authority. This was followed by two further pieces of research. Our work was designed to focus on decision-making in admission to care and how the results could influence the development of social services departments' (SSDs') child care strategies. The results, as we hope to illustrate, portray not only a continuance of problems in child care practice, but also, if anything, a slightly more disturbing picture than original DHSS research.

The studies

The three studies were conducted between August 1986 and June 1987 and examined child care cases from 1985 onwards. In Seaside and Newtown the research concerned only children aged 10 and over. The two studies used the same research methods once all children admitted to care during a period of a year had been identified. The two routes used to obtain information were first, a detailed file search, and second, an interview with the social worker responsible for each child admitted to care. In the file search basic information was extracted, including how long the child was known before admission occurred, whether any alternatives were tried in an attempt to avoid the admission and where the child was initially placed. In Innercity, the study was of more limited duration and included children of all ages. A file search of a sample of cases where children had been admitted to care between 1985 and 1987 was undertaken and this was backed up by discussions with social work managers and specialist workers.

It should be stated that we are aware of some of the limitations to our work. We did not interview parents and children, conduct visits with social workers or look very closely at work with children who were not admitted to care. This was not only due to the specifications of the funding agencies, but also because our central concerns were with social workers' official actions and the question of whether and how the basics of child care legislation and policy were being implemented.

The route to care

An effective child care system is one in which decisions are made on the basis of accurate information. Many authorities, including Seaside, Newtown and Innercity collect statistics only on the numbers of children received into care under their respective legal categories. While such information enables the authority to provide the Department of Health with their annual returns, it does little to enable resource planning. There is also a possibility that legal categories reflect what legal recourse is open to the social worker rather than the reason for admission. In our file search we started by trying to ascertain the actual reason for admission. Such information is obviously essential if resources are to be targeted towards problems.

Table 4.1 shows that the main reason for admission to care is the breakdown of family relationships and communication, that is the beyond parental control and abuse/neglect groups. Therefore the problems presented pre-care are not intangible but are directly related to the problem-solving expectations that might be made of social workers in SSDs. However, it is vital to ascertain the

Table 4.1   Category on entry to care

Category	Number of admissions		
	Seaside (all admissions)	Newtown (all admissions)	Innercity (sample of admissions)
Abuse/neglect victim	13	17	14
Offender	8	23	7
Non-school attender	1	2	0
Beyond parental control	27	17	20
In need of care	6	1	3
Other	3	6	0
Total	58	66	44

length of time between referral and admission to care so that it can be determined whether there is the opportunity for preventive work on these problems to be undertaken. In all studies there was often a fairly long history of contact with SSD between the initial referral and admission to care – just under half the young people in Seaside and nearly three-quarters in Newtown had been known to the department for more than a year.

It was difficult to pinpoint the major influence on the decision to admit a child to care. There was some evidence that intensity of demands from parents/children was the deciding factor, particularly in cases where there was a breakdown in family relationships. Many parents were clear over a long period of time that removal of the child was the only solution to the family's difficulties: this finally occurred as a result of increased demands rather than being due to any visible deterioration in the child's behaviour. Certainly where the problems were clearly stated at the time of referral, social work action appeared only to delay the initial request and there was great inconsistency in decision-making over reception into care.

Alternatives to care

The children who entered care in these three studies were rarely strangers to the department, and while the actual admission may have been precipitated by a crisis, there was sufficient time before that point to consider alternative intervention strategies. The most striking finding in all studies was the number of children for whom no alternative, for example child and family guidance, had been tried – about half of the children admitted in Seaside and Newtown and well above this number in Innercity.

The interventions of social workers themselves were not ignored when considering the avoidance of reception into care. However, in all studies, it was rare to find case recording in files that detailed exactly what work had been undertaken with a family, that is there was little indication of the purpose of the visit, methods of work used and evaluation of any progress towards problem-solving. The general impression gained from the majority of files was, at best, one of the social workers providing rather a vague support to adolescents and their families, and, at worst, the mere monitoring of misfortune.

It was not possible during the studies to observe social workers in action, but discussion with them about the children they were responsible for gave us no reason to believe that it was a lack of time that resulted in poor case recording. In fact, if anything, recording was longer than necessary as it included a considerable amount of information unrelated to the stated problems of referral. Overall, little planned intervention seemed to be offered by social workers in an attempt to avoid reception into care, although comparatively few cases were unknown before admission occurred.

It is difficult to surmise why alternatives are not better explored. An obvious answer would be that the resources on offer are not those which social workers require, but this idea is invalidated by the fact that in Seaside and Newtown, when asked in discussion whether admission could have been avoided with better resources (of any type and with no financial constraints), practically all social workers felt that it could not. It may be, however, that social workers' answers reflect the eventual crisis nature of many admissions, and that by the time a preventive resource is offered, it is already too late to avoid reception into care. Certainly in discussions, social workers frequently seemed resigned to the fact that admission was inevitable and felt that they were fighting a losing battle. In some instances, part of this battle was with other professionals who proposed reception into care: in the absence of clear alternatives, social workers bowed to this pressure.

What occurred on entry to care

As the DHSS-sponsored research points out, social workers often put more emphasis on the justification for admission than on what should happen when a care episode commences, and this was true in all our studies. In discussions with social workers in Seaside and Newtown, we asked them what they felt could be achieved by a reception into care, and were surprised by the limited range of replies given to such an open-ended question. The majority of answers were along the lines of 'to provide a safe place', 'to give parents and child a break from each other' or simply 'to enable a full assessment to take place'. It is probably not inaccurate to suggest that in cases where social workers were uncertain where to turn next, if a crisis occurred then the admission was legitimised by stating that a full assessment was needed.

In both Seaside and Newtown, discussions with social workers indicated that well over 90 per cent of practitioners involved at the point of reception into care felt that the initial placement was an appropriate one. In view of the fact that so many of the admissions took place following a crisis and the difficulty in matching needs with resources in such situations, this is, at first glance, very surprising. However, when the responses to the question concerning the purpose of the placement outlined are considered, then if social workers' aims are limited, it follows that the type of placement obtained is of lesser importance.

A striking similarity in all three studies was the lack of precision in long-term planning. In very few cases was there any indication of how, or an estimation of the time needed, to achieve the end objective. This is perhaps partly because, as Fruin and Vernon point out in their study of social work decision-making, 'although social workers used the vocabulary of planning, the plans they stated were not necessarily the outcome of a conscious planning process' (Fruin and Vernon 1985: 79).

Discharge from care

It should be noted that well over half of the young people in each sample returned home within six months. The most significant pattern occurred among the beyond parental control group in Seaside where about three-quarters of the teenagers left care within this time period. However, it was often very difficult to ascertain why children returned home, although there were several cases where a family decision for an older teenager to return home was imparted to the social worker at a later date. Even where decisions were made formally the reasoning behind them was often very unclear, and there were few references in recording to any change in the situation that had brought the child into care in the first place.

Why change is needed in the care system

Having looked at three departments in very different areas, we believe that the results of our studies provide clear evidence of continuing problems in local authority child care work (for a more detailed description of the research data, see Kerslake and Cramp 1988). The main conclusions are as follows.

1 Although children are usually known to departments for some time prior to admission, in a large number of cases no alternative services (other than the social worker's own intervention) are offered to try and avoid reception into care.
2 Social work intervention rarely focuses on the initial problems presented to the department. Instead the social worker provides vague support to the family rather than trying to tackle specific difficulties.
3 Care episodes usually occur as a result of a 'crisis' and are therefore unplanned.
4 There is frequently much more emphasis on the justification for admission than on what should happen once a care episode commences.
5 Children are often discharged home when there is no apparent change in the situation that brought the child into care in the first place.
6 In a few instances, there is evidence of incompetence either through files being lost or through statutory reviews never being completed.

The brief findings described above are the result of looking at case files and asking structured questions of social workers. However, in the course of our work a large amount of contextual material also came to light.

First, there is the multiple effect. Once 'set off' down an inappropriate course of action, each problem becomes a consequence of previous decisions and means a further deviation from the norms of good practice. Therefore, because few alternative agencies are used, there is little opportunity for external gatekeeping mechanisms to offer a detached view of the admission to care process. As a consequence, social workers are left with the burden of preventive work, which becomes untargeted, unstructured and increasingly based on 'firefighting'. This in turn leads to crises which produce unplanned admissions. Because admissions are unplanned, young people tend to rapidly move from being the victim of family turmoil to being the problem for the care system, which can easily lead to unplanned drift from one placement to another. Finally, discharge occurs either when placements cannot be found or a child becomes old enough to 'drift' out of care. While the above represents a caricature of the whole system and obviously does not occur to all children, it is frequent enough to be the most common route through the care system in our sample.

Second, in all three departments, decision-making inevitably meant decisions about individual cases. Although social workers collect large amounts of information about children and families, there are few attempts to categorize information into a format which could inform departmental decision-making and no attempts to use known research findings as a means of targeting intervention. Consequently one department was planning a considerable investment in a new psychiatric-based resource for adolescents, yet had no accurate data on the need for such a resource.

Third, while all three agencies would undoubtably agree that they needed additional resources, there was no evidence that the problems we described were directly caused by a lack of either funding or social worker time. Indeed, it might have been expected that if resources had been in short supply greater evidence of targeting would have been seen. Instead it is probable that child care services act as a drain on other areas of social services provision.

Therefore the overall context of the care system is one where the initial lack of targeting, structure and creativity leads to a later sequence of re-active decisions from admission to discharge. The system consumes considerable resources but with few measures of effective outcomes and rewards for good practice. It was sad to see that one social worker who had recently qualified at first had structured case notes with clear plans, which deteriorated to the norm within months of working in the department.

At the time of the research we saw few prospects of widespread implementation of new models of child care. At least two of the three departments, like many others, tended to see child care problems as being primarily caused by external forces such as lack of resources, poor training and/or complicated legislation. In addition, where the need for change was perceived, incremental change was invariably preferred to something more radical.

Since then, the Griffiths Report (1988) and the accompanying legislation, albeit with staged implementation, has changed the managerial climate within many SSDs. Given the extensive restructuring required in the next couple of years, it seems unlikely that departments could sustain two managerial systems

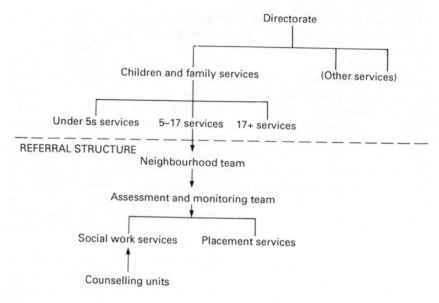

Figure 4.1   Organizational structure

– one for child care and one for community care. In addition, the Children Act 1989 is going to require greater monitoring by management if implementation is not going to result in more strain on resources.

The model described below was developed prior to the Griffiths Report. None the less, we feel it still has considerable relevance and appropriately mirrors a complimentary system for child care service delivery.

The model

As can be seen from Figure 4.1, the basic model divides work with children and families into three sectors:

1 pre-school services (under 5s)
2 family services (aged 5–17)
3 adult counselling and support services (aged 17+).

Most of the remainder of this section will deal with services in the 5–17 category, although reference will be made to work in the other two sectors. The age boundaries refer to the age of the primary client (the child), although we recognize many of the services offered to families and those in the 17+ age group operate at the interface between child and community-care services.

The model comprises three different tiers of service, the first providing a generic service, and the others dealing only with children and young people (other client groups would have their own assessment and monitoring and social work services teams).

Role of the neighbourhood team

All work would initially come into the neighbourhood teams, which would serve all SSD clients. The idea is that neighbourhood teams should only serve a small area/population and that each team would have about six members. Apart from a team co-ordinator, these may be a mixture of case-managers, social workers and community workers. The underlying assumption is that many problems could be dealt with at a local level by voluntary action and local agreements. Workers would try to involve the neighbourhood in resolving problems. For example with juvenile crime, the first duty would always be to see if a local response could be developed either by crime prevention, the involvement of volunteer workers or a reparation scheme. Work at this level would also seek to involve other local organizations such as churches and community associations in responses to child care problems. To 'pump prime' services, each team would control a small decentralized budget.

There would be three criteria for passing work to the next level of service:

1 it requires statutory intervention
2 it needs specialist resources outside the neighbourhood
3 it involves contact between non-SSD agencies external to the neighbourhood.

Role of the assessment and monitoring team

The assessment and monitoring team are central to achieving a good child care system as they perform a key 'gatekeeping role'. Assuming that one or more of the above criteria are met, the assessment and monitoring team would be asked to make a detailed assessment. If they felt the case did not require any of the above types of services, they could then pass it back to the neighbourhood together with details of their assessment. In certain circumstances it may be appropriate for the assessment and monitoring team to suggest that a worker from the social work or placement services acted as a consultant to a neighbourhood worker if that was the only way of avoiding the use of statutory intervention or a specialist service. But assuming that further intervention is necessary, the assessment and monitoring team would take case responsibility. Certain work would be handled by the team directly, for example court reports and the court staffing functions, child care reviews. Only through this team could access to non-neighbourhood services be given. The idea is that workers would not only control access to services but also minimize statutory involvement.

Once the assessment and monitoring team had carried out an assessment, if services were required that the team could not provide then an examination would be made of what might be available in their third tier, that is social work or placement services. First, a meeting would be held with the services that might be required. There would then be a second contract meeting with the client(s) resulting in a detailed contract being produced which laid out what services were to be used, how they would be co-ordinated, what expectations and targets should be set, how these should be monitored and a date for a meeting of everybody involved to review the contract and progress made. Case accountability at all times would remain with the assessment and monitoring team. The main principle behind the assessment and monitoring team controlling the contract-making process is to ensure that services would be targeted to problems rather than becoming generalized.

Some consideration would need to be given as to whether these functions were handled by one large assessment and monitoring unit or by a mixture of smaller teams, given the different sizes both geographically and demo-graphically of SSDs. What is important is that if divisions are made, each subsection should work to the same guidelines and principles to ensure standardization of the gatekeeping function across the department.

The role of the work and placement services team

The social work services sector could provide a range of services grouped into units, for example a youth counselling unit, a children's counselling unit, a community services unit (summer playschemes, and so on) and a family counselling service. Such units could involve voluntary sector provision, co-operatives of staff working to contract for the council, or existing workers directly employed in one of the four units. The significance of this structure lies not in the basic units but in the flexible teams that could be created within them. Thus small teams of workers could be created to tackle specific problems and then regrouped when the focus of need shifted. The emphasis would be on a worker's particular social work skills and how they might be used to tackle specific problems.

Because the monitoring and legal aspects of child care are contained in the second tier of services, this frees the social work sector to move away from a monitoring role into one that is much more proactive and directed towards the resolution of problems and difficulties. It is hoped that the social work services could combine the flexibility and professionalism of many specialist voluntary counselling agencies with the stability, planning and resources that local government can provide.

The placement services sector would also provide a flexible range of responses, the aim being to offer support to families and children in conjunction with the social work services, as requested and co-ordinated by the assessment and monitoring team. Currently it is difficult for fostering and residential resources to take this family and client support role because social work rarely intervenes to change what is happening within a family. This reactive approach assumes, and in a way by its non-interventionist nature predicts, family breakdown, which then leaves the placement sector to pick up the pieces.

Changing the nature of the other two sections should also change the type of service that a placements section would be called upon to provide. Our model assumes that when families run into difficulties there is often a stage when counselling help alone is not enough but full permanent care away from the family is not necessary. This form of care needs to be with people familiar to the family, child and adolescent, available at a time when crises are occurring and time limited to prevent drift into long-term services. It also needs to emphasize the importance of the family's continuing involvement and responsibilities. Intervention such as 'respite care' (using foster parents) and 'tracking' (using former residential workers), would be appropriate for a number of the children who currently end up in the permanent care of the local authority and predicts the possible role 'accommodation' might perform when the Children Act 1989 is implemented.

We recognize that, even given these new levels of provision, there would still be some need for more long-term foster care, and in some rare instances care in a residential establishment (where placement either in the tracking scheme or foster care was not appropriate). Access to such resources should be either only by legal request or when the assessment and monitoring team can demonstrate that no other placement is possible.

Other aspects of the model

So far we have said little about the other 'two arms' to this sector. In the case of services in the under 5s category, a similar model could be developed, although it would need to take account of the greater service provision role for this category. With regard to the 17+ age group, at the moment SSDs have few statutory responsibilities although this will change with the implementation of the Children Act 1989. Certain categories of work fall obviously into this area, for example after-care and home finding, and support to voluntary agencies. It is also important to recognize future potential changes to services that might occur with any increasing role that social services might assume with regard to AIDS. Therefore, even though there is currently not a wide range of 17+ provision, it is important to create a model which can retain credibility in the light of service changes.

We are aware that the model we suggest is not perfect in every detail, for example work would need to be done on the boundaries of confidentiality between the assessment and monitoring team and the social work services sector. Nevertheless, our desire was to design a system for delivering services that was likely to offer stronger control of the system than at present and an improved quality of social work practice by separating care and control.

Our model has three distinct advantages. First, if offers social workers greater freedom, specialization and responsibility but at the same time sets higher expectations. At the moment it seems absurd that in many departments social workers have the power to make major decisions over other people's lives, which can incur vast expenditure for the department, yet individually have no direct expenditure powers or responsibilities. Equally some staff can take seven years to qualify as social workers yet work at tasks that would hardly demand an educational ability beyond GCSE. Our model gives workers the freedom either to practise social work or control the system, but it also sets expectations and monitors their achievements. Second, by the use of contracts, services can be expanded or contracted as finance allows. Where services are not available their absence is visible because the work of the assessment and monitoring team makes it obvious. Currently because services are not always visible, cuts tend to fall only on what can be seen, regardless of the appropriateness of the incision. Finally, the model is both proactive and 'consumer sensitive' with the features outlined below.

1 The basis of both organizational control and intervention with clients is contractual. Such contracts spell out clear expectations, goals and responsibilities. As a consequence the consumer is clear about the role of a particular worker.
2 The consumer becomes involved in discussions at the contract-making stage about what services are available, and the particular 'package' which is put together from the social work services and placements sector.
3 If the consumer is dissatisfied with the 'package', there is an opportunity to discuss new options at the regular review of the contract held by the assessment and monitoring team. Reviewing the contract on a regular basis also makes it very visible whether progress is being made.
4 Because they are freed from the monitoring and legal aspects of child care, the social work sector can move into a more proactive role with the opportunity to respond quickly to any new 'need' which arises, for example, working with perpetrators in cases of sexual abuse.

We recognize there may well be other models which could achieve the same objectives. However, we are clear that simply imploring social workers to do better will achieve few long-term gains unless the organizational structure and context in which they practise matches the tasks and functions they are expected to perform. The structure should prove highly attractive to social workers, with its clear divisions in roles and responsibilities. It allows for an easy transfer of staff from one section to another as an aid to preventing 'burn out' and potentially offers a model of practice that can take social work in child care into the 1990s.

References

DHSS (1985) *Social Work Decision-Making in Child Care*, London: HMSO.
Fruin, J. and Vernon, D. (1985) *In Care: A Study of Social Work Decision-Making*, London: National Children's Bureau.
Griffiths, R. (1988) *Community Care: Agenda for Action*, London: HMSO.
Kerslake, A. and Cramp, J. (1988) *A New Child Care Model: The Evidence for Change*, Social Policy Paper no. 14. Pub. Social Services Research and Development Unit, Bath University.

5
Family centres

Hilary Walker

Family centres appeared on the social work scene in the early 1970s. Expansion and development have continued steadily, despite a comparative lack of research, evaluation or written material – critical or otherwise. This chapter will explore the history of family centres outlining the social and ideological trends which contributed to their growth and development. I shall discuss the wide range of provision now made under the umbrella title 'family centre' and consider current pressures towards a more treatment-oriented style of working. Through analysis of the institutions of the family and motherhood, I shall explore some practice dilemmas for family centre work and suggest alternative approaches. Finally the implications of current staffing policies will be explored. My analysis is based on eight years' experience of working in family centres (encompassing both local authority and voluntary organization provision), a survey of the literature on family centres and a developing understanding of the fundamental importance of race, class and gender issues for the future of social work and care. Underlying the necessarily brief exploration contained in this chapter is concern about the future direction of family centre work and the style of services offered to families.

Background and history

There is no agreed definition of a family centre – it has tended to mean whatever those setting it up want it to mean. However, writers on family centres tend to agree on the following characteristics. The work of family centres is focused on the whole family unit – generally parents and children but possibly also including the extended family. Centres see their task as preventing family breakdown and are committed to strengthening family functioning through the provision of support or improvement of parenting skills. Family centres may be either a day or a residential facility (or both). They are most often located in neighbourhoods displaying a high incidence of factors associated with social and environmental problems and receptions into care. Many place importance on user participation, are responsive to local need, are seen as resource centres and adopt flexible approaches to family work (SSI 1988; Phelan 1983; Holman 1988; Warren 1990; De'Ath 1985).

A comparatively recent phenomenon, family centres began to be developed in the 1970s, mainly by voluntary organizations. Most (84 per cent), however, including those set up by local authorities, were established in the 1980s (Warren 1989). During the 1970s those voluntary organizations which had traditionally provided residential care for children were casting around for a new field of activity. Local authority demand for places in children's homes had decreased as fostering became the preferred option for children in care. It was expedient for voluntary organizations to use their former children's homes to accommodate individual, innovative projects. Other factors contributing to family centres being the chosen direction were a belief that day care for young children should not be provided for the children unless work was also carried out with their parents; a general trend towards parental involvement; and the deterrent effect of the high cost of day care (Phelan 1983).

Underpinning the development of interest in concentrating on the whole family and on improving parenting skills was the ideology of the 'culture of deprivation' expounded by Keith Joseph in 1972. His thesis was that inadequate child-rearing practices were transmitted from one generation to the next, thus creating a hard core of emotionally and intellectually deprived people, unable to take advantage of education, ill-equipped with work skills, lacking morality and unable to form stable relationships (Holman 1988). It was necessary, he argued, to break the cycle through preventive work. His suggestions were birth control, education services to prepare children for adulthood, day-care experiences to stimulate development and social work intervention to improve parental behaviour. Clearly family centres were ideally placed to take on the latter two tasks. Joseph's speech was heavily criticized and later research suggested that such transmission was by no means automatic (Cannan 1986; Madge and Rutter 1976; Brown and Madge 1982). However, the 'common-sense views' it seemed to represent had a powerful ideological effect and have since been reproduced in various guises (such as for example the recent increased use of the term 'underclass').

Other broad policy directions in social work and social care have contributed to the impetus for developing family centres. There has been an ongoing interest in the traditional family, its maintenance and support, together with concern about the single parent family (Brook and Davis 1985; Deakin and Wicks 1988). In addition there has been a general trend towards community and neighbourhood-based work (NISW 1982); a concern to expand preventive approaches to child care work (Holman 1988); a shift towards community-based rather than institutionally based care (A. Walker 1982); a questioning of the usefulness of full day-care provision for children at risk; and a growing recognition of the importance of parental involvement in the care, education and development of children under 5 (Pugh and De'Ath 1986).

The evolution of individual family centres has been a process of assimilating some or all of these policy perspectives into their philosophy and development. In many instances, children's homes or day nurseries were turned into family centres, inheriting the associations and expectations of the building's previous function. Staff groups were often expected to take on new and different tasks with little or no retraining for their new role.

There has been little evaluation of the effectiveness of family centres by the agencies who developed them (SSI 1988). However, while they are generally agreed to be 'a good thing', the reasons why are more difficult to establish. Holman (1988) claims that the value of family centres managed by voluntary organizations is that they provide help and preventive services without stigma. The Social Services Inspectorate (1988) survey concluded that family centres represent an encouraging step towards the improvement in the quality of community care and family services. De'Ath (1985) found that self-help family centres reduced isolation, gave support in crises, were a springboard to new experiences for families, provided opportunities for children to play, enjoy activities and go on outings – resulting in parents who were less stressed. Certainly those who work in family centres, and many users, seem to be consistently enthusiastic about their value. In this chapter, rather than question the usefulness or effectiveness of family centres, I shall discuss some issues underlying family centre work that are often obscured by this consensus. Because they connect with practice dilemmas, their articulation and exploration should help clarify the future direction of family centre work.

Family centres now

A survey by the Family Centre Network (Warren 1989) suggests that currently there are 495 centres nationally. They are provided and managed by a range of bodies from large, well-established voluntary organizations such as NCH and Barnardo's, to small self-help community groups; from local authority social service or education departments to health authorities – and by partnerships made up of any of these bodies. Family centres vary enormously in their orientation and approach – from clinical assessment and treatment, to general support services; from therapy to community work. A variety of methods and approaches are used within family centres – psychotherapy, family therapy, group work, individual counselling, direct teaching of parental skills, hygiene, home and child management, parent and toddler groups' play sessions. Some have a health orientation and concentrate on family planning, screening, and immunization; others are concerned with child development through play and stimulation, encouraging parents to be involved in the day's activities. Others aim primarily to meet the parent's needs believing this will in turn improve parenting. Many offer a mix of all these approaches, aiming to provide a range of positive experiences for parents and children. Different criteria are applied to decide who can use family centres. Some centres accept only 'at risk' families referred by other professionals; some expect families to be self-referring; some take children off the local day-care waiting-list; some have open-door policies – any family can use the centre at any time. Some family centres offer part-time day care, some full time, others none. Some include residential provision. Most appear to focus on families with children under 5, but others cater for all ages, including adolescents. Different policies operate on issues of parental attendance, involvement, participation and management. Variants and mixes of all these approaches exist both within and between different centres (Gill 1988; Warren 1990).

Tensions can exist within family centres between direct service provision and a treatment or therapeutic orientation. Service provision recognizing that parenting is a demanding, isolating and stressful experience, encompasses activities intended to provide support. These might include advice, day care, toy libraries, discussion groups, crèches – any service parents choose to use. In contrast a treatment-oriented approach targets particular parents or families identified as requiring surveillance, monitoring and some change. Attendance may be compulsory (or veiled compulsion); parents may therefore be ambivalent towards the opportunities presented by the centre and anxious about the stigma of attending.

Here the 'ideal types' have been presented – in practice the differences will rarely be as clear cut and these potentially contradictory styles often exist within one centre. The lack of research on family centres limits the information available about the numbers of different types of centre and makes it difficult to identify the direction of current developments. An impressionistic view is that the trend is towards treatment-oriented family centres concentrating on families where abuse has taken place. This connects with Warren's (1989) estimate that nearly half of all centres carried out intensive work with families. Since family centre expansion has mirrored other social work developments, an examination of these should provide further indications of current directions. The most significant shift in social work is the increased attention and concern focused on child abuse, both physical and sexual, and child protection work (Parton 1985; Parton and Parton 1988/9). That this is reflected in family centre developments therefore seems likely.

The current concern of child protection work has been described as the assessment of dangerousness, so as to identify those high-risk families where legal action or therapeutic control and surveillance are necessary. In contrast for those deemed to be low risk, preventive work is not given priority (Parton and Parton 1988/9). This connects with the two groups delineated in the Children Act 1989 – those children deemed to be 'in need' and others. For those identified as being 'in need' the local authority must provide preventive services including family centres 'as they consider appropriate' (Schedule 2, para. 9). For other children there is no obligation to make provision. The development of family centres has already resulted in a loss of day-care places as a general supportive service, especially for working mothers. Specialist provision targeted on a few has taken preference over more broad-based services (Eisenstadt 1986; Castledine 1983; Parton and Parton 1988/9; B. Walker 1988). This trend is set to continue as financial constraints on hard-pressed local authority social services budgets dovetail neatly with the direction of social work thinking. The limited resources will be targeted on families in which children have been identified as being at risk. But resources for broad-based preventive work in the form of useful and universal services for parents and children are less likely to be available. This could lead to family centres being restricted in the help and support they can offer to a wide range of families and less able to adopt community work approaches. Those required to use centres may feel stigmatized and labelled.

The family—gender, race and class

It is both self-evident and generally agreed that the focus of work within family centres should be the family. Yet little or no critical attention is given to the institution of the family within family centre literature. It is taken for granted that it is 'a good thing'. Yet essential to an understanding of some practice dilemmas in centres and the key to the progress of family work is, I suggest, a critical understanding of the family and related issues of gender, race and class.

The traditional nuclear family continues to be held up as the universal ideal in social work and social policy despite mounting evidence of both a wide variety of family structures and of women's (and often children's) less than satisfactory experiences within it (Brook and Davis 1985; David 1985). Recent research into and analysis of the family has highlighted the following issues. Within the family there is inequality between men and women; women tend to be financially dependent on men and to have less available disposable income (Popay 1989). Inequality exists in respect of the division of labour – women are expected to take major responsibility for the management of the home, domestic chores and child care and for looking after other dependants, even though they may also be in paid employment (Hamner and Statham 1988). The family and society's assumptions and arrangements for the family reinforce male domination and patriarchal power relations. In many instances this is played out within the family through the use of violence towards wives (Wilson 1983; Dobash and Dobash 1980). A *World in Action* survey reported in *The Observer* (25 February 1990) found that 28 per cent of wives surveyed were hit by their husbands. It is against this background, and primarily within the family, that children are socialized into their gender roles. Given recent developments in our understanding about the relationship between child (sexual) abuse and families which adhere to traditional sex roles, including unquestioned male superiority (Glaser and Frosh 1988) this should be an area of concern for family work. However, for many, the family is also a source of strength, emotional intimacy, comfort and support. Women will have different perspectives of the family, dependent on their material experience. For example black women are more likely to see it as a source of support and strength in the face of racism (Dominelli 1988).

In the context of welfare services the family really means women – for it is them upon whom the state relies for the care of dependants, both old and young. The attention of the state is focused on them if things go wrong (Wilson 1977; David 1985). When family centres say they are concerned with the functioning of families and good parenting, this really means 'fit mothering'. Both support and critical attention are directed to mothers when families present problems.

For many working-class women motherhood is carried out in the material context of poverty, bad housing and poor health (Hamner and Statham 1988). Many experience isolation and mental health problems related to their role and responsibilities within the family (Graham 1984). Many live in poverty, some despite household income being adequate, because their husbands hand over insufficient money for the running costs of the home (Popay 1989).

Most analysis of the family has been carried out by white feminists and academics. Black women point out that their experiences cannot be subsumed in this account and that for them traditionally the family has been a support and strength against the oppression of slavery and the racism of white society (Williams 1989). Further, while the white family is celebrated, the black family is pathologized: for example Afro-Caribbean mothers are criticized for their high use of day care because they are out working, while Asian mothers are criticized for not using day care and for being confined to the home (Carby 1983; Bryan *et al.* 1985). Neither is the rich and diverse variety of black family forms recognized, understood or valued (Dominelli 1988).

This brief examination of the family raises many issues that do not feature in the literature or discussions on family centres. Here I am able to consider only some of the implications for practice. Family centres need to consider what role they play in reinforcing gender inequalities and the implications of this for the adults and children who use them. Does the centre implicitly accept that in most families mothers care for the children and focus their attention on women? Or should the centre challenge that assumption and insist on the active involvement of men and, if so, on what terms? Should the centre challenge other divisions of labour and resources within the family in the interests of the mental and physical health of the mothers with whom they work? What messages about gender inequalities are conveyed to the centre users by staff, both male and female: specifically do male workers actively refuse to take on traditional male roles, expectations and privilege? Should the family centre operate as a sanctuary for women to be on their own away from men in 'safe space' where they can develop systems of mutual support and strength? Eisenstadt (1986) tells of a group of women within a family centre who chose not to have male staff involved in the 'drop-in' and made no efforts to increase fathers' use of it.

I suggest that decisions about the involvement of men might depend on the style of family centre. If the provision consists of helpful, non-stigmatizing services designed to support mothers, build their confidence, encourage them to question and challenge their roles and experiences and give them new opportunities, then perhaps it is appropriate that work is targeted upon women. In this context any educational work with women aimed at improving parenting should include challenging the social context of motherhood (David 1985). However, if the centre is concerned with diagnosis and treatment of faulty family functioning, then there should be insistence on attendance by male partners – otherwise responsibility for family problems and their resolution continues to rest with mothers. Further, any work with the whole family should incorporate an understanding of, and a challenge to, gender inequalities.

Family centres need to consider their working assumptions about the 'normal' family and how they respond to and deal with the variety of family forms with which they come into contact. This is of particular importance when working with black families who have received insensitive and racist treatment from welfare agencies because of their lack of conformity to the 'traditional white nuclear family' (Dominelli 1988). In his survey of family centre literature, Warren (1990) found that little attention was paid to race issues and suggests this is a neglected area. The Social Services Inspectorate report noted that staff lacked the confidence to deal with race issues, limiting their 'ability to provide an ethnic-sensitive service' (SSI 1988: 7). If family centres are to continue to develop useful services it is essential that the work takes on an overtly anti-racist approach that goes deeper than the provision of multicultural toys and the celebration of festivals, to a real understanding of the past and present experiences and concerns of black families.

A related consideration is highlighted by the articulated experiences of the pathologized families in the black community, but relevant also to families labelled as inadequate or problem. Family centres need to challenge their practice to establish whether they focus on the alleged deficiencies of the family or recognize, build on and support its strengths. While theory and practice in early childhood education have acknowledged their past devaluing and under-estimation of working-class mothers' teaching abilities and its signifi-cance in the cognitive development of young children (Tizard and Hughes 1984; Smith 1980), social and family centre work thinking have not developed in parallel. Given the multidisciplinary nature of much family centre work, it is unfortunate that this insight from education has not been incorporated into practice.

The material context of working-class mothering outlined above also requires a considered approach from family centres. Can centres ignore the poverty of the women and children attending the centre? What practical help, if any, is it appropriate to provide? Should family centres campaign around issues such as housing policy or improvements in child benefit? At present, many centres operate a 'back-door' compensatory approach to the poverty and deprivation experienced by families but are rarely explicit about this. So, for example, they may ensure that children and mothers get a reasonable meal each day, organize low-cost outings, jumble sales and clothes sales at bargain prices, and give help in kind if a mother is without food, milk or nappies. This approach has difficulties. It fails to tackle inequalities in the family budget. Without clear guidelines within the centre it can lead to a lack of consistency with staff feeling 'conned' and users not responded to in an equitable manner. It provides short-term aid to families using the centre but cannot recognize or help other families in the local community facing similar problems. Neither does it confront wider issues of poverty wages and low levels of state benefits.

Family centres are increasingly concentrating their attention on child abuse and child sexual abuse work, including surveillance and monitoring of families. In order to be able to develop this, they need to develop a framework for practice which acknowledges the connection between abuse and power relationships within the family. This could include preventive approaches such as models for working with all young girls which enable them to develop as confident, assertive and powerful people, less likely to be victims, and encouraging boys to behave in less sexually stereotyped ways.

The needs of children and the needs of mothers

Two assumptions lie behind family centre practice – that it is helpful and constructive to work with both parents and children together, and that the needs of all family members can be met in this way. Yet in practice family centre workers experience tensions and contradictions suggesting the issues are not so straightforward. For example staff often find it easier to spend their time and energy on caring for the children who attend the centre rather than dealing with and involving parents. A member of staff interviewed by Holman commented 'it is much easier to help the children, they are ripe to learn. . . . We are practically all trained in child-care and that's the easy part of the job' (Holman 1988: 128). Indeed the initial career choice of many staff in family centres was to work with children and this is their area of expertise. Understandably they are naturally more drawn to working with the children rather than taking on the more complex issues presented by adults. Occasionally concern for children develops into antagonism and hostility towards the mothers, particularly if staff, attached to and involved with children, don't like the way their mother treats them. 'We nursery staff generally thought we could do a better job of looking after the children than their mothers. Therefore we ignored them' (B. Walker 1988: 27). One explanation for this (suggested by Eisenstadt 1986) is that workers with low status (such as family centre staff) may need to find a group who know less than them so as to bolster their self-esteem – in this instance mothers.

Alternatively family centre staff may focus their attention on parents to the neglect of children. This can provide different job satisfactions: there is more status in work with adults and at least you can have a sensible conversation with them. Yet many staff lacking experience in work with adults may become overwhelmed by the concerns they take on. Coming up against, perhaps for the first time, the social, economic and emotional deprivation experienced by many women who use family centres can be a powerful and unsettling experience. For some staff the issues raised will have painful connections with their own lives and backgrounds – this may inhibit their ability to work effectively with parents.

In family centre practice a balance between parents and children is often very difficult to achieve. A further pressure can be competition between parents and their children for staff time and attention. Indeed many mothers who have found 'sanctuary' in the centre, and who have many needs unmet within the family, may resent the concern for the children and want the care themselves (Holman 1988). Staff will experience these potentially conflicting priorities as taxing and demanding. New and David (1985) provide a way of understanding this apparent conflict between mothers and their children. They suggest that motherhood is currently defined in such a way that if the needs of women are met it is thought to threaten the interests of their children. Being a mother is assumed to be about self-sacrifice and denial, if children are to be properly cared for. However, they assert, this definition can and should be challenged. This could be done by shifting relationships between men and women particularly in the areas of child care and work. Policy measures such as increased child benefit and free universal child care would enable such changes. The effect would be to alter mothers' relationships with their children as they would not be seen as in opposition to women's needs or preventing them being met. Within family centre practice this understanding of motherhood might be used to guide practice. Staff could acknowledge and recognize the implications of these tensions for their everyday work.

With users they would be able to explore the current experience of motherhood and consider alternatives. This connects with the development of a woman-centred practice advocated by Hamner and Statham (1988). Its key elements are liking, valuing and accepting women and the problems they bring; resisting pathologizing their behaviour; recognizing the reality of the experience of motherhood; encouraging and enabling mothers to make time and space for themselves. Family centres wanting to adopt this approach would need to explore and challenge their current understanding of motherhood and its implications for their practice. This should enable them to develop an alternative style of work based on a new definition of motherhood that respects the needs of both women and children.

Staffing concerns: tasks, training and prospects

Finally I shall raise some issues concerning the staffing of family centres which have also implications for their future development and prospects. The Social Services Inspectorate report notes that staff were often 'expected to change role or do work for which they were not equipped, trained or inclined' (SSI 1988: 10). Some effects on the work of family centres of the lack of retraining for day nursery and children's home staff have been discussed above. Warren (1989) provides some limited information about the qualifications of staff. The NNEB (nursery nurse training) was probably the most commonly found qualification; about one-third of centres in his sample employed a few staff with either a CQSW or CSS. Other training and qualifications represented included teaching, PPA, nursing, youth work, residential care, community work and a few with childminder or volunteer backgrounds. While this range of staff adds richness and diversity to the provision in family centres, many staff are under-equipped to deal with the wide range and complexity of the tasks expected of them. For example the Social Services Inspectorate (1988) report noted that staff were required to construct treatment plans, record progress, work with parents, carry out home visits and negotiate with other professionals – all areas of practice which have, until recently, been the province of field social workers. Indeed family centre staff are also often at the front line of the detection, surveillance, monitoring and management of child abuse and child sexual abuse work – dealing with the feelings and reactions of both parents and children. Many staff have little or no training or background in working with adults. The day-care setting places particular demands on them. Their responses and behaviour are frequently exposed and subject to scrutiny from both colleagues and users. The boundaries between professional and personal issues are less clear than in a fieldwork setting, and often under pressure. Staff need to be sensitive, responsive, flexible and innovative.

Yet the pay and conditions of family centre staff are rarely consistent with the demands and expectations of the work. Pay levels and the status of family work are generally low – like most work done by women and with women and children. Salary scales fall well below those of field social workers and are often lower than those of day-care workers with young people (for example intermediate treatment work – mostly with adolescent boys) and adults. There is no recognized and arguably no appropriate qualification for family centre work. In-service training could be used to develop expertise in areas of work where staff are lacking knowledge and experience. For example a focus on working with adults for child care workers and a concentration on young children for those with a social work training. However, such opportunities have not generally been available. For main-grade family centre staff there is currently no clear route to career progression and a diminishing number of secondments to professional social work training. The introduction of National Vocational Qualifications in Residential, Domiciliary, Day Care and Under Sevens settings may provide expanded opportunities for this group of staff to gain recognition for skills, knowledge and competency developed in the workplace. However, the concrete outcomes of the scheme cannot yet be predicted.

The levels of support and supervision offered to family centre staff are variable. Although no hard evidence appears to exist, experience and observation suggest that formal supervision is rarely structured into the programme and task maintenance is more valued than exploration of the tensions, conflicts and demands of the work. In dealings with other agencies and field social workers family centre staff often feel insufficiently recognized and valued. Their contributions at case conferences may be given little weight – though they might well have had more contact with the family than other professionals present. Information relevant to an understanding of the family is often not passed on to the family centre by other agencies, signalling an undervaluing of the work carried out there. Staff can begin to internalize the low status attached to themselves; in turn this can have a negative effect on their work with children and mothers.

The future development of family centre work will require recognition of the work of staff financially and professionally and the opening up of career possibilities and quality in-service training. Through supervision staff need the opportunity to examine their responses to families. This would include an exploration of what they have in common with mothers, particularly around gender issues. The significance of differences between staff and users, and their effects, will also need to be addressed – for instance around race, culture, sexuality, class, poverty and (un)employment. The opportunity to consider and acknowledge the emotional impact of the work on them – pain, pleasure, rewards, frustrations will also be important for family centre workers. For women staff, personal matters concerning their own relationships particularly with men and children; issues about their self-esteem and life-style may be raised by this exploration. An appropriate, safe and supportive environment should be available to enable awareness and understanding of these connections.

Conclusion

If family centres are to develop a coherent role and purpose within social work and care provision they will need to consider the challenges posed in this chapter. This should include adopting an approach to the family that integrates an understanding of the material experiences of the oppressions of class, race and gender. It will mean being alert to the implications of current trends away from broad-based preventive help towards the targeting and surveillance of families deemed to have failed. It will need to incorporate a consideration of the effect on the development of good practice of current staffing policies. Without these, family centres are in danger of drifting into a narrow, stigmatizing, coercive role and function focused on families who have failed, rather than providing an enabling and empowering, broad-based service for families requesting support.

References

Brook, E. and Davis, A. (1985) *Women, the Family and Social Work*, London: Tavistock.
Brown, M. and Madge, N. (1982) *Despite the Welfare State*, London: Heinemann.
Bryan, B., Dadzie, S. and Scafe, S. (1985) *The Heart of the Race*, London: Virago.
Cannan, C. (1986) 'Sanctuary or stigma', *Community Care* 22 May: 14–17.
Carby, H. (1983) 'White women listen!' in Centre for Contemporary Cultural Studies, *The Empire Strikes Back*, London: Hutchinson.
Castledine, L. (1983) 'The new right on nurseries', *Bulletin on Social Policy* 14: 34–6.
David, M. (1985) 'Motherhood and social policy: a matter of education?', *Critical Social Policy* 12: 28–43.
Deakin, N. and Wicks, M. (1988) *Families and the State*, London: Family Policy Studies Centre.
De'Ath, E. (1985) *Self-Help and Family Centres*, London: National Children's Bureau.
Dobash, R. E. and Dobash, R. *Violence Against Wives*, London: Open Books.
Dominelli, L. (1988) *Anti-Racist Social Work*, London: Macmillan.
Dominelli, L. and McLeod, E. (1989) *Feminist Social Work*, London: Macmillan.
Eisenstadt, N. (1986) 'Some feminist issues', in N. Browne and P. France (eds) *Untying the Apron Strings*, Milton Keynes: Open University Press.
Gill, O. (1988) 'Integrated work in a neighbourhood family centre', *Practice* 2, 3: 243–55.
Glaser, D. and Frosh, S. (1988) *Child Sexual Abuse*, London: Macmillan.
Graham, H. (1984) *Women, Health and the Family*, Brighton: Wheatsheaf.
Hamner, J. and Statham, D. (1988) *Women and Social Work*, London: Macmillan.
Holman, B. (1988) *Putting Families First*, London: Macmillan.
Madge, N. and Rutter, S. (1976) *Cycles of Disadvantage*, London: Heinemann.
New, C. and David, M. (1985) *For the Children's Sake*, Harmondsworth: Pelican.
NISW (National Institute of Social Work) (1982) *Social Workers: Their Roles and Tasks*, Barclay Report, London: Bedford Square Press.

✗   Parton, C. and Parton, N. (1988/9) 'Women, the family and child protection', *Critical Social Policy* 24: 38–49.

Parton, N. (1985) *The Politics of Child Abuse*, London: Macmillan.

Phelan, J. (1983) *Family Centres*, London: Children's Society.

Popay, J. (1989) 'Poverty and plenty', in *Women and Poverty*, Thomas Coram Research Unit/University of Warwick, Coventry.

Pugh, G. and De'Ath, E. (1986) *The Needs of Parents*, London: Macmillan.

Smith, T. (1980) *Parents and Preschool*, London: Grant McIntyre.

SSI (Social Services Inspectorate) (1988) *Family Centres*, London: Department of Health.

Tizard, B. and Hughes, M. (1984) *Children Talking*, London: Fontana.

Walker, A. (1982) *Community Care*, Oxford: Basil Blackwell.

Walker, B. (1988) 'More than childminders', *Community Care* 11 February: 26–8.

Warren, C. (1989) 'Family centre survey', *Family Centre Network Newsletter* 2: 7–10.

—— (1990) 'Parent advocacy in family centres', unpublished M. Phil thesis, Southampton University.

Williams, F. (1989) *Social Policy: A Critical Introduction*, Oxford: Polity.

Wilson, E. (1977) *Women and the Welfare State*, London: Tavistock.

—— (1980) *What is to be Done About Violence Against Women?*, Harmondsworth: Penguin.

6
Analysing policy–practice links in preventive child care

Pauline Hardiker, Ken Exton and Mary Barker

In 1987 we were commissioned by the DHSS to undertake a feasibility study of policies and practices in preventive child care. The study was in four parts (Hardiker *et al.* 1989):

1 a *literature review* of preventive concepts and methodologies in child care and related areas, such as crime and health care
2 an analysis of *policy* formulation and implementation in preventive child care in two social services departments
3 a study of preventive child care *practices*
4 an *evaluation* of the above.

This chapter describes the approach we adopted to the second part of this study – the analysis of preventive child care policies in two social services departments (SSDs).

Conceptual frameworks

There are two theoretical traditions in policy studies (Ham and Hill 1984; Webb and Wistow 1987). In the bureaucratic/rational tradition, organizations are tools to serve a purpose and policies are statements of the agency's intent. Policies are discrete phenomena formulated through rational processes, and policy implementation follows a relatively unilineal course. This is associated with a top-down approach to policy. The interactionist tradition, on the other hand, attributes policies to individual members rather than to organizations. Policies are a set of interrelated decisions (or non-decisions) which incrementally produce a stance towards the organization and its purposes. Policy processes are fused in a seamless web of informal actions. This is viewed as a bottom-up approach to policy (Lipsky 1980).

Critics of the bureaucratic tradition argue that policy goals are rarely formulated as discrete phenomena. They are complex, multiple, conflicting, ambiguous and sometimes displaced (Smith and May 1980; Booth 1988). The interactionist position prefers a pragmatic, problem-solving approach because the search for optimal policies is too costly. Artificial distinctions between ends and means are created, as when the terms 'policy vacuum' and 'implementation gap' are used in policy evaluation. Critics of interactionism argue that it assumes consensus, is conservative in its approach to options, and relates to fine-tuning rather than fundamental decisions (Smith and May 1980; Booth 1988). If policy is defined as a stance or seamless web of day-to-day decisions, it is also difficult to identify what it actually is.

Any policy researcher is thus faced with dilemmas regarding both the nature of policy and ways of analysing it. Webb captured these succinctly:

> this only serves to highlight one of the great mysteries of social services policy-making. We can conceive of policy as intent and discuss planning and budgeting. We can also conceive of policy as outputs and talk of field decisions and resource allocations. What we cannot do at present is to explain how, if at all, these two worlds of social services decision-making interact.
>
> (Webb 1979: 114)

Webb (1979) and Ham and Hill (1984) suggested that very little empirical research had addressed the mysteries of the links between these two worlds of decision-making. Packman found the links very difficult to decipher in her study of policies on admission to care:

> There were common difficulties in identifying what the policy actually was, and how it linked with practice in each department.
>
> Grasping 'policy', like grasping 'decisions', was a matter of trying to capture something that was multidimensional, constantly moving and, furthermore, something that often appears ghostly and insubstantial in outline and detail.
>
> (Packman 1986: 147; 13)

A Social Services Inspectorate study of home help services in eight local authorities also found contrasts and conflicts between official policies and front-line decision-making:

> Home help organisers frequently had no knowledge of any formal policy, and talked of 'policy' as a set of informally transmitted understandings and assumptions, rather than anything written down. In certain SSDs . . . there was conflict between emerging formal policy and these understandings and assumptions.
>
> (DHSS 1987: 10–11)

A hiatus between formal and informal policies may be inevitable if these are analysed from either a bureaucratic or an interactionist perspective. Such approaches fail to address the ways that organizations daily reconcile divergent understandings and demands in order to produce the outputs of policies. A different approach to policy analysis seemed to be called for, but where could this be found?

We undertook a very selective review of the literature in our search for an alternative approach. Barrett and Hill (1984) expounded and integrated, interest group perspective, in which policy was viewed as a political process of negotiation, bargaining and compromise. Dunleavy (1981) referred to systems of ideological corporatism which operated in policy communities to generate a unified view of social problems (e.g. a medical model of child abuse) across diverse groupings. Ham and Hill (1984) suggested that macro and micro levels of policy could be explained in terms of structural features of society, such as classes, the state and capitalism. Whitmore (1984) developed a multilevel model of formulation/implementation processes, in which different interest groups addressed child abuse policies. The levels included the policy paradigm; monitoring framework; resource dependencies; administrative systems; and fieldworker–client interfaces. This model may have greater purchase on child abuse policies than those in preventive child care, the regulatory framework being institutionalized more firmly in respect of the former than the latter.

These frameworks did not suggest a way forward, since they indicated lines of inquiry which were too macro or ambitious for our purposes. However, Webb and Wistow suggested clues. They defined policy as 'authoritative statements of intended courses of action which provide a framework for detailed decision-making' (Webb and Wistow 1987: 124). Policies are seen as expressions of consciously articulated choices. They are not necessarily imposed deterministically from above. Webb identified a further link in the chain by defining the policy process as 'the entire process of control by which broad objectives are successively translated into specific guidelines for action' (Webb 1979: 99).

Policy is located at points where authoritative intentions and workers' actions are brought together. This accorded with our view that a middle-range level of analysis might avoid the problems generated by the separate pursuit of bureaucratic and interactionist approaches. The respective influence of managers and front-line workers can be studied as empirical questions in relation to specific examples of policy. This approach treats policies as identifiable social phenomena even though they may be heterogeneous, partial, unclear or contradictory. Room is allowed for the analysis of practitioners' contributions to policies.

We decided to adopt a midway approach to policy analysis but had not located our perspective in a theoretical tradition. Systems approaches to organizations helped us in our thinking here (Silverman 1970; Elliott 1980). In order to survive in their environments, organizations 'need' to exchange problems for resources or to convert inputs into outputs. These processes are facilitated by various structures: interdependence between different parts, such as production and marketing or services and resources; boundaries between the organization and its environment, such as social service committees or arrangements for client access. The effect of these structures and processes may be viewed as a series of balancing acts or a managed equilibrium, which adjust authoritative intentions and front-line activity.

Systems approaches suggest ways of thinking about complex social units in terms of parts rather than wholes and processes rather than causes. The respective functions of different parts and the degrees of influence of various processes can be treated as empirical questions to be studied. So this became our mid-way perspective, though we now had to find a means of operational-izing these somewhat abstract ideas.

Signposts for analysis

The approach adopted encouraged us to forsake the elusive search for policy as a holistic, totally graspable phenomenon. Webb and Wistow (1987) suggested the following signposts for the analysis of social services policies.

1 *The broad frameworks addressed*   residential or community care, child abuse or juvenile delinquency, prevention or permanency planning.
2 *Political control and direction*   party political influence and the speed of change in policies.
3 *Methods of organizational control*   governance policies which identify principles of organization in respect of the role of the state and social planning and monitoring procedures.
4 *Arenas for negotiation*   between members, officers and trades unions.
5 *Policy streams*   degrees of coherence, conflict and contradiction between services and resources.
6 *Non-decisions*   action not taken, decisions not documented, disseminated or incorporated into strategic objectives.

These signposts provided a basis for operationalizing research questions:

1 Do SSDs have policies which offer a framework for prevention, or does such a framework have to be found elsewhere, for instance in policies for families and community services?
2 Do policies reflect an identifiable political stance in respect of the role of the state in preventive services?
3 Do policies identify mechanisms of control over implementation, such as monitoring procedures?
4 Do policies locate arenas for negotiation through consultation machinery?
5 Are mechanisms for linking policy streams specified, such as virement in relation to services and resources?

Hopefully these questions would locate various systems in social services departments whereby authoritative intentions and practices are brought together. The approach did not claim to offer an exhaustive analysis but highlighted relevant dimensions of the policy process. Perhaps by this stage we had turned our research problem into a researchable project, but methods had now to be selected to pursue our empirical questions (Whitaker *et al.* 1989).

Principles of selection for policy analysis

Two considerations emerge from the previous sections: first, that policy cannot be fully grasped by researchers, so some limits to the search have to be set;

second, that policies are multidimensional, so several methods of analysis are needed. We chose the following principles to guide our inquiry.

Methods of triangulation

A systems approach indicates that methods have to be found to capture ways in which authoritative intentions and workers' practices are interrelated. Signposts for analysis suggest that relevant dimensions of policy would not be located in one form: a strategic document or a fieldwork decision. *Methods of triangulation*, using pluralist sources, might meet these rubrics (Smith and Cantley 1985):

1 statistical analysis
2 documentary analysis
3 interviews with officers at different levels in the organization
4 observations of critical decision-making arenas
5 participation in policy processes.

Comparative method

Another way of penetrating our subject would be to compare different places simultaneously or the same place recurrently through the use of the *comparative method* (an established social science technique). We studied two social services departments (Cityshire and Townshire) simultaneously, and also pursued a historical perspective. Inter-departmental comparisons in policies were sought and two divisions within each department (comprising eight areas) were selected to draw intra-departmental comparisons. We had also undertaken a project in the two Cityshire divisions five years earlier, so selective use was made of this data to make temporal comparisons (Hardiker and Barker 1986).

Boundary for search

Since policies were studied retrospectively, decisions had to be made on limiting the search by choosing a starting-point for historical analysis; data sources also had to be selected, as we were offered open access to every potentially relevant document in the two SSDs. On the basis of guidance from managers, insider knowledge and perusal of documents, the *boundary for search* was set at 1982, when significant policy changes were initiated. The year 1983 represented a watershed in both departments. Since then, some policies had become stabilized, others had been extended, ignored or abandoned, and new policies had evolved. These policy processes could not be grasped solely through documentation because policies were sometimes implemented ahead of or without documentation, and those documented were not always implemented.

Lateral sources of data

Although it is important to stress the partial nature of policy research, attempts should be made to ensure that principles of selection do not distort through narrowing the field of inquiry too much; this is a tall order! Our insider knowledge and participation in policy processes provided additional sources of information.

Some of this insider knowledge derived from our former employment and from students' practice placements. These *lateral sources of data* had to be used carefully. For example through membership of the Labour party, we were aware of some of the relevant political processes influencing Cityshire's child care strategy, but we had to ask questions about these rather than rely on our previous knowledge. Practice teachers indirectly engaged in child care were helpful observers of the policy processes, for example the demise of the Community Programme in Townshire. One member of the research team participated in the policy process through membership of the Prevention Assignment Group in Townshire.

Data retrieval and reduction

Any search for policies inevitably generates masses of paper and data. Methods of *data retrieval and reduction* were devised to track relevant policy papers and decisions and to document materials available, needed and collected. A framework for reducing these data also had to be devised. This focused initially on philosophy and value-base, strategic objectives and implementation procedures. Subsequently data were coded in relation to the signposts for analysis outlined above.

Validity

The bureaucratic tradition may rely too heavily upon official policy statements, whereas the interactionist perspective may trust too much participants' perceptions of policy processes. A multi-method approach, exploring several dimensions of policies, may help to identify ways in which authoritative intentions and practices are linked. We were still left with the problem of *validity* in respect of researchers' interpretations, especially since we necessarily made several imaginative connections between diverse sources and types of data. We discussed our understandings with officers in the two SSDs, who found them acceptable, though they were not necessarily the final arbiters of our analysis. We are moving into realms of epistemology here and believe that researchers can never know policy completely.

Methods of data collection and analysis

We now discuss methods for collecting and analysing data in policy research. Data were collected from a variety of sources using a range of methods.

Pilot study

Child care policy documents were retrieved and collated from six Midlands SSDs, one authority in the north-east and the London Boroughs Children's

Regional Planning Committee. This exercise illustrated the wide variation in this type of documentation. First, preventive policies were more or less selective; some focused on services for adolescents, while others spanned the whole career of children in and out of care. Second, some documents were more comprehensive than others, identifying values and principles, strategic objectives and operational procedures, whereas others merely summarized legislative powers. One department produced no policy statements claiming that policy was unified by a shared belief in family care. This exercise encouraged us further in our view that policy analysis should not rely exclusively on documentary sources.

From a bureaucratic/rational perspective, it would be relatively easy to illustrate ways policy statements fail the test of comprehensive rationality. From an interactionist perspective, practitioners might be asked about the content of policies and their instant recall would probably be variable; this would not necessarily accurately reflect their understandings of policies.

The pilot study taught us that policy statements have limited value to researchers unless they are analysed in relation to their political and organizational contexts. First, these documents are multifunctional: rhetorical or legitimizing statements of value; strategic outlines of objectives; pointers to implementation procedures. Second, policy researchers need to use a middle-range level of analysis to tap ways in which authoritative intentions influence practices. Third, other influences on policies need to be identified and analysed: undocumented decisions, ongoing developments, external pressures.

Collation and analysis of policy documents

In Cityshire and Townshire a range of documents (official policy statements, committee minutes and working party reports) was collated. These were analysed initially in relation to

1 *Framework*   were the target groups adolescents or children in and out of care?
2 *Prevention*   was this a discrete theme or included under family support services?
3 *Function*   were the policy documents statements of value, strategic objectives or procedures?

Interviews with managers

Group interviews were conducted with managers for several purposes:

1 to locate the range and variety of relevant documents to be retrieved
2 to discuss their perspectives on policies and processes
3 to explore our interpretations of policies derived from documentary analysis
4 to brief participants about the nature of the feasibility study
5 to explore issues about access, sampling and definitions
6 to provide feedback and discuss findings

The importance of these meetings is worth highlighting. Managers were sent briefing notes in advance, and we structured the discussion around these notes. Researchers must concentrate very hard when undertaking such interviews, as managers are usually working to a tight schedule and interviewers have to keep a grasp of extremely complex issues which they cannot therefore fully comprehend. Careful briefing is essential.

Interviews with fieldworkers

Thirty-two social workers were interviewed regarding one of their preventive child care cases and asked questions about preventive policies; other workers (aides, intervention team practitioners and officers in family centres) were interviewed in relation to these cases. Again, we were ever conscious of the need to be disciplined and parsimonious in our use of practitioners' scarce time.

Observations of critical events

Reception into care panels, reviews and case conferences were important arenas for the translation of policies into practices. Six observations were undertaken: three panels, two case conferences and one review. We took notes during these events and completed the observation schedule subsequently.

These methods operationalized relevant dimensions of policies and unravelled some complexities of untidy and ever-changing scenes.

Selected findings

We now describe some discoveries about preventive child care policies in Cityshire and Townshire.

Broad frameworks

There were some differences in the frameworks for prevention. Cityshire's child care strategy was primarily concerned with adolescents, especially those in residential care, whereas Townshire's policy was addressed more broadly to children and their families. The strategic objectives in Cityshire were to reduce the numbers of children admitted to and remaining in care. Services were to focus on children with severe problems and interventions were to target children on the threshold of care using task-centred methods (Goldberg *et al.* 1985). The objectives in Townshire were more comprehensive and focused on services for children over the child care career. Preventive services were also seen somewhat differently. In Cityshire prevention was identified through a range of family support services, including family aides, increase in the preventive aid budget and day care schemes. Prevention would be reinforced through strict gatekeeping of receptions into care. Townshire's policies were defined more broadly as the prevention of family breakdown through keeping children in their own communities.

There was no discrete policy statement on prevention in Cityshire, as this was incorporated into strategic objectives relating to diversion and to targeted, rather than needs-based, intervention. Prevention was identified discretely in Townshire: first, the prevention strategy was directed towards those children and their families where there was likelihood of damage or breakdown increasing the risk of admission to care; second, primary and secondary levels of prevention were identified and prevention through collaboration was seen as an important part of the strategy. Services were specified in terms of a continuum of care rather than strict gatekeeping of receptions into care.

Both authorities referred to changes in the functions of residential provision. Children's resource centres were to be used in Cityshire to provide local family services in order to prevent admissions to care; children's centres in Townshire were to provide a broader range of services, less precisely defined in terms of gatekeeping of admissions to care.

Though prevention was identified more sharply in Townshire than in Cityshire, some managers in both departments defined prevention rather loosely as any work undertaken with children not in care. The problem with such a broad definition is that it fails to differentiate between different types of preventive work and excludes some of the preventive activity undertaken when children are in care. We therefore developed a fourfold classification of levels of prevention:

1 *primary*   universalistic services for population groups
2 *secondary*   targeted service for early risk groups
3 *tertiary*   targeted services for 'heavy end' risk groups
4 *quaternary*   work undertaken to rehabilitate children to their parents.
(Aldgate *et al*. 1989)

Political control and direction

Both departments shared the view that interventions should be the minimum required to enable families to care for their children. Townshire's documents described this residualist approach rather precisely:

> The SSD is not a community work agency with responsibility for the provision of equal opportunities or facilities for all the population. Its preventive strategy is directed towards those children and their families where there is likelihood of damage . . . or breakdown bringing them into care. . . . Departmental initiatives . . . are aimed at prevention of damage or breakdown among the most vulnerable, and a real connection must always be apparent to legitimate officers' involvement.

A senior manager in Cityshire expressed a similar perspective:

> SSDs are powerful instruments intervening in people's lives, and the powers they have need to be executed with the maximum degree of caution and sensitivity. . . . We conned ourselves in the 1970s and made outrageous claims regarding what SSDs could do. . . . Once children, young people and families with certain types of problems are referred, the

hooks go in and a whole series of other processes start, which are not necessarily the most appropriate.

The source, speed and direction of policy changes also differed in the two departments, though this was not evident from strategic policy documents. Cityshire was on the crest of radical changes in its child care strategy, whereas developments in Townshire were evolutionary. Previous officer-led developments in Cityshire recommended an evolutionary mode spanning about ten years. These recommendations were rejected by local authority members who were actively shaping child care policies in a different direction, influenced by initiatives in juvenile justice (systems concepts, avoidance of net-widening, importance of diversion). Prevention was defined in terms of strict gatekeeping of admissions to care and the development of alternatives to residential provision. The fast pace and member-driven nature of these developments was influenced by the Labour group's anticipation of its loss of political control. The changes were not accurately reflected in strategy statements and some developments were not documented at all, such as the abandonment of children's resource centres in favour of less net-widening intervention teams. Preventive services began to adopt a common, highly selective and targeted approach to service delivery. This created tensions between needs-based practices and the new policy which was perceived by some practitioners to be too rigid and controlling. It also took time to develop the new range of provisions, and some resources were withdrawn (residential places) before others (day care and family aides) were in place.

Service developments in Townshire were more evolutionary and officer-led. The approach tended to be through preparing a knowledge-base rather than a position statement, and strategic statements consolidated rather than blazed a trail. The system of assignment teams plus consultation processes were the bedrock of policy-making, and this department instituted a Prevention Assignment Team to work in tandem with our research project.

Methods of organizational control

These systems relate to ways organizations survive in their external and internal environments. First, governance policies include the role of the state in welfare, and it was changes in this area which surprised us most. In the 1960s and 1970s there was a strong commitment to a major role for state services and social planning, and institutional needs-based models of welfare flourished (Wilding 1986; Webb and Wistow 1987; Booth 1988). By the late 1970s these policies had been reversed except in relation to resource controls (McCarthy 1989). The moves towards residualism and the developments in diversionary policies in the two agencies need to be seen in this wider political context. Processes by which SSDs convert inputs into outputs as they address their external environments are important dimensions of organizational control. This is not an entirely deterministic process – top-down or bottom-up – but a flexible, precarious and dynamic one shaped by the relative influences of members and officers.

Second, internal systems for monitoring were identified in the child care strategies. Control over implementation in Cityshire was allocated to a centrally based child care resources team; several devices were envisaged, including social surveys, statistics on panel decisions, reviews of services and a computerized database. Further controls were instituted through key managerial appointments, the creation of middle-management child care appointments and use of social information systems. Townshire also developed monitoring systems, including member seminars, reviews, independent research evaluations and a range of procedural documents. A county-wide database was eventually established to generate data on the careers of children in care and trends in caseloads; this agency was also developing tighter systems to control some of the psychosocial variables in fieldwork decisions.

The remaining signposts for analysis will be illustrated briefly, since we hope we have presented sufficient evidence that this approach to policy analysis generated useful material. First, in relation to arenas for negotiation, the consultation process in Cityshire was foreshortened, largely because of the member-driven nature of policy developments. The process was more protracted in Townshire, in line with the more evolutionary officer-led nature of policy development. Second, policy streams in respect of services and resources were kept in tandem in both agencies. Stringent efforts were made in Cityshire to vire resources released from residential provisions into community services, especially following a change in political control, and a report of the District Audit Service confirmed this outcome. Similarly policy streams were harnessed in Townshire through virement. Policies in both agencies identified implications of strategies for related services: education, probation, youth and voluntary sectors. Third, frameworks not addressed in policies may be areas of non-decision; for instance, family casework was not specified in either department, though managers argued that these methods became more focused and targeted than hitherto. Child protection was not specified as a discrete area in the policies, though children services in both agencies were affected by increasing child abuse referrals; child care strategies were turned on their head in relation to child abuse, where net-widening interventions were evident.

Concluding findings refer to ways in which authoritative intentions and workers' practices were harnessed. Systems for external and internal control in agencies are relevant. For example central government controls on local authority spending certainly shape the boundaries of social services permitted and required endeavours, and statistical procedures monitor fieldwork decisions in relation to strategic objectives. Observations of critical decision-making arenas also illustrate these processes: panels depicted the tight gatekeeping procedures in Cityshire compared with the continuum of care in Townshire, both of which were in line with strategic objectives. Case conferences showed ways in which prevention is much more complex in relation to child abuse, so decisions concern multidimensional and net-widening rather than diversionary procedures. Finally, social workers' perceptions illustrate the impact of authoritative intentions upon practices: social workers' answers to questions about preventive policies differed between Cityshire and Townshire; the former referred more frequently to preventing admissions to care, whereas the latter identified a wider variety of policies. These agencies had apparently been relatively successful in communicating their preventive policies to front-line workers.

Practices in relation to a wider sample of eighty-five cases also reflected differences in the strategic objectives of the two departments. The research design had identified a group of families whose problems were serious and whose needs were great. Comparatively the Cityshire sample had more statutory involvement and more problems of older children; Townshire identified a wider range of problems, including more child abuse and neglect and more families receiving informal support services. The two agencies also differed in terms of throughput; the Cityshire sample was more concerned with inappropriate entry into care, with monitoring and with the prevention of agency dependency, whereas Townshire social workers had more aims in relation to a wider range of problems and used a wider variety of services. Reviewing outputs, workers in both agencies thought their aims would be achieved in less than one year in about one-third of the cases (though for the majority the timespan was longer); as most of these preventive cases were high risk and high need, the strategic objectives of the departments were apparently beginning to have an impact upon the work undertaken, in terms of targeted, focused and time-limited interventions.

We have tried to convey in this section an account of some ways in which our approach to policy research succeeded in helping us to grasp some elusive dimensions of complex policy processes and to begin to analyse ways in which these were implemented across different negotiating arenas. It should be remembered that our project was a feasibility study; in this type of research the best way of showing that methods are feasible is to use them. Perhaps we even began to penetrate some of the mysteries regarding ways in which authoritative intentions and fieldworkers' decisions interact!

In retrospect

Accounts of research invariably portray the process as more tidy, linear and holistic than it can possibly be. Policy research was new to us so we could not rely on tried and tested methods as we did in our studies of preventive practices. We floundered at many points but trusted the research process. Such trust is justified only if certain canons of research are respected: work on the conceptual framework, read the literature, devise relevant methods of data collection and analysis, constantly engage with the data.

What we would have done without the signposts in Webb and Wistow (1987) it is difficult to know; we had read this book earlier without illumination. Alternative conceptual frameworks would undoubtedly have offered other ways of understanding the data. A relevant conceptual framework has to be found if research is to succeed though this should not be selected *a priori*.

Though the agencies studied were changing and reorganizing during the project, we felt then that we had some grasp of their structures and dynamics. This is no longer so. When we return to the agencies now, our field research seems somewhat distant; staff have changed, teams reorganized, new specialisms developed, and the departments are facing the challenges of the new Children Act and *Care in the Community* (1990). We think we can safely conclude that the preventive sections of the Children Act 1989 in relation to children in need and family support services will not be translated into strategic objectives in SSDs in any simple form. To attempt to do so would freeze the process and omit significant realities. Policies are formulated and implemented in many forms and at different levels in SSDs, and this will be so as they begin to meet the promises and challenges of the Children Act 1989 (Department of Health 1990).

References

Aldgate, J., Pratt, R. and Duggan, M. (1989) 'Using care away from home to prevent family breakdown', *Adoption and Fostering* 13, 2: 32–7.

Barrett, S. and Hill, M. (1984) 'Policy, bargaining and structure in implementation theory: towards an integrated perspective', *Policy and Politics* 12, 3: 219–40.

Booth, T. (1988) *Developing Policy Research*, Aldershot: Gower.

Department of Health Social Services Inspectorate (1990) *Child Care Policy: Putting it in Writing – A Review of English Local Authorities' Child Care Policy Statements*, London: HMSO.

—— (1990) *Care in the Community*, National Health Service and Community Care Act, London: HMSO.

DHSS (1987) *From Home Help to Home Care: An Analysis of Policy, Resourcing and Service Management*, London: Social Services Inspectorate.

Dunleavy, P. (1981) 'Professions and policy change: notes, towards a model of ideological corporatism, *Public Administration Bulletin* 36: 3–16.

Elliott, D. (1980) 'The organisation as a system', in G. Salaman and K. Thompson (eds) *Control and Ideology in Organizations*, Milton Keynes: Open University Press.

Goldberg, E. M., Gibbons, J. and Sinclair, I. (1985) *Problems, Tasks and Outcomes: The Evaluation of Task-Centred Casework in Three Settings*, London: Allen & Unwin.

Ham, C. and Hill, M. (1984) *The Policy Process in Modern Capitalist Society*, Brighton: Wheatsheaf.

Hardiker, P. and Barker, M. (1986) *A Window on Child Care Practices in the 1980s*, Leicester: School of Social Work Research Report.

Hardiker, P., Exton, K. and Barker, M. (1989) *Policies and Practices in Preventive Child Care: Feasibility Study*, Leicester: Report for the Department of Health.

Lipsky, M. (1980) *Street Level Bureaucracy*, New York: Russell Sage Foundation.

McCarthy, M. (ed.) (1989) *The New Politics of Welfare*, London: Macmillan.

Packman, J. (1986) *Who Needs Care? Social Work Decisions about Children*, Oxford: Basil Blackwell.

Silverman, D. (1970) *The Theory of Organizations*, London: Heinemann.

Smith, G. and Cantley, C. (1985) *Assessing Health Care: A Study in Organisational Evaluation*, Milton Keynes: Open University Press.

Smith, G. and May, D. (1980) 'The artificial debate between rationalist and incrementalist models of decision-making', *Policy and Politics* 8, 2: 147–61.

Webb, A. (1979) 'Policy-making in social services departments', in T. Booth (ed.) *Planning for Welfare*, Oxford: Basil Blackwell/Martin Robertson.

Webb, A. and Wistow, G. (1987) *Social Work, Social Care and Social Planning: The Personal Social Services since Seebohm*, London: Longman.

Whitaker, D. S. and Archer, J. L. (1989) *Research by Social Workers: Capitalizing on Experience*, Study 9, London: Central Council for Education and Training in Social Work.

Whitmore, R. (1984) 'Modelling the policy/implementation distinction: the case of child abuse', *Policy and Politics* 12, 3: 241–67.

Wilding, P. (ed.) (1986) *In Defence of the Welfare State*, Manchester: Manchester University Press.

7
Blinded by family feeling? Child protection, feminism and countertransference

Janet Sayers

Feminism has done much to expose the frequent blindness to the sexual inequalities and abuses of family life resulting from our longing for it to be ever-loving and conflict-free. Yet there are also forces seeking to undo such blindness. This chapter is about three such forces within current child protection work: first, those unleashed by recent child abuse inquiries, second, feminist exposure of the prevalence of incest, and third, recent psychoanalytic attention to countertransference. I shall end with some of their implications for undoing the defences that otherwise so readily blinker social work in this area.

Recent inquiries into child murder

All three of the most heralded recent inquiries into child murder – Kimberley Carlile, Jasmine Beckford and Tyra Henry – draw attention, and thereby seek to undo the blindness to child abuse resulting from what Dingwall *et al.* (1983) call the 'rule of optimism' whereby social workers feel bound 'to think the best of parents' on the assumption that natural instinct guarantees the universality of parental love, that appearances to the contrary notwithstanding all parents essentially care for their children.

In the Kimberley Carlile case, Martin Ruddock, the already over-burdened social work manager involved, evidently fell back on this assumption in the absence of anybody to take on the case and given social work training that not unnaturally engenders a co-operative rather than inquisitorial stance toward clients. An anonymous phone call reported neighbours' worries about Kimberley – about a 4-year-old who seemed to be being beaten she cried so pitifully. Ruddock's colleagues – Olive Swinburne and Marilyn Streeter –

immediately followed up the phone call with a home visit. But they were fobbed off from seeing Kimberley by her parents' apparent concern for her, by their saying they did not want her wakened after a tiring shopping expedition. Not that Ruddock did not return a couple of days later. Finding the Carliles out he left a letter insisting on the children being medically examined. This prompted Kimberley's stepfather, Nigel Hall, to ring social services. He complained of Kimberley's rejection of him and consequent bad behaviour – even eating her own shit – resulting in him occasionally shaking and smacking her. Despite this, and Ruddock's image of Kimberley as 'withdrawn, sallow, pasty and still' on an unscheduled family visit to social services, this was readily eclipsed by Ruddock's picture of them all on leaving:

> parents holding children by the hand, children leaping around in the car as they got in, laughing, shouting and playing happily with each other. It was almost an archetype for a happy family scene.
>
> (London Borough of Greenwich 1987: 111)

Insistence on medical examination now gave way to attempts at gentle persuasion. No wonder, implies the inquiry: Ruddock cherished a happy memory of the family's stage-managed social services visit, and was all too willingly reassured a month later by Hall letting him see the children even though this was only through a small glass panel above their bedroom door. This was his last sighting of Kimberley. Two months later she was dead.

The Jasmine Beckford inquiry likewise seeks to expose the blinding of social workers by optimistic belief in the family, in this instance by a belief that any defects can be readily put right through material provision and supportive casework. Social workers Gun Wahlstrom and Diane Dietmann became involved following Jasmine's and her younger sister Louise's hospitalization after being severely injured by Morris Beckford in August 1981. The inquiry implicitly criticizes both social workers for failing to notice, as child abuse expert Joan Court observed, that although Jasmine played happily in the hospital she 'became watchful and completely quiet, in a state of "frozen watchfulness"' when her mother, Beverley Lorrington, visited (London Borough of Brent 1985: 92). Likewise the inquiry drew attention to the social workers overlooking the implications of Morris and Beverley visiting the girls only spasmodically in hospital, Beverley's emotional flatness, and her lack of concern for the children as compared to her considerable concern to get rehoused.

Instead Wahlstrom and Dietmann early set themselves the task of reuniting the girls with their parents as though belief in family love could wipe the slate clean of their abuse. Both social workers also seemed blinded by family feeling for Beverley and Morris. Certainly there was much in both parents' history to excite such sentiment. Morris, born in Jamaica, was left there by his parents till he was 9. When eventually reunited with them in England they so severely beat and neglected him – even banishing him to sleep in an outhouse – that he was taken into care. Similarly Beverley was deserted as a 6-month-old baby by her mother, only later to be beaten by her father and stepmother.

So taken up were both social workers with trying to right the wrongs the parents had themselves suffered as children, and their current housing difficulties, claims the inquiry, they entirely lost sight of their daughters' needs. Not a single entry in all their copious notes was devoted to either girl. Instead, soon after their parents were rehoused, they were returned home and supervision relaxed immediately Jasmine began day nursery. Nor did supervision increase when her attendance dropped both here and at nursery school. Wahlstrom readily accepted Beverley's account of Jasmine's non-attendance. Indeed so much did both social workers believe all was all right in the family, despite the stress introduced by Beverley's then pregnancy with her third daughter Chantelle, they pressed for revocation of the Care Order on Jasmine and Louise. Yet, as subsequent post-mortem examination showed, Jasmine was even then being severely abused again. But Wahlstrom saw nothing, not even on a home visit only four months before Jasmine's death. As the inquiry puts it, she 'lamentably failed to see what was crying out to be seen, namely, a grossly undernourished, limping child' (London Borough of Brent 1985: 292). Hoodwinked by overweening faith in the family to which we all so readily succumb, and by Morris's play-acting to this belief – dressing Jasmine in cover-all clothes and propping her up against the furniture – Wahlstrom recorded 'all three children appeared well and happy' (London Borough of Brent 1985: 126).

Last Tyra Henry. Social worker Avon Pailthorpe first became involved in the case following Tyra's older brother Tyrone's hospitalization after being stupefied and blinded by his father Andrew Neil. Tyrone was taken into care, and Tyra was made the subject of a Care Order at birth. She was assigned to the care not of her mother, Claudette, but of her grandmother, Beatrice Henry.

Like Beatrice, Pailthorpe was also a mother of several children including a mixed race adopted daughter not much younger than Claudette. It was as though, the inquiry implies, Pailthorpe took over Beatrice's role, indeed wrote her off, and sought to mother Claudette instead (London Borough of Lambeth 1987). Blinded by this parenting focus to the provisions of the Care Order, indeed she always dissented from them, Pailthorpe sought to enable Claudette to become independent of Beatrice. This included arguing for Claudette's separate housing so she could learn to look after Tyra on her own even though this breached the Care Order's requirement that Tyra stay with her grandmother. Pailthorpe's mothering focus not only lost sight of the overriding need to protect Tyra from her father, but also lost sight of the need to involve him in planning for her care even if only to explain to him why he could not have access. So preoccupied was Pailthorpe with helping Claudette prove herself able to mother Tyra independently of Beatrice she entirely overlooked the dangers of this, given that with Andrew's release from custody Claudette was likely to return to him. Pailthorpe neither heeded evidence of their being together again, nor that Tyra was no longer living with Beatrice but with Claudette and Andrew. Within days he had killed her.

As a result of inquiries into such deaths and their exposure of social work blindness to child abuse bred of family feeling and mothering parents to the neglect of the children involved, a much more confrontative approach has developed. Illustrative is the work of Peter Dale and his colleagues (1986b).

They criticize the focus of previous US and NSPCC work on 're-parenting' the parents of children at risk, of seeking to make good problems stemming from the parents' own deprived and abusive childhood. Instead Dale's team insist on social workers attending first and foremost to the child, not the parents. Only then will they work with the family. They will only institute family therapy aimed at keeping or returning the child to the family provided the child is seen, and the parents recognize their direct or indirect, collusive responsibility for past abuse, and for preventing its recurrence. Furthermore Dale's team seeks to puncture the myth of the family – of the universality of parental love – that so often blinds social workers to child abuse by emphasizing that sometimes parents really do not want their children home.

Not that this approach is without its own blind spots. It treats child abuse as a matter of individual deviance and responsibility, thereby neglecting the general abuses and inadequacies of family life stemming from male social dominance and from lack of adequate state support services for the family such as day nurseries (Parton and Parton 1989). Dale's 'over-confident, even dogmatic, assertions' also involve wilful myopia bred of craving for 'certainty in an uncertain and stressful area of work' (Stevenson 1989: 172). Nevertheless the confrontative rather than wait-and-see approach Dale advocates now characterizes much social work with non-accidental injury as well as with sexual abuse, to which I shall now turn.

Feminism and child sexual abuse

The history of social work with sexual as with other kinds of abuse is chequered with 'now you see it, now you don't'. Its visibility, as demonstrated by Linda Gordon (1989), varies with family attitudes. She points out that the prevalent post-Second World War belief in the family as essentially harmonious and conflict-free so blinded social workers to its sexual abuses that any such violation was either overlooked or misattributed to the work of strangers.

Psychoanalysis contributed to this. Not that Freud was always blind to incest. Quite the reverse. In 1896 he argued that all cases of hysteria stem from repressed memory of being sexually abused as a child by a nurse or governess, or by an older sibling themselves victim of such abuse. By 1897 he reported that many of his patients attributed their symptoms to having been sexually abused by their fathers in infancy. Indeed he wondered whether his own father was not also culpable. Nor was Freud alone in such speculation. Concern about incest was then widespread – this paralleling feminist campaigns of the time about the abuses done to women by sexual inequality in marriage, education and politics.

Certainly some sought to keep such realities in the closet. The sexologist Krafft-Ebing (Jones 1972: 179), who chaired Freud's 1896 'seduction theory' paper, denounced it as 'a scientific fairy tale'. The next year, following his self-analysis after his father's 1896 death, Freud adopted the same viewpoint. Blinded as it were by grief for his father he now refused to believe that fathers were as often guilty of sexually abusing their children as his patients indicated.

Instead he now increasingly argued that hysteria and neurosis are the effect not of memories but of fantasies of abuse constructed out of the child's own incestuous impulses and their repression into the unconscious.

No wonder social workers, once alert at the time of the late-nineteenth-century feminist movements to the realities of child sexual abuse, now lost sight of it, especially as psychoanalysis increasingly informed their practice, and as feminism declined after women won the vote. Incest, when recognized, was now characterized as a quaint habit of the rurally isolated far away from the urban middle-class family life of social work and psychoanalytic ideology. Nor was the widespread prevalence of child sexual abuse immediately redis-covered with the revival of feminism in the late 1960s. Social workers, femin-ist and otherwise, continued to overlook incest not least because of the extremely heavy mandatory prison sentences exacted of its perpetrators.

The rediscovery of incest arguably resulted from a further development in feminism – namely the setting up of women's centres. This resulted in the discovery of the prevalence of wife-battering, and in the establishment of women's refuges and rape crisis help-lines through which many women felt able to come forward to tell others, now with some hope of being believed, of the abuse – including sexual abuse – they suffered both as adults and chil-dren. This resulted in the formation of Incest Survivors' Groups. These in turn led to increasing publicity being given to child sexual abuse. Autobiogra-phies and semi-autobiographical accounts of such abuse – including *Cry Hard and Swim* (Spring 1987) and *The Unbelonging* (Riley 1985) – enabled yet further women to recognize what they had previously failed to see, namely their own and others' history of abuse. Sylvia Fraser (1987), for in-stance, recounts how her previously repressed memory of being sexually abused by her father as a child came to light only following the disclosure of a friend's sexual abuse, this itself being an effect of increased feminist-inspired attention to such wrongs.

This attention has likewise led social services departments to appoint child abuse consultants, as did Cleveland in appointing Sue Richardson to just such a post in June 1986. Adopting very much the post-Beckford confrontational approach to child abuse recommended by Peter Dale, Richardson insisted on looking child protection issues squarely in the face: 'I want clarity about the framework,' she says, 'I don't like things being left in the shadow of sus-picion' (Campbell 1988: 121).

Having again uncovered the widespread existence of child sexual abuse, doctors and social workers, otherwise blinkered by normative equations of sex with penile penetration of the vagina, became alert, as Freud did in the early 1890s, to the perverse, non-genital character of such abuse. This in turn made way for the anal dilation test now used in its diagnosis.

Not that the forces against seeing what was there to be seen did not con-tinue to operate. In Cleveland these included opposition from parents, police and the Labour MP Stuart Bell. And, of course, this culminated in yet another inquiry which, in a sense, reversed the conclusions of those into the deaths of Carlile, Beckford and Henry (Butler-Sloss 1988). For it argued in favour of parental rights: this in turn informed the Children Act 1989.

All four inquiries, however, drew attention to the otherwise often over-looked stress on social workers of child protection work. As social worker Christopher Horne, quoted in the Cleveland inquiry, observes:

> it has been possible to accept the nature of this abuse as something which happens in families when certain strains, stresses and predisposing factors are present. It is possible in this sense, for a worker to 'understand' the abusive behaviour. However, in working with sexual abuse, I believe I am not untypical of colleagues in finding great difficulty in understanding in this same way ... [working with sexual abuse is] a different and demanding task not only because of the problems of multi-agency working or of medical conflict but because of the nature of the activities involved. For example, the idea ... of someone inserting tea in the vagina of a child aged 7 ... represents a shock to the sensibilities of all who hear it.

(Butler-Sloss 1988: 73)

It is such shock, involving as it does both continuities and discontinuities with social workers' own family feelings and desires, that I shall now consider through an account of recent developments in psychoanalysis toward bringing such 'countertransference' issues into the light of day.

Countertransference, psychoanalysis and child protection

Freud drew attention to the way patients transfer, and are thus blinded to the reality of the analyst by feelings stemming from their families of origin. He also pointed out that, in becoming embattled with the patient's resistance to becoming conscious of such family feelings, the analysts' feelings about their own family are thereby revived. He recommended that such 'countertransference' feelings call for further analysis of the analyst, presumably so as better to keep such feelings in check. In effect Freud no sooner opened the door on analysts' own family feeling than he encouraged them, like fathers, to shut out such feeling – to keep a stiff upper lip. The result was to draw a veil over the countertransference feelings evoked in analysts and other helping professions by their work by implying that to give way to such feeling is 'unmanly', unprofessional, pathological, and cause for therapists themselves to be treated.

Today, however, psychoanalysts are much more ready to recognize such feelings. This is largely thanks to a shift in psychoanalysis from a father-centred to a mother-centred theory and practice initiated, as I have explained elsewhere (Sayers 1991), by the work of women psychoanalysts such as Karen Horney and Melanie Klein. Whereas Freud focused on the ways his patients' difficulties stemmed from unconscious feelings about the father's sex and power as transferred on to him in analysis, his women followers and critics found themselves paying much more attention to the formative effects of early mothering and its vicissitudes so much was this transferred on to them in therapy by virtue of their sex. Klein also drew attention to the way patients often disown and project unwanted feelings into the analyst just as the child does into the mother.

Her analysand and student, Paula Heimann, in turn took up this idea to suggest that the countertransference might not only reflect unresolved family conflicts from the analyst's own past, but also reflect feelings induced in the analyst by the patient's own projections. As such it provides important information about the patient's feelings. Far from being pushed away, therefore, the countertransference should be examined as a way of better understanding the patient.

As a result of these women analysts' work, men analysts became more willing, indeed often eager, to recognize what Freud had so often overlooked – namely the extent to which patients treated him not only as a father but also as a mother in therapy. This in turn resulted in yet greater willingness by analysts to attend to countertransference feelings induced in them by their patients as in mothers by their babies. Another of Klein's analysands and students, Wilfred Bion, for instance valorized the countertransference as a means whereby the analyst holds, contains and digests the patient's projected feelings thereby making them more bearable just as, Bion hypothesized, the mother contains the baby's feelings – say of discomfort and rage – so that it is more able to bear and thereby own to these feelings without damagingly splitting them off and projecting them into the mother.

Attention to the countertransference – once left in the shade by Freud disparaging it as indicative of pathology in the analyst – has accordingly now become respectable within psychoanalysis. This has in turn helped enable social workers likewise to see what was previously hidden and unconscious, namely the feelings about their own families evoked by work with those of their clients.

As a result several distinct countertransference reactions to child abuse have now been identified. Alan Carr (1989) details five. First, the overwhelming feeling, often in young social workers still seeking to become independent of their own families, of wanting to rescue the child to the neglect of the client parents' possible strengths and abilities. Second, identification with parents understood as victims of a hostile social world elicited in social workers insecure about their own parenting – a feeling that can blind them to the child's needs. Third, the wish to rescue the mother from a seemingly persecuting man – a wish often found in men with difficulties accepting their own sexual and aggressive impulses, or in women who feel oppressed by a man and who thereby perceive or misperceive the client mother as similarly oppressed. Either way the social worker's eyes are thereby opened to the mother's plight at the cost of overlooking her possible complicity in the child's abuse. Fourth, and much rarer, is the wish to rescue the father occurring in men social workers who feel isolated and misunderstood. Last is the burn-out reaction of wanting to retaliate against the client's family, as against the social worker's family of origin, for disappointing and frustrating their attempts to help.

Not only have developments in psychoanalysis helped recognition of the extent to which social workers' feelings about their own families can be stirred up by, and inform their child protection work both for good and ill. Feminist attention to sexual inequality has also resulted in greater awareness of the possibility of sex differences between social workers in the family feelings elicited by child abuse and the sexual inequalities involved given the different identification by sex with either the father's power or the mother's subordination in the family bred of men's social dominance outside it. Carr certainly draws attention to this sex difference. So too do Howe *et al.* (1988). They demonstrate that assessment of families as abusive is affected not only by whether the professionals involved were abused themselves as children but also by their sex.

Nowhere is this more likely to be important than in work with sexual abuse. Sex differences are less obvious in the countertransference reaction of social workers to non-accidental injury perhaps because, as Gordon (1989) and others point out, women are often as culpable as men on this score. Not that family ideology does not still equate mothering with caring femininity thereby blinding men and women social workers – as in the Beckford case – to maternal as well as paternal abuse, albeit feminism has begun to expose this (see e.g. Migutsch 1985).

Sex differences between social workers are more marked however as regards sexual abuse which mostly involves violation of daughters by fathers or stepfathers. Women social workers may be unwilling to adopt the masculinist confrontational approach advocated by Dale in working with non-accidental injury. But perhaps they are more willing than men to recognize and confront sexual abuse both in their own and their clients' lives especially now that feminism has helped reveal it and the general patriarchal abuse of women therein involved.

By the same token women social workers may be less self-critical, as the aggrieved sex, about their countertransference reactions to sexual abuse now that it is not so often attributed to maternal failure and neglect. Certainly men are now more self-critical in this sphere. Stephen Frosh (1987), for instance, argues that the sexual inequality leading us to recognize emotional vulnerability more readily in women than men leads to sexuality often becoming the sole avenue whereby men express their otherwise denied need of emotional closeness along with the defensive, triumphant, rejecting and degrading feelings thereby involved. This, he suggests, in turn gives rise to reaction formation in men social workers against such feelings in their sex, and an urgent need to atone for its wrongdoing. Men social workers may accordingly impulsively act out such reactions rather than contain, process, and think through the child's and parents' feelings that also need taking on board in arriving at a considered rather then impulsive course of action.

Alternatively as David Mann (1989) points out, men workers can become embroiled, because of their sex, in countertransference identification with the child's abuser. He gives an example of just this process, of finding himself identifying with the child's sexually abusive, aggressive brother when the co-therapist – who had become the wicked mother in the patient's eyes – was absent. Others too (e.g. Gardner 1990) indicate the dangers of both men and women therapists being likewise drawn into abusing the victims of child abuse.

Psychoanalytic readiness to recognize such countertransference reactions, once obscured by Freudian patriarchalism, has also resulted in therapists and social workers being more aware of such reactions in working with physical abuse and neglect. Krell and Okin (1984), for instance, point out that abused, neglected and unwanted children can evoke feelings of hostility or ambivalence in the social worker. Reactions to abusive parents, they say, can include disgust, anger, dislike, hopelessness, sympathy, guilt and a sense of vicarious pleasure in the parents' mistreatment of a child that social workers themselves find unlikeable. Abusive parents can also elicit otherwise repressed feelings in the social worker of grandiosity, condescension, control or even sadism leading in turn to fear of the parents' retaliation. Failure to recognize these feelings, or recognizing them only impulsively to act them out, can result in avoidance of the case, drift or over-hasty decision-making (see also Pollak and Levy 1989). Similarly others have recently pointed out how general feelings of exhaustion and loss of confidence – burn-out – can also adversely affect decision-making in child protection work (McGee 1989).

Recent psychoanalytic attention to the countertransference has also rendered more visible ways such feelings affect group as well as individual social work processes. Roger Bacon (1988), for instance, describes a case conference about a 5-year-old boy, Robert. The middle child of three, Robert suffered severe emotional abuse and neglect resulting, amongst other things, in his becoming incontinent. During the conference it emerged that the social workers had the omnipotent fantasy of being able to destroy Robert's family with their knowledge of it – a fantasy they extruded into Robert, who thereby became entirely unlovable in the team's eyes. Hence, claims Bacon, its failure to enter Robert's name on the child abuse register, so little did the team want to work with him. As a result they also overlooked the family's strength in recognizing the problem and wanting to change.

However far-fetched this new attention to social workers' countertransference reactions in group as well as individual settings, those outside psychoanalysis are also now more alert to this aspect of child protection. The Tyra Henry inquiry, for instance, draws attention to the way group dynamics influenced decision-making in this case, namely through the way Avon Pailthorpe's perspective prevailed in case conferences because others invested omniscience in her on account of her experience of fostering and multiracial issues (London Borough of Lambeth 1987). Similarly Olive Stevenson, chair of the recent Wandsworth child abuse inquiry (London Borough of Wandsworth 1990), points out how social work in Cleveland was hampered by those who felt child sexual abuse requires removal of alleged victims from their parents holding sway over those who, although not necessarily subscribing to this view, went along with it so much were they swept away by the anxiety, anger, and distress aroused by sexual abuse.

Packman and Randall (1989) point out that the chaos of abusing families often engenders similar chaos in social work teams dealing with them. An illustration, from Dale *et al.* (1986a), is the case of Sandra, sexually abused by her father. Her case elicited two highly polarized attitudes in the team. This in turn produced paranoia and distrust like that occurring in Sandra's family itself. The result was drift and delay in taking measures to protect Sandra so much did the team, like her family, want to avoid conflict – in the team's case between entrenched dogmas drawn from systems theory and feminism.

Implications and conclusion

However entrenched, social work, feminism and psychoanalysis, as I have sought to demonstrate in this chapter, have done much recently to lift the lid off family feelings that both motivate and obstruct effective child protection. To conclude: what are some of the implications for improving social work practice in this area?

At the group level, the Tyra Henry inquiry recommends that case conferences be chaired by an independent party, not by the key worker's supervisor as in the Henry case, so as to help obviate such meetings being dominated by one, possibly highly subjective, viewpoint (London Borough of Lambeth). For the same reason, namely to counter the bias of family feeling engendered in each individual worker by child abuse, Dale *et al.* (1986b) recommend that social workers operate collectively as a team rather than individually. Not that they overlook that teams can also reflect subjective processes occurring within the families with whom they work. But, they argue, provided such countertransference feelings are not impulsively acted out but instead reflected upon they can provide useful information about the family, thereby enhancing rather than hindering effective practice. Team and inter-agency meetings may be sufficient to render such processes conscious. If not, Dale recommends bringing in an independent consultant to identify otherwise damagingly unconscious countertransference processes operating within the group. Furthermore his team also insists on firm management guidelines to prevent child protection becoming morassed in the family feelings and conflicts it elicits (see Dale *et al.* 1986a).

But what about the more day-to-day situation of individual social work with abusive families? Greater recognition of the damage done by the personal feelings aroused by such work has resulted in more value being given to supervision. The Beckford inquiry asserts its importance in balancing the key worker's subjective feelings through the supervisor insisting on having objective data and information (London Borough of Brent 1985). Others also emphasize the need for supervision to provide a space for social workers to look at, and talk through the feelings their work engenders. However, this is constrained by supervisors often being so obviously stressed themselves that supervisees feel loath to burden them yet further with their own problems. Or they fear lest in thus unburdening themselves they appear unprofessional and thereby stymie their chances of promotion.

Nevertheless, recent social work literature on child abuse strongly urges more supervision and consultation as a means of better managing the stress involved (see e.g. Cooper and Bell 1987; Glaser and Frosh 1988). As John Simmonds (1988) points out, however, it is not sufficient simply to introduce further supervision, team and case conference organization, and line manage-ment procedures. Certainly the procedural obstacles to recognizing child abuse and the countertransference feelings it evokes need to be undone. But we also need to recognize, so as to challenge, the psychological defences and ideological obstacles to such recognition as indicated in the above account of ways that the blinding of social work to child abuse by subjective longings and ideological belief in the family as essentially harmonious and conflict-free has been exposed by recent developments in social work, feminism and psychoanalysis.

References

Bacon, R. (1988) 'Counter-transference in a case conference', in G. Pearson, J. Treseder and M. Yelloly (eds) *Social Work and the Legacy of Freud*, London: Macmillan.
Butler-Sloss, E. (1988) *Report of the Inquiry into Child Abuse in Cleveland 1987*, Cm 412, London: HMSO.
Campbell, B. (1988) *Unofficial Secrets*, London: Virago.
Carr, A. (1989) 'Countertransference to families where child abuse has occurred', *Journal of Family Therapy* 11: 87–97.
Cooper, D. and Bell, D. (1987) *Social Work and Child Abuse*, London: Macmillan.
Dale, P., Davies, M., Morrison, T. and Waters J. (1986a) 'The towers of silence: creative and destructive issues for therapeutic teams dealing with sexual abuse', *Journal of Family Therapy* 8: 1–25.
Dale, P., Davies, M., Morrison, T. and Waters, J. (1986b) *Dangerous Families*, London: Tavistock.
Dingwall, R. Eekelaar, J. and Murray, L. (1983) *The Protection of Children: State Intervention in Family Life*, Oxford: Basil Blackwell.
Fraser, S. (1987) *My Father's House*, London: Virago.
Frosh, S. (1987) 'Issues for men working with sexually abused children', *British Journal of Psychotherapy* 3: 332–9.
Gardner, F. (1990) 'Psychotherapy with adult survivors of child sexual abuse', *British Journal of Psychotherapy* 6, 3: 285–94.
Glaser, D. and Frosh, S. (1988) *Child Sexual Abuse*, London: Macmillan.
Gordon, L. (1989) *Heroes of their Own Lives: The Politics and History of Family Violence*, London: Virago.
Howe, A. C., Herzberger, S. and Tennen, H. (1988) 'The influence of personal history of abuse and gender on clinicians' judgments of child abuse', *Journal of Family Violence* 3, 2: 105–19.
Jones, E. (1972) *Sigmund Freud Volume I*, London: Hogarth.
Krell, H. L. and Okin, R. L. (1984) 'Countertransference issues in child abuse and neglect cases', *American Journal of Forensic Psychiatry* 5: 7–16.
London Borough of Brent (1985) *A Child in Trust: The Report of the Panel of Inquiry into the Circumstances Surrounding the Death of Jasmine Beckford*, London: Borough of Brent.
London Borough of Greenwich (1987) *A Child in Mind: Protection of Children in a Responsible Society: The Report of the Commission of Inquiry into the Circumstances Surrounding the Death of Kimberley Carlile*, London: Borough of Greenwich.
London Borough of Lambeth (1987) *Whose Child? The Report of the Panel Appointed to Inquire into the Death of Tyra Henry*, London: Borough of Lambeth.
London Borough of Wandsworth (1990) *Report into the Death of Stephanie Fox*, London: Borough of Wandsworth.
McGee, R. (1989) 'Burnout and professional decision-making', *Journal of Counselling Psychology* 36, 3: 345–51.
Mann, D. (1989) 'Incest: the father and the male therapist', *British Journal of Psychotherapy* 6, 2: 143–53.
Migutsch, A. (1985) *Punishment*, London: Virago.
Packman, J. and Randall, J. (1989) 'Decision-making at the gateway to care', in O. Stevenson (ed.) *Child Abuse*, London: Harvester Wheatsheaf.

Parton, C. and Parton, N. (1989) 'Child protection, the law and dangerousness', in D, Stevenson (ed.) *Child Abuse*, London: Harvester Wheatsheaf.

Pollak, J. and Levy, S. (1989) 'Countertransference and failure to report child abuse and neglect', *Child Abuse and Neglect* 13: 515–22.

Riley, J. (1985) *The Unbelonging*, London: Women's Press.

Sayers, J. (1991) *Mothering Psychoanalysis: Helene Deutsch, Karen Horney, Anna Freud, Melanie Klein*, London: Hamish Hamilton.

Simmonds, J. (1988) 'Thinking about feelings in group care', in G. Pearson, J. Treseder and M. Yelloly (eds) *Social Work and the Legacy of Freud*, London: Macmillan.

Spring, J. (1987) *Cry Hard and Swim*, London: Virago.

Stevenson, O. (1989) *Child Abuse*, London: Harvester Wheatsheaf.

Strean, H. S. (1988) 'Effects of childhood sexual abuse on the psychosocial functioning of adults', *Social Work* 33, 5: 465–7.

8
Race, social work and child care

Mark R. D. Johnson

Social workers are accustomed to being 'damned if they do, damned if they don't'. As Franklin (1989) argued in the first issue of the *Yearbook*, press coverage of child abuse cases characterized social workers as simultaneously indecisive and ineffectual, and as authoritarian bureaucrats who pay little attention to civil liberties. This he suggested was one of those moral panics which are generated at times when 'traditional values and social institutions momentarily lose their credibility' (Franklin 1989: 4). In 1989 the issue of transracial adoption was to form the core of another moral panic affecting the practice of social work.

With the advent of 1992, British nationality and the national self-identity has become a constant leitmotiv of politicians and press alike. Antipathy to ethnic minority settlers in Britain was expressed by the former Conservative party chairman, Norman Tebbit, in April 1990, in his coinage of the so-called 'cricket test' for national identity (*Observer* 22 April 1990: 18); a further expression of xenophobia led to the resignation in July 1990 of the Secretary of State for Trade and Industry, Nicholas Ridley, following criticism of what he perceived to be characteristics of German culture (*Spectator* 14 July 1990: 5, 8). It would seem that the issue of race which was so topical in the 1960s has returned.

One of the ways in which that uncertainty is being explored is through the situation of children. Much of the present furore has centred upon schools, with stories of children 'forced to learn' nursery rhymes in Punjabi or Urdu: but the issue has also been a live one for social workers concerned with the situation of children in care. Indeed the new provisions of the Children Act 1989 place a statutory duty upon them to 'have due regard to' the racial origins, culture and language of the child and parents. Specifically in Part III (Section 22) 'Local Authority Support for Children and Families', the Act states that

In making any . . . decision a local authority shall give due consideration . . . to the child's religious persuasion, racial origin and cultural and linguistic background.

(Children Act 1989: 18)

The same terminology is repeated in Part VIII (Section 64) in discussing Registered Children's Homes, while Schedule 2 (Section 11) extends these provisions by stating that

Every Local Authority shall, in making any arrangements (a) for the provision of day care within their area, or (b) designed to encourage persons to act as local authority foster parents have regard to the different racial groups to which children within their area who are in need belong.

(Children Act 1989: 110)

In this chapter I shall seek to lay out some of the implications of that 'due regard'.

Race and adoption: a political issue

The ramifications of considering the role of race and culture in adoption and fostering go beyond questions about the welfare of the children alone, although clearly that is the principal concern of most parents and professionals. At a political level, however, it raises questions about the nature of race: what is the position of the child of a 'mixed race marriage', and about the relationship between black and white in society. As a guest writer observed in the *Voice* 'Viewpoint' column, 'They [whites] took our land, don't let them take our children' (*Voice* 13 March 1990). Since white children are rarely if ever placed for fostering in black homes, it is a legitimate question for black communities to ask whether they are in fact 'donors' of children for white couples. Some observers, and certainly individuals in the community, note that transracial adoption became common in the USA after the 1950s, as white birthrates fell. The factors behind that fall are complex, including the greater availability of safe and effective methods of contraception and abortion and perhaps the increasing acceptability of single parenthood. Additional factors, such as the impact of relative affluence and changing life-styles, along with costs and means of child care, also contributed to this reduction in supply of white babies, and black–white differentials in social and economic conditions magnified rather than diminished the gap in fertility rates. A similar pattern developed in Britain in the 1960s (Gill and Jackson 1983: 2) although subsequently the fertility rates for those of Afro-Caribbean origin in Britain have fallen to less than those of 'whites', albeit with a considerable growth in the number of babies being born and described as 'of mixed origin' (Haskey 1990: 35). Asian birth-rates are still relatively high, although now falling sharply, but historically few Asian babies have been placed for adoption or fostering. The focus has therefore been on the situation of those of 'West Indian' origin. Indeed Afro-Caribbean resistance through the development of placement strategies for black children has been growing since the mid-1970s. However, it is only recently that a similar sort of awareness has seemed to develop in the British African community (*Socialite* 29 September 1989), and indeed that the issue has seemed at all relevant to the Asian community. Following the events of summer 1989, when the 'moral panic' over white parents and transracial placement hit the headlines of the press (Johnson 1990), the situation would appear to have developed considerably.

Not all the controversy has stemmed from white British parents concerned about their own 'cultural identity'. In the case of the adoption and fostering of children from minority backgrounds much of the development of pressure has arisen from the growing assertiveness of black (Afro-Caribbean and Asian) communities. These have become conscious that they have been serving as suppliers of progeny to a white society which has otherwise sought to deny their cultural and socio-economic contributions. In recent years, matters appear to have come to a head, and it seems appropriate to review the situation. There are also new trends to be taken account of. As the supply of healthy black British children has been denied to white would-be adopters, and perhaps as a gut reaction to exposure in the media of the situation of 'Ceauşescu's Orphans' in Romania, the practice of inter-country adoption has reappeared (Editorial 1990). This has included well-publicized adoptions from Latin America and India. As yet, however, it is perhaps too early to comment upon this trend, but it may be worth considering what the implications of that practice may be for those children and indeed for social workers.

Historical approaches to black children

The controversy over the situation of children of ethnic minority origin in British society has been central within debates over 'British Race Relations' (Carter *et al.* 1987). The stereotypes evoked were as 'an alien wedge posing an unprecedented threat to the British way of life' (Carter *et al.* 1987: 16). Thus the Liverpool Group of the Conservative Commonwealth Association described how 'Hundreds of children of negroid or mixed parentage eventually find their way to the various homes to be maintained by the corporation, to be reared to unhappy maturity at great public expense' (Liverpool Group 1954, cited by Carter *et al.* 1987). With the growth of New Commonwealth settlement in Britain following the Second World War, such concern over the 'misuse' of children's homes by black parents was to intensify. This initially occurred in the context of a supposed pattern of West African parenting (Ellis 1971). It also drew attention to 'deviant' West Indian family structures (Fitzherbert 1967). Allied to this was a long-standing concern among British authorities regarding the situation of children of 'mixed race', a group which has historically been seen by welfare professionals as 'at risk'. Early attention was paid to the need to find non-residential care settings for black children, as they were perceived as 'hard to place' even during the early 1960s when adoption and fostering reached a peak never since attained. Commonly concern was expressed over the specific needs of such children, notably in respect of physical issues such as skin and hair care (see for example Community Relations Commission (CRC) 1976), but very rarely in relation to self-identity.

Later attention switched more specifically to the continuing presence of disproportionately large numbers of minority children in care. Also attention increasingly focused on the factors that prevented fostering and adoption placements for them. Many of the studies, such as that of Foren and Batta (1970) or McCulloch *et al.* (1978) were largely concerned with documenting this over-representation. Others sought to facilitate the practice of transracial adoption and fostering (Edgar 1974; CRC 1975; Jackson 1976) following the established practice developed in the USA. Interestingly a DHSS bibliography (1979) of the period consisted almost entirely of US references. Then as now, 'transracial' meant almost exclusively 'black child – white parents' even if British law did not expressly forbid the reverse as was the case in certain states in the USA. Legal sanctions did enter the picture, briefly, with a Commission for Racial Equality (CRE) 'Formal Investigation' into the refusal of one children's home to accept black placements (CRE 1979). But it was clear that legal sanctions alone would never produce a satisfactory solution to the problems of the agencies. It is perhaps surprising that it took so long for agencies to remedy the lack of willing adopters of black children by finding black foster homes. The reasons for this are probably to be found in stereotyped views of the suitability of such homes, based upon assumptions about social disadvantage, 'West Indian' marriage patterns and single-parent families and a blindness to the potential contribution of minority groups (Arnold 1982: 100). The search for black families for black children had to await developments in the 1980s, when the practice of transracial placement was beginning to come under question (Laurance 1983).

Given this and other insensitivities to the feelings of the black community, it is scarcely surprising that certain black authors saw social work as a 'bane to the West Indian Community' (Gibson 1979). Therefore the growing assertiveness of the community, and of black social work professionals, led to demands for changes in child care policy, and in attempts to set up alternative means for finding black families for black children (Small 1983a). There had been earlier attempts: the 'Soul Kids Campaign' of the late 1970s (Association of British Adoption and Fostering Agencies (ABAFA) 1977) met with slight success. Few resources were dedicated to the search, and most campaigns were clearly dependent upon the energy and commitment of key individuals, often with personal experience of the issue (Small 1983b; Schroeder and Lightfoot 1983). It was not until this grassroots activity had proved the viability of such a strategy, and the political climate had changed, that the mainstream services began to reconsider their apparently unquestioning support for transracial placement. It is, however, clear that it took both a demonstration of practicality and political will to bring this about. A breakthrough was the agreement of Lambeth Council in London to set up an experimental New Black Families Unit in conjunction with the Independent Adoption Service. This was extended from three to four years but then absorbed by the council following problems of collaborative working. However, it did demonstrate the possibilities for successful recruitment of black families, and the wherewithal by which this could be achieved (Arnold 1982: Arnold and James 1989).

Contemporary controversies and developments

Some commentators have observed that the 1980s were a period when 'get tough anti-racism' really got underway (Jervis 1990). Certainly the formation of ABSWAP (the Association of Black Social Workers) in 1983 was a significant development in the social work field. Inquiries into a series of tragedies such as the cases of Tyra Henry, Jasmine Beckford, Kimberley Carlile, and the refusal of an official inquiry into the case of Beverley Lewis, indicated a continuing confusion, not to say embarrassment among the profession, about the situation of black children 'at risk' of abuse. Those outside it, however, have never scrupled to attack, and while the anti-racist lobby grew during this period, it was also countered with increasing vigour. Agencies such as the right-wing Social Affairs Unit (*New Society* 15 May 1987: 5) used the issue of black children in care as another stick with which to beat 'extremist and doctrinaire' left-controlled authorities by publishing the report, *Denying Homes to Black Children* (Dale 1987). This appeared to argue that transracial or transcultural adoption was of positive benefit to children of minority origin. However, it failed totally to address the issue of cultural or ethnic diversity in society, going as far to state that 'race signifies nothing' (Dale 1987: 26).

More recently it is possible to discern the government paying some attention to the notion of Britain as a multicultural and multiracial society. For example in the Community Care White Paper:

> The Government recognises that people from different cultural backgrounds may have particular care needs and problems. Minority communities may have different concepts of community care and it is important that service providers are sensitive to these variations. Good community care will take account of the circumstances of minority communities and will be planned in consultation with them.
>
> (DoH 1989: 10–11)

Even among the few departments that have committed themselves to promoting equality of opportunity in service provision, policy implementation is still in its early stages. Ten years on from the publication of the ADSS/CRE (1978) report, which found that responses were 'patchy, piecemeal and lacking in strategy', there is still little evidence that social services departments are doing much more than making ad hoc arrangements (CRE 1989: 5). Perhaps this lack of strategy is why authorities have seemed unprepared for the legal challenges to policy which emerged as soon as attempts were made to enforce the new determination for 'appropriate placement' – and why all too often the 'tabloid media' have found so much to exploit.

Policy and the press

During August 1989 the press, notably the *Daily Mail* and *Daily Express*, gave front-page headlines to an Appeal Court backing of Croydon Borough Council's removal of a child from a white foster mother who had cared for the child from six days after its birth, and his placement with 'a West Indian couple' for adoption. The case was complicated by the 'mixed race' origins of the child, his mother's mental illness and father's imprisonment, and the remarriage of the (divorced) foster mother. Following the failure of her appeal against the decision (*Guardian* Law Report 1989), the strictures of David Mellor, the minister of state responsible (*Community Care* 5 October 1989), and the upholding of that decision on appeal to the House of Lords, (*Daily Telegraph* and others 2 and 3 November 1989), it became apparent that the press were loath to abandon 'the spicy combination of race, social workers and babies' (*New Statesman and Society* 1 September 1989). Much of the debate picked up the issue of 'transracialness' for children of 'mixed race origin'; a problem also for the parents of such children who wish to value both the white and the black parents' contributions (*Community Care* 5 October 1989; *Caribbean Times* 6 October 1989; *Voice* 28 November 1989). Other commentators observed that irrespective of such considerations, these children would be seen as black by most of society (*London Standard* 10 November 1989), and must learn the techniques for survival in a racist society (*Social Work Today* 21 September 1989; *Voice* 13 March 1990). Almost all reportage agreed that the primary factor must be the child's best interests, but some saw speed of placement and stability as of primary importance (*Social Work Today* 31 August 1989; *Asian Herald* 6 October 1989; *Guardian* 1 March 1990). Many examples were put forward, as academic research had suggested (Tizard and Phoenix 1989; *Community Care* 5 October 1989), of where white parents had done a 'good job' in bringing up black children (*Coventry Evening Telegraph* 9 February 1990). These included the clearly honest and heartfelt testimony of some black children themselves (*Sunday Correspondent* 5 November 1989), but it is now apparent that the tide of professional opinion has moved on.

The popular press have continued to regard these issues as 'good for a story', doing probably no little harm to what was once called 'good race relations' in the process. Few took as balanced an approach as that adopted in the *Independent* (28 October 1989). While there was an implicit assumption in much of the writing that Black equalled African or Afro-Caribbean, during 1989 the coverage of the issue was 'enlarged' to include the situation of children of Asian origin (*Daily Star* and *Daily Mail* 31 October 1989), although it would appear that there was at that time less concern expressed by Asian religious community groups over this (*New Life* 17 November 1989; Manzour 1989). Subsequently debate among Asian groups has developed, and a television programme (*East*, BBC TV, 11 June 1990) discussed at some length the possible reasons why Asian parents might be loath to adopt children from local authority care. Not unreasonably attention was drawn in that discussion to the particular difficulties of matching not only on 'skin colour', but also by religion, language and indeed caste. Surely if attention has to be paid to the best interests of the child, then the particular concerns of the cultural community to which that child belongs, and wherein marriages are likely to be arranged, must also be an issue. But at the same time, children interviewed for the programme made the telling point against transracial adoption that however loving the home, it is immediately apparent to onlookers that the black child – whether Afro-Caribbean or Asian – is not living with his or her natural parent(s). This capacity for the immediate assessment of 'otherness' is rarely as obvious for white children. It is hardly surprising that black children in such a situation often feel exposed, vulnerable and insecure. What is surprising is that those who pontificate about the 'greater need of the child for love and security' (see e.g. Black 1990) have apparently failed to recognize the new forms of jeopardy that transracial placement may create.

The issue has also concerned a sector of Britain's black population which has more rarely been considered of late. Further to discussion in Parliament about the Children Bill, and a TVS television documentary, the issue of West African patterns of fostering was raised. This had appeared to lay dormant since the publication of a number of studies in the 1970s (Ellis 1971; 1977; Ellis *et al.* 1978), which seemed to indicate an excessive use of private fostering arrangements.

> This readiness to place the children in the homes of private families has led to the popular belief that this practice is merely an extension of patterns in the cultural background of the [West African] students.
>
> (CRC 1975: 16)

This professional concern now re-emerged with the added threat of the contemporary panic regarding child abuse (*Guardian, Daily Telegraph* and *Morning Star* 23 October 1989; *Daily Express* 2 November 1989). Clearly the use of private fostering agencies, the pattern of child care now followed by many West African families in Britain, is no guarantee of greater sensitivity, or a way of avoiding censure. It might appear that little has changed in public attitudes since those early days, although perhaps there is a greater sensitivity among professionals and certainly less excuse for them to express ignorance of the issues (McGrath 1989).

At long last, furthermore, some of that greater awareness is also emerging in research and has been present in a number of studies of child placement. For the first time in twenty-five years, some national statistics on the background of children entering care have been collated in a study by Bebbington and Miles (1989). They observe that (perhaps not surprisingly) a background of deprivation is the most significant 'risk factor'. When this is taken into account, the reputed over-representation of children of Afro-Caribbean descent in care disappears. However, those of 'mixed race' remain more than twice as likely to enter formal care, although the report does not enlighten us as to why this occurs. What that study also does not address is the fate of children once admitted. Rowe and Hundleby (1989a; 1989b) attempted to get behind the statistics, and discovered substantial gaps in our knowledge in this area of policy. In particular they found 'staggering differences' in local authority policy. It is their belief that most Afro-Caribbean children enter care for relatively short periods, while those of 'mixed parentage' experience both longer and more frequent placement and are also more likely than whites to be placed for adoption. Once again, however, they felt unable to comment on outcomes, and observed that 'in spite of our large overall numbers, we found that sub-groups of Afro-Caribbean, African, Asian and mixed-parentage children were often too small for definite conclusions to be reached' (Rowe and Hundleby 1989a: 13). A more focused study, looking at only 'healthy black pre-school children' awaiting adoption, reflected the impressions of the public debate that 'the objectives of speedy placement and same-race placement often pull in different directions' (Chambers 1989). If, however, the findings of the two research projects cited earlier are correct, then a preoccupation with adoption may be misleading. Clearly the problems are centred upon the greater shortage of appropriate short-term foster parents, and perhaps of suitable preventive activity (Barn 1990).

Children's identity and the effects of policy

Few social workers would disagree that it is preferable for any child to spend the minimum amount of time in residential care. An increase in the number of foster-places would self-evidently assist in bringing this about. However, even a foster placement can lead to a degree of uncertainty and insecurity which may adversely affect the child. The question that then has to be asked is whether the deleterious effects of a 'transracial' placement outweigh those of remaining 'in care': an issue just beginning to be discussed by those who have experienced it (Mallows 1989). For some proponents there is no doubt, and Children First has made considerable impact with its campaigning around this issue. They do not seek to deny that some individuals 'have suffered badly as a result of being placed in white families – families who have failed to nurture healthy attitudes towards ethnic identity' (Children First 1990: 1). However, these are contrasted, as in the newspaper stories cited above, with examples of 'those black people who have grown up in white families and who are successful in their careers, happy in their personal lives and are at ease with people from all ethnic backgrounds' (Children First 1990: 1). Clearly such people exist! What is not clear is the effects upon those who subsequently are *not* 'successful in their careers', whether because of racism endemic in the employment market, misfortune or personal reasons. Children First accept that damaged lives do exist, but they maintain that 'none of the empirical research carried out into the outcome of transracial placements offers any support for the view that it is damaging to children' (1990: 1).

In opposition to this view the research of the Commission for Racial Equality can be cited. They unequivocally state that 'experience has shown that transracial placements may result in a child from an ethnic minority group becoming confused and negative about her/his colour or racial origins' (CRE 1990: 3). They agree that 'research has been inconclusive', but argue that most of the transracially adopted children studied were living in 'predominantly white middle-class areas' (CRE 1990: 6) and had suppressed their racial identity. While those successful children studied were possessed of strong self-identity and confidence – characteristics we are led to assume come from growing up in such neighbourhoods – the problem is never addressed of what will happen to such people in later life when they meet personal racism and discrimination, as it is certain they will. As the new director of BAAF (British Agencies for Adoption and Fostering), Chris Hammond, observes,

> Our concern is for the wider needs of children, which often only become significant as they grow older and start to separate from their families . . . difficulties have arisen as the child approaches adolescence and becomes more aware of issues such as racism.
>
> (Hammond 1990: 53)

Anecdotal evidence from the author's personal experience testifies to the different ways in which black families in middle-class 'white highlands' experience and avoid racism, and the impact upon their children of discovering that cruder forms of racism exist in less genteel neighbourhoods, that they are not elsewhere sheltered by the good respect in which their families may be locally held. This dilemma was identified for American practitioners in the early 1970s by Chestang: 'The black man is not a marginal man but a bicultural man . . . he lives in both the larger society and in the black society' (1972: 103). Chestang also questioned whether white parents could equip the black child for the 'inevitable assaults' which the child would come to encounter simply on the basis of skin colour. Similarly Chimezie (1975) stressed the need for the black child to learn psychosocial skills for survival in a racist society. This, he concluded, was just as true for those of mixed racial origin. 'To say that it is doubtful to which race the mulatto [*original terminology*] belongs is a naive statement that does not recognise the definition of a black person in this society' (Chimezie 1975: 298). In the same article, questioning the 'psychosocial need of white adoptive parents to adopt black children' he observed that

> individual white adoptive parents may harbor the thought that they are 'saving' the black child from black upbringing – one dimension of the so-called 'rescue fantasy'.
>
> (Chimezie 1975: 296)

Even where that ethnocentricity was not so overtly found, he doubts whether the parental action was entirely altruistic – since in his opinion almost all consciously motivated human actions serve selfish needs – and hence white parents are from the outset in a poor position to teach the child the survival skills needed in a racist society.

Specifically Chimezie maintains that white adoptive parents skirt around the issue of racism, either by ignoring it or by appearing to believe it is part of a more general system of oppression and therefore not something requiring specific challenge or coping strategies. Although the opponents of racial matching have sought to deny that there are 'life skills' specific to black communities, the day-to-day experience and testimony of many black people, including those in white families, is such that these experiences are real to them. Furthermore, there are too many well-documented and attested cases of black children seeking to 'whiten' themselves to be dismissed as a modern myth. One of my own students reports:

> I know of a current case of a 9-year-old boy who after attempting to bleach his skin physically using Domestos bleach and a scrubbing brush is

now receiving psychotherapy. He has since been removed from his white foster parents (who contested the move) and has been placed with black foster parents.

(personal communication)

The practitioner has to balance such immediate experience and anecdotal evidence against the studies of Simon and Altstein (1987), Tizard and Phoenix (1989) and Gill and Jackson (1983), which may be summarized as stating that, 'on balance we could not prove any serious harm to self-esteem, or any measurable difference in awareness of blackness' (author's interpretation). But this has to be weighed by the practitioner concerned with the welfare of an individual child, and clear evidence of benefits arising from same-race placement (Heywood 1990). Within this setting too, other dimensions must be considered. For example the reactions of family members such as aunts, grandparents and siblings to adopted black children joining 'their' family. Considerable stresses can arise from this, as they have been seen to do in the extended families of 'mixed marriages'. It is true that the Simon and Altstein (1987) study did ask about the remainder of the family, but none the less it seems more concerned with the parents' feelings and the relationship of child to parent, while appearing to ignore the reaction of 'significant others' in the family. That study also failed to contribute to our understanding of the ability of the child to function in society. They omitted to interview virtually all of those children who had left home for college or an independent life. Equally none of the British research studies of transracial placement has followed the adoptees beyond their teenage years.

Criticisms have been levelled at the methodology used by such studies (Rowe 1990; Small 1986). Doubts exist regarding the validity of 'doll choice studies', that is do children identify with dolls, or even photographs of other children? These doubts and criticisms combined with certain inconsistencies within the argument raise the whole question if there is no harm done by sticking with transracial adoption, there cannot be any serious harm to be risked by changing, either! Indeed there is reason to suppose that other benefits may come from a widening of the potential placement market and a strengthening of the black community's 'parity of esteem' in being regarded as 'fit to foster'. However, it seems likely that academic argument will continue over the merits of the case until sufficient numbers of 'in-racial' placements have occurred to establish that policy's impact. Or, as Chimezie wrote in the mid-1970s, that until empirical studies are made 'of the adult personalities of white-raised Blacks, placements of black children should not proceed as if it had already been ascertained that transracial adoption is beneficial' (Chimezie 1975: 299). An alternative test might also be suggested for the validity of the 'transracial' argument, since some schemes are now finding it easier to recruit black carers than Whites:

Whether those professionals who deny that any harm results from transracial placement have the same attitude to white children being so placed is a question which does not so far seem to have been addressed.

(Shaw and Hipgrave 1989: 16)

During preparation for the writing of this chapter, only one such reported case was found: practitioners are invited to reflect upon their feelings in the matter.

Conclusion

While the academics and researchers debate, progress has been made. Most significantly at the start of 1990 the Health Minister (Virginia Bottomley) appeared to have bitten on the bullet and accepted the (new) conventional wisdom (*Independent* 30 January 1990). Current policy guidelines, enshrined in a Circular from the Department of Health, state clearly that

> it may be taken as a guiding principle of good practice that, other things being equal and in the great majority of cases, placement with a family of similar ethnic origin and religion is most likely to meet a child's needs.
>
> (Utting 1990: 3)

Furthermore, it is implicit that local authorities are expected to make determined efforts to recruit both long-term and short-term caring families from all appropriate groups represented in their areas; to train their staff in ethnic sensitivity; and to recognize that those of 'mixed ethnic origin' should be 'helped to . . . take a pride in both or all elements in their cultural heritage' (Utting 1990: 4). The responsibility for this, of course, will fall primarily upon social workers, and it may be assumed especially upon black staff. At least they can now point to the growing body of good practice literature, including the official guidelines of the Inspectorate to support them. These will help those concerned to insist that it is the responsibility of all their colleagues to be aware and competent to support black families involved in adoption and fostering. What is more, the Circular is quite explicit that there is a legal duty upon departments to ensure that the guidelines are followed. Regrettably the evidence found by the CRE suggests that remarkably few have developed adequate policy guidelines in this field (CRE 1990). Media reactions and resistance notwithstanding (*Daily Mirror* 6 February 1990; *Birmingham Post* 5 March 1990), it is clear that in future, and with the additional force of the Children Act 1989, those local authorities who continue to neglect their responsibilities in seeking to place black children with appropriate black families will be in breach of their statutory duties. May we wonder how long it will be before such an approach appears in the delivery of other services?

Acknowledgement

I should particularly like to thank Nancy Johnson and Janet Thenacho for their comments and assistance with the development of this paper. The Centre for Research in Ethnic Relations is a national research centre funded by the Economic and Social Research Council.

References

ABAFA (Association of British Adoption and Fostering Agencies) (1977) *Working with West Indian Applicants in Fostering and Adoption*, Soul Kids Campaign Report,

London: ABAFA reprinted in J. Cheetham (ed.) (1981) *Social and Community Work in a Multi-Racial Society*, London: Harper & Row.

ADSS/CRE (1978) *Multi-Racial Britain – The Social Services Response*, London: Association of Directors of Social Services/Council for Racial Equality.

Ahmad, S., Cheetham, J. and Small, J. (1986) *Social Work with Black Children and their Families*, London: Batsford.

Arnold, E. (1982) 'Finding black families for black children in Britain', In J. Cheetham (ed.) *Social Work and Ethnicity*, London: Allen & Unwin.

Arnold, E. and James, M. (1989) 'Finding black families for black children in care: a case study', *New Community* 15, 3: 417–25.

Barn, R. K. (1990) 'Black children in local authority care: admission patterns', *New Community* 16, 2: 229–46.

Bebbington, A. and Miles, J. (1989) 'The background of children who enter local authority care', *British Journal of Social Work* 19: 349–68.

Black, D. (1990) 'What do children need from parents?', *Adoption and Fostering* 14, 1: 43–51.

Carter, B., Harris, C. and Joshi, S. (1987) *The 1951–55 Conservative Government and the Racialisation of Black Immigration*, Policy Paper 11, Centre for Research in Ethnic Relations, Warwick University, Coventry.

Chambers, H. (1989) 'Cutting through the dogma', *Social Work Today* 21, 6: 14–15.

Chestang, L. (1972) 'The dilemma of biracial adoption', *Social Work* 17, 3: 100–5.

Children First (1990) *Transracial Adoption: The Issues*, London: Children First in Adoption and Fostering.

Chimezie, A. (1975) 'Transracial adoption of black children', *Social Work* 20, 4: 296–301.

CRC (Community Relations Commission) (1975) *Fostering Black Children*, London: CRC.

—— (1976) *Afro Hair and Skin Care*, London: CRC.

CRE (Commission for Racial Equality) (1979) *Barlavington Manor Children's Home: Report of a Formal Inquiry*, London: CRE.

—— (1989) *Racial Equality in Social Services Departments*, London: CRE.

—— (1990) *Adopting a Better Policy: Adoption and Fostering of Ethnic Minority Children – The Race Dimension*, London: CRE.

Dale, D. (1987) *Denying Homes to Black Children: Britain's New Race Adoption Policies*, Research report 8, London: Social Affairs Unit.

DoH (1989) *Caring for People: Community Care in the Next Decade and Beyond*, Cm 849, London: HMSO.

DHSS (1979) *Bibliography B117: Transracial Adoption*, London: Library of the DHSS.

Dutt, R. (1989) *Community Care – Race Dimension*, London: Race Equality Unit, National Institute for Social Work.

Edgar. M. E. (1974) 'Black children, white parents', *Child Adoption* 78, 4: 35–9.

Editorial (1990) 'Inter-country adoption', *Adoption and Fostering* 14, 1: 1–2.

Ellis, J. (1971) 'The fostering of West African children in England', *Social Work Today* 2, 5: 9–11.

—— (1977) 'Differing conceptions of a child's needs', *British Journal of Social Work* 7, 2: 155–71.

Ellis, J., Stapleton, P., Biggs, V. (1978) *West African Families in Britain: A Meeting of Two Cultures*, London: Routledge & Kegan Paul.

Fitzherbert, K. (1967) *West Indian Children in London*, London: Bell.

Foren, R. and Batta, I. (1970) 'Colour as a variable in the use made of a local authority child care department', *Social Work* 27, 3: 10–15.

Franklin, B. (1989) 'Wimps and bullies: press reporting of child abuse', in P. Carter, T. Jeffs and M. Smith (eds) (1989) *Social Work and Social Welfare Yearbook 1*, Milton Keynes: Open University Press.

Gibson, A. (1979) *Social Work: A Bane to the WestIndian Community*, London: WestIndian Concern (Caribbean House).

Gill, O. and Jackson, B. (1983) *Adoption and Race*, London: Batsford.

Guardian Law Report (1989) 'Adoption of a child of mixed race', *Guardian* 8 September: 39.

Hammond, C. (1990) 'BAAF and the placement needs of children from minority ethnic groups', *Adoption and Fostering* 14, 1: 52–3.

Haskey, J. (1990) 'The ethnic minority populations of Great Britain: estimates by ethnic group and country of birth', *Population Trends* 60: 35–8.

Heywood, S. (1990) 'Putting same race placement policy into practice', *Adoption and Fostering* 14, 2: 9–10.

Jackson, B. (1976) *Adopting a Black Child*, London: Association of British Adoption and Fostering Agencies.

Jervis, M. (1990) 'The decade of gloom and boom', *Social Work Today* 21, 17: 14–15.

Johnson, M. R. D. (1990) 'Health and social services: a matter of controversy', *New Community* 16, 2: 288–95.

Laurance, J. (1983) 'Should white families adopt black children?', *New Society* 30 June: 499–501.

Liverpool Group (1954) *The Problem of Colonial Immigrants*, Conservative Commonwealth Association Liverpool Group, Cabinet Papers 124/1191.

McCulloch, J. W., Batta, I. D. and Smith, N. J. (1978) 'Colour as a variable in the children's section of a local authority social services department', *New Community* 7, 1: 78–84.

McGrath, S. (1989) 'Guide to placing Black children in care', *Social Work Today* 14 September: 32.

Mallows, M. (1989) 'Abercrave weekend: exploring the needs of transracially adopted young people', *Adoption and Fostering* 13, 3: 34–6.

Manzour, K. (1989) 'Fostering a Muslim identity', *Muslimwise* 8 December: 7.

Rowe, J. (1990) 'Research, race and child care placements', *Adoption and Fostering* 14, 2: 6–8.

Rowe, J. and Hundleby, M. (1989a) 'Child care: placement patchwork', *Community Care* 14 September: 11–13.

—— (1989b) 'Child care measure for measure', *Community Care* 21 September: 23–5.

Rowe, J., Hundleby, M. and Garnett, L. (1989) *Child Care Placement Patterns and Outcomes*, London: British Agencies for Adoption and Fostering.

Schroeder, H. and Lightfoot, D. (1983) 'Finding Black families', *Adoption and Fostering* 7, 1: 18–21.

Shaw, M. and Hipgrave, T. (1989) 'Young people and their carers in specialist fostering', *Adoption and Fostering* 13, 4: 11–17.

Simon, R. J. and Altstein, H. (1987) *Transracial Adoptees and their Families: A Study of Identity and Commitment*, New York: Praeger.

Small, J. (1983a) *Black Children in Care: Evidence to the House of Commons Social Services Committee*, London: Association of Black Social Workers and Allied Professionals.

—— (1983b) 'New Black families', *Adoption and Fostering* 6, 3: 35–9.

—— (1986) 'Transracial placements: conflicts and contradictions', in S. Ahmad, J. Cheetham and J. Small, *Social Work with Black Children and their Families*, London: Batsford.

Tizard, B. and Phoenix, A. (1989) 'Black identity and transracial adoption', *New Community* 15, 3: 427–37.

Utting, W. B. (1990) 'Issues of race and culture in the family placement of children', Circular CI(90)2, London: Social Services Inspectorate, Department of Health.

9
Drug problems and social work

Geoffrey Pearson

Drug misuse has not been a central focus of concern for British social work, except for the small number of social workers employed in specialist agencies such as drug dependency units, or those working in 'street agencies' in the voluntary sector (Dorn and South 1985). During the course of the 1980s, however, Britain's drug problems took a sudden turn for the worse in the form of a sustained heroin epidemic (Pearson *et al.* 1986; Pearson 1987a; Dorn and South 1987; Parker *et al.* 1988; MacGregor 1989). As a consequence drug-related problems are likely to have made an increasing impact on the work of social workers, especially those working in the Probation Service. There is also some evidence of increasing concern about drug-related issues in child care and child protection work. Even so, it probably remains true that with the exception of probation officers, problems of drug misuse make an uneven impact on the routine workloads of social workers and that this is therefore an area of continuing uncertainty.

The aim of this chapter is to review this field and its policy contexts. While heroin misuse has been the central concern of the 1980s, this has given way in some areas to the illicit use of tranquillizers, with evidence of a growing pattern of cocaine use adding a new uncertainty. The risk of accelerated HIV infection among intravenous drug users has brought about a rapid policy shift. Drug misuse is therefore a problem area of extreme fluidity, and one which places a number of challenges before social work. As a first step, it will be necessary to outline the background of British drug control policy which has often been the subject of misunderstanding (Pearson 1990).

The 'British system': sixties breakdown?

Britain has been something of a late developer in terms of problems of drug misuse. It is true that in the nineteenth century opium use was widespread, where it became associated with the problem of 'infant doping' through the use of patent medicines marketed under names such as 'Soothing Syrup', 'Mothers' Quietness', 'Nurses' Drops' and 'Pennyworth of Peace' (Berridge and Edwards 1981). In the twentieth century, however, it was Britain's drug problem itself which seemed to go to sleep for many years. In contrast with North America where patterns of heroin and cocaine use had been long established (Courtwright *et al.* 1989) there were few signs of serious drug misuse in the early post-war period. In his authoritative review of trends in heroin misuse in Britain, Spear (1969: 254) pointed to 'the first signs of an emerging drug sub-culture' in the mid-1950s, although it remained quite tiny and was almost entirely centred on jazz clubs in the West End of London, together with other clubs catering for foreign sailors and soldiers.

Since the 1920s and the recommendations of the Rolleston Committee, Britain had adopted a policy whereby drug addicts were to be regarded as sick rather than as criminals, allowing medical practitioners to prescribe drugs such as morphine and heroin to addicts in regulated doses (Ministry of Health 1926). Once again this stood in sharp contrast to the strict prohibitionist policy of the USA, where under the leadership of Harry Anslinger the Narcotics Bureau had hounded both drug addicts and doctors who advocated prescribing methods as criminals and degenerates (Courtwright *et al.* 1989). As a result of these deep shades of contrast, both in terms of policy and problems, an argument gained ground that it was because of the success of the so-called 'British system' of maintenance prescribing that Britain had failed to develop either a serious problem of illicit drug misuse or its associated pattern of criminal activity and trafficking (Schur 1964).

A certain amount of concern in the late 1950s, however, had prompted the government to convene an inter-departmental committee chaired by Sir Russell Brain. The committee advised that although the number of known addicts had increased from 260 in 1954 to 454 in 1960, the illicit trade in dangerous drugs remained 'so small as to be almost negligible' (Ministry of Health 1961: 9). Consequently the Brain Committee saw no need to rethink the assumptions of the Rolleston era and the right of medical practitioners to prescribe dangerous drugs to their patients.

Even so, there was a persisting current of anxiety surrounding the use of amphetamines ('purple hearts', 'pep pills' and 'mother's little helpers') by young people; as a result of these kinds of concerns the Brain Committee was reconvened within less than four years. In its second report the Brain Committee reaffirmed its general stance that the addict 'should be regarded as a sick person . . . and not as a criminal', and also dismissed fears that illicit trafficking had become a major problem (Ministry of Health 1965: 6–8). What was regarded as a significant difficulty, however, was that a small number of doctors in London were prescribing huge amounts of heroin to patients who were under their care. In one case, a doctor had prescribed 600,000 tablets of heroin (that is 6 kilograms) in a single year. The same doctor had prescribed 900 tablets (9 grammes) to an addict, and three days later a further 6 grammes to the same patient who had allegedly 'lost' the heroin in an accident.

It is hardly a matter for surprise that these findings caused a public scandal, nor that the second Brain Committee recommended that tighter restrictions should be placed on doctors' rights to prescribe dangerous drugs. The committee's central recommendation was that specialist treatment centres should be established, at least in the London area, and that only medical staff working in these centres should be allowed to prescribe drugs such as heroin and cocaine to addicts. More generally doctors were to be placed under a statutory obligation to notify the Home Office of addicts who came to their attention.

The government accepted these recommendations, albeit in a somewhat leisurely and hesitant manner, so that the new drug treatment centres (or 'clinics' as they are more usually known) were opened in 1968. In the mean time controversy had continued to surround the issue of drugs. In 1965 former Prime Minister Harold Macmillan's grandson had died from an overdose in Oxford. A couple of years later, Mick Jagger of the Rolling Stones was jailed for the possession of a small amount of amphetamine sulphate. 'Flower power' and 'psychedelia' had also arrived, with immense publicity surrounding the celebration of LSD (*d*-lysergic acid diethylamide) by the Beatles and their *Sergeant Pepper* album. And from California's Haight Ashbury, there had been the fiasco of the 'Summer of Love' in 1967 . . . with abundant evidence of 'bad trips', 'flash-backs' and unwary adolescents crashed out on 'speed' (amphetamines) (Davis and Munoz 1968).

There was thus a heightened sense of crisis about drug problems in the late 1960s, fuelling an unrelenting moral panic as anti-Vietnam War protest spread across student campuses, through and beyond the dramatic revolt of May 1968 in Paris. Undoubtedly these background events helped to shape the perception of what was at stake in Britain's change of drug policies. Certainly there had been an upturn in heroin misuse, with a five-fold increase in the number of known addicts in the course of the 1960s. Even so, in 1968 there were still fewer than 1,000 heroin addicts undergoing treatment in Britain, of whom only 147 were located outside London (Home Office 1968: 25). The number of doctors found guilty of over-prescribing by the second Brain Report, moreover, had been 'not more than six' (Ministry of Health 1965: 6). What was widely acclaimed as the breakdown of the 'British system' might therefore seem, on reflection, to have been no more than a storm in a teacup (Pearson 1990).

The 1980s heroin epidemic: enter the dragon

During the 1970s Britain's drug problems stabilized themselves to a large degree. The new clinics, as described in some detail by Stimson and Oppenheimer (1982), experienced a certain amount of initial difficulty in negotiating their role – which encompassed the sometimes conflicting functions of treatment and control. In the clinics the prescribing of heroin to addicts rapidly passed out of fashion, to be replaced by the substitute drug methadone either in an injectable or linctus form. On the street the 'flower power' and 'hippie' movements came and went, with a decline in the popularity of potentially hazardous psychedelics such as LSD. Although cannabis continued to gain ground in popularity, there were few innovations in the British drugs scene. The one notable development was that in some parts of the country there was a modest growth of an injecting drug subculture, involving a highly dangerous phase of poly-drug use which mixed amphetamines and barbiturates, although this went largely unnoticed except in specialist professional circles (Jamieson *et al.* 1984). In the late 1970s there was also some evidence of spillage on to the street market through the over-prescribing of opioids such as Diconal (known colloquially as 'dikes', 'dikeys' or 'pinkies') which became a preference drug in some localities (Advisory Council on the Misuse of Drugs 1982; Pearson *et al.* 1990).

At some point between 1979 and 1981 there was a dramatic sea change as heroin came to be available in cheap and plentiful supply from the south-west Asian region bordering on Iran, Afghanistan and Pakistan. The 'new' heroin was in a smokeable form, and came to be associated with the practice of 'Chasing the Dragon' – heating the drug on metal foil and inhaling the fumes – thereby allowing many of the new heroin users to circumvent the formidable cultural barrier against self-injection (Pearson *et al.* 1986; Pearson 1987a; Burr 1987; Parker *et al.* 1988).

The habit spread like wildfire in many towns and cities, including any number where heroin misuse had been previously quite unknown: Manchester, Liverpool and the Wirral peninsula in Merseyside, Glasgow, Edinburgh and elsewhere. In those areas where injecting drug subcultures (often around 'speed' and 'barbs') were already in place, the new 'brown' heroin could be rendered soluble for injection purposes by acidifying the powder with a 'Jiff' lemon, citric crystals or a drop of vinegar. In other areas, 'chasing' remained the dominant pursuit. But this was only one of the ways in which the new heroin problem suffered from local and regional diversity. Research in the North of England in the mid-1980s established that the problem was not only much more severe to the west of the Pennines than to the east, but that it also varied substantially from one town to another and between different neighbourhoods within any given town or city (Pearson *et al.* 1986).

Some of this local diversity could be explained by reference to the uneven development of distribution networks, and hence the local availability of the drug. In other cases, it might have been because of enduring patterns of local resistance within drug subcultures towards the use of a 'hard' drug such as heroin. One highly significant variation, however, was the way in which the heroin epidemic assumed its most intense form in areas suffering from the highest levels of unemployment, social deprivation and housing decay (Pearson *et al.* 1986; Pearson 1987b; Parker *et al.* 1988; Giggs *et al.* 1989).

This association of heroin misuse with employment was by no means a straightforward, causal relationship (Pearson 1987b). It was nevertheless real. The new heroin problem thereby came to interact with a whole host of other social difficulties, as it began to settle like a shroud around those already embattled communities where the infrastructure of jobs and housing was in the process of being wrecked by Thatcher's disastrous monetarist experiments of the early 1980s.

The scale of this calamity should not be under-estimated. Detailed research in the Wirral peninsula has indicated that whereas in 1980 there were fewer than 100 people using opiates, by 1987 there were some 5,000 regular heroin users (Parker *et al.* 1988: 76). Nation-wide the Advisory Council on the Misuse of Drugs (ACMD) 1988: 13) reached an estimate of 'between 75,000 and 150,000 misusers of notifiable drugs in the UK during 1986'. Quite apart from the impact on health and social services, heroin epidemics on this scale have widespread knock-on effects on the wider community, particularly in the form of property crime by which heroin users commonly sustain their habits (Parker and Newcombe 1987; Johnson *et al.* 1985). Problems of crime and the fear of crime are, once again, experienced in their most intense form in the poorest neighbourhoods (Hough and Mayhew 1985).

One further consequence of the heroin epidemic is the likelihood of accelerated HIV/AIDS transmission through high-risk practices such as sharing injecting equipment. Again, there is considerable local and regional diversity in the known levels of HIV seroprevalence among intravenous drug subcultures in Britain. In Edinburgh, sometimes known as the 'AIDS capital of Europe', rates of HIV infection among intravenous drug users were already in excess of 50 per cent by the mid-1980s (Robertson *et al.* 1986). This is reflected in sharp differences between the characteristics of people known to be HIV seropositive in Scotland as against the rest of the United Kingdom. Whereas in the rest of the UK, 52 per cent of those known to be HIV positive in 1987 were homosexual or bisexual males, in Scotland the figure was only 15 per cent. By contrast, whereas only 7 per cent of those known to be HIV positive in the rest of the UK were intravenous drug users, in Scotland they accounted for 57 per cent. Finally, the male to female ratio of people known to be HIV positive had experienced a dramatic alteration: in the rest of the UK it stood at 15:1, but in Scotland it had been reduced to 2.5:1 (Scottish Home and Health Department 1988).

Set against this woeful combination of problems flowing from the 1980s heroin epidemic, the government response has been pitiful. While drug enforcement efforts have been quite rightly strengthened and brought under a new system of co-ordination through the National Drugs Intelligence Unit, the Central Funding Initiative announced by the Department of Health amounted to a mere £17 million over three years to develop massively over-stretched services (MacGregor 1989). In addition, a few million pounds have been thrown at a series of mass advertising campaigns – with little or no evidence that mass media drug campaigns work, but with more than a hint of suspicion that they provided a presentational front to demonstrate to the public that the government really cared (Power 1989). Where there has been an occasional glint of light it has been passed over in a deafening governmental silence. Most notably the brave and radical proposals of the twin reports of the Advisory Council on the Misuse of Drugs on *AIDS and Drug Misuse* (ACMD 1988; 1989) appear to have been largely ignored. The Advisory Council's overall position was that 'HIV is a greater threat to public and individual health than drug misuse' (ACMD 1988: 1). This led to a series of recommendations about how to encourage larger numbers of drug users to make contact with services by making these services less threatening and more 'user-friendly'. The

Advisory Council's recommendations make abundant good sense, but met with a frosty ministerial response (Newcombe 1988). More generally, in fact, there has been a lack of governmental attention to detail. Amidst the general disarray of higher education policy, it is hardly surprising that there has been a massive neglect of the education and training needs of a variety of generalist professionals whose work brings them into contact with problems of drug misuse (ACMD 1990). In the specific context of social work, of course, the Central Council for Education and Training in Social Work frittered away most of the 1980s in a foolish political miscalculation whereby, in pursuit of its deservedly ill-fated QDSW fiasco (Jones 1989; Parsloe 1990), it was imagined that the government was about to heap an additional £40 million per year upon its plate. Meanwhile, the defenceless and the weak groan beneath an unceasing stream of cuts to housing benefits, child benefit, social security payments, health and social services provision and much else. The legacy of the 1980s has piled up a policy agenda of such proportions that it will require the strength of Hercules to clear before the end of the century. Enter the social worker . . .

The impact of drug problems on social work

There is little in the way of clear evidence of how problems of drug misuse impact on social work, other than workers in specialist 'street agencies' in the voluntary sector (Dorn and South 1984; 1985). If we set this to one side, the blunt truth of the matter would appear to be that contact with problem drug users by social workers is extremely uneven. In part, this reflects the uneven geographical distribution of drug problems themselves. The more general impression, however, is that drug problems surface only indirectly within a social worker's routine workload, rather than being a direct focus for intervention.

For example for a probation officer they will arise (admittedly quite regularly in some areas) through routine work with offenders whose more general difficulties might (or might not) be drug related. Similarly in a social services department it will be typically in the context of a routine child care inquiry that it 'comes out in the wash' that one or more of a child's parents are experiencing problems with drugs. In psychiatric settings, on the other hand, illicit drug problems might show themselves in the form of 'dual diagnosis' (that is mental disorder and drug dependence) although the question of 'dual diagnosis' is much less remarked upon in Britain than it is in North America. In medical social work, to take one final example, drug misuse might emerge when a patient suffering from back-pain has been self-medicating and developed a dependency as a consequence.

It would be difficult to pretend, however, that drug misuse is a major concern for social workers in most settings. Research in the North of England in the mid-1980s established that probation officers were much more likely to have contact with heroin users than social workers in social services departments (Pearson *et al.* 1986; Parker *et al.* 1988). This tendency was also reflected in a survey of the numbers of clients with drug and alcohol-related problems known to social workers, probation officers and health visitors in the London Borough of Hammersmith and Fulham (Laister and Pearson 1988). On average, social workers and health visitors had slightly fewer than one known problem drug user per caseload, whereas probation officers on average knew of seven problem drug users. The greater impact of drug and alcohol misuse on probation workloads has also been confirmed by a more recent Inner London Probation Service survey (ILPS 1990). The ILPS survey also found wide variations between different boroughs: whereas on average 12 per cent of all probation clients had a history of heroin use, this varied between 6 per cent to 30 per cent; with all alcohol and drug misuse combined accounting for 29 per cent of caseloads London-wide, varying from 19 per cent to 52 per cent in different boroughs.

The Hammersmith and Fulham survey found that alcohol-related problems were generally a more commonly encountered difficulty than illicit drug misuse for social workers. Clients experiencing difficulties with medically prescribed tranquillizers might also have been reliably expected to make a larger impact on workloads, but tranquillizer use had been excluded from the remit of the survey. A couple of matters of detail are worth noting. Surprisingly perhaps, health visitors reported that problem drinkers were twice as likely to experience child care difficulties than problem drug users. Where social workers were concerned, there was also significant evidence of drink problems among those in mid-life and among elderly people. Illicit drug problems were therefore of relatively minor concern, with the exception of the Probation Service. Indeed on the basis of this evidence it would be difficult to justify the allocation of extra resources to drug problems (whether in terms of personnel or training) given their modest impact on routine workloads. Why might this be so?

Given that social workers tend to work among the most disadvantaged families and communities, coupled with what has already been said about the ways in which drug problems tend to be concentrated in the poorest neighbourhoods, it might be anticipated that social workers would have much more regular contact with problems of drug misuse. One aspect of the slightly haphazard way in which social workers come across drug problems is that they might not be sufficiently well attuned to recognize them, by virtue of their education and training (ACMD 1990). It is equally possible, of course, that many social work clients successfully attempt to hide their patterns of illicit drug use from social workers – perhaps because they fear that their children will be taken into care. One woman who ran a self-help group for women drug users on a notorious inner London housing estate put the matter this way:

> Social services? They know nothing about drug problems round here. You go to see them, happen to mention you like a bit of a puff [smoke cannabis] now and again, whatever . . . Bzz . . . Bzz . . . Bzz . . . Bzz . . . [gestures as if she were writing something down] . . . Next thing you know, your kids are in care. People aren't stupid, you know. Social workers know nothing.

Key areas of work: child protection and social work with offenders

Suspicion towards statutory agencies such as this reflects a more general tendency for drug users to fight shy of social workers (Parker and Chadwick

1987). It is a suspicion with a rational core. Following the widely publicized 1986 Law Lords ruling in the Berkshire case where a care order had been made on a baby born to a drug-using mother, it is reported that a number of local authorities adopted procedures by which the children of drug-using parents were placed automatically on the child protection register (Association of Metropolitan Authorities 1989: 4).

The controversy surrounding the Berkshire case has a number of implications. It tended to reinforce unhelpful stereotypes that drug users inevitably lead chaotic life-styles which make it impossible for them to provide adequate child care. While this can sometimes be true, it is by no means universally true. Rosenbaum's major research study of women heroin users found that with proper support women could successfully combine motherhood and addiction, and also that drug use could be a means by which women dealt with routine difficulties in caring for other people – which is also reflected in Graham's research on women who smoke during pregnancy (Rosenbaum 1979; 1981; Graham 1976; 1987).

The wider context is that female drug users tend both to be more hidden than male drug users, while also being regarded as more defiled and polluted by virtue of their drug misuse (Ettorre 1989). Moreover, service provision has often not been organized in ways that are 'user-friendly' towards women (Drugs Alcohol Women Nationally (DAWN) 1985). Although there is a developing experience of good practice where issues of child protection and drug misuse coincide, it remains true that this is an area of confusion for social workers which is largely unexplored on a systematic basis (Dubble *et al.* 1987; Kearney 1987; Kearney and Aldridge 1989). It is nevertheless entirely likely that this will be an area of growing concern, particularly in view of the heightened awareness of HIV and AIDS within the field of service provision for drug users and their families. We have already noted the view taken by the Advisory Council on the Misuse of Drugs (1988: 1) that 'HIV is a greater threat to public and individual health than drug misuse'. Consequently the major thrust of its policy recommendations are that, if successful efforts are to be made to work with drug users so as to change behaviour and minimise the risks of HIV transmission, they must first be brought into contact with a helping agency. Indeed, one of the Advisory Council's recommendations in its first report on *AIDS and Drugs Misuse* was that

> If drug misusing parents are not to be deterred from seeking help, Social Services Departments should work hard to ensure that drug misuse *per se* is never, and is never seen as, a reason for separating parent and child.
> (ACMD 1988: 33)

Without quarrelling in any way with this recommendation, it is one hedged about with all manner of difficulties. A clear lead from government would appear to be necessary, if both social workers and the courts are to heed this warning. There is obviously always going to be some element of risk in allowing parents who misuse dangerous drugs to continue to care for their children under supervision at home. Given the steady flow of child protection scandals, social workers themselves might be in need of some element of protection, best offered by clear ministerial guidance and support, from being pilloried by judges and the press when things sometimes go wrong.

In the case of work with offenders with drug-related problems, matters are somewhat different in that the Home Office (1988; 1990a; 1990b) has brought forward recommendations by which to reduce the reliance on custodial sentences for 'less serious' offenders by expanding community-based programmes involving 'punishment in the community'. Where offenders with drug-related problems are concerned, it is proposed that community programmes might involve a package including the requirement to enter a course of treatment. The Green Paper, *Punishment, Custody and the Community*, which initially floated these ideas, expressed them in the following terms:

> the chances of dealing effectively with a drug problem are much greater if the offender can remain in the community and undertake to cooperate in a sensibly planned programme to help him or her come off drugs. Such a programme would aim, in the first instance, to secure a transition from illegal consumption to a medically supervised regime designed to reduce the harm caused to the individual by drug taking and would be based on a realistic plan for tackling the addiction in the context of his or her other problems. The process might well take time, but the programme could be varied as progress was made.
>
> (Home Office 1988: 13)

Here the Home Office proposals would seem to be directly in line with the views of the Advisory Council, which has also advocated an extension of non-custodial programmes (ACMD 1989: 61). The risk of HIV transmission within the prison system, both through the sharing of injecting equipment and high-risk sexual behaviours, is now clearly established (Rahman *et al.* 1989; Prison Reform Trust 1988; Carvell and Hart 1990). The Advisory Council has consequently grasped the nettle of the need to tackle sentencing patterns:

> The evidence we have received so far indicates that little or no thought is currently being applied to the specific question of whether the advent of HIV-disease should influence prosecution and sentencing practice for drug misusers, and if so how. There appears to be an unchallenged assumption that the presence of asymptomatic HIV-disease should make no difference to a person's sentence. In view of the potentially serious consequences of imprisoning people who are infected with HIV, we are disturbed that no policy is being actively formulated on this.
>
> (ACMD 1989: 63)

These lines of thinking offers a real window of opportunity for the development of social work and related services for drug offenders. Law enforcement at a low level is a means by which drug users can be encouraged to take up treatment options at an earlier point in their drug-using careers than they might otherwise do. Drug users invariably discover the motivation to seek help under one form or another of subtle compulsion, whether from family, friends, social workers or the law (Gilman and Pearson 1990). The careful deployment of low-level enforcement, coupled to such strategies as arrest-referral schemes, diversion programmes, and non-custodial options of different descriptions, can therefore provide a positive and humane means of getting to grips with the life-styles of problem drug users.

However, the Home Office proposals have not always seemed to be a welcome departure, if judged from the response of the National Association of Probation Officers, where they are seen as a direct assault on the traditions of the probation service (NAPO 1988). There are undoubtedly going to be difficulties in implementing some aspects of these proposals, specifically as they refer to offenders with drug-related problems (Standing Conference on Drug Abuse (SCODA) 1990). More generally it is most unfortunate that the Home Office, by way of deference to that section of the Conservative party back-benches who see 'alternatives to custody' as a disguise for loose permissiveness and a threat to the 'manly' virtues of their law-and-order enthusiasms, has put its position forward under the slogan 'punishment in the community'. This is, in any way of thinking, a somewhat decorous use of the word 'punishment'.

As I write, it is difficult to foresee the exact outcome of this contest, other than that some form of provision will be brought forward in a Criminal Justice Bill in the autumn of 1990 which will include much good sense together with a clutter of frills and irrelevances which play to the gallery – such as curfews, 'combined orders', and electronic tagging. The probation service will be changed in some ways, not all of them bad. A more co-ordinated partnership with voluntary sector drug agencies would be an important step forward in the response of health and social services to problems of how to manage sometimes difficult and damaged people in the community. It is no different in many ways from the responsibilities placed upon the community by the major closure programme of mental hospitals. It is in this sense an attempt to curb the excessive reach of the Victorian institutions – asylums and prisons – handed down to us as crumbling monuments to late-nineteenth-century civil engineering and civic architecture, and now cluttered with late-twentieth-century problems.

Defining a policy agenda: harm reduction, multi-agency work and the limits of social work intervention

In a paradoxical way the emergence of HIV and AIDS which has threatened to redouble the stigmatization of already marginalized groups such as homosexuals and drug users, has also blown gusts of fresh air through the policy debate on drug misuse. Maintenance prescribing of substitute drugs such as methadone, which became unfashionable with many doctors during the 1970s and 1980s, is now firmly back on the agenda. There has been an expansion of facilities such as syringe-exchange schemes, together with outreach work with prostitutes, and innovative attempts to exploit methods of communication such as comics in order to encourage high-risk and hard-to-reach groups to rethink their patterns of drug use and sexual behaviour (Monitoring Research Group 1988; Plant 1990; Gilman 1988). There nevertheless remains much to be learned about how to engage effectively with drug misusers on questions such as needle-sharing, where the practice can often involve expressions of group solidarity, friendship and loyalty (McKeganey 1989). Friendship is invariably the context within which initial experimentations with drugs begin, and is also an important factor in subsequent patterns of help-seeking (Pearson *et al.* 1986; Pearson 1987a; Drug Indicators Project 1989). Informal networks must also count as an issue in the vastly unexplored area of developing drug services which are relevant to the needs of black and other minority ethnic groups (Gabe and Thorogood 1986; Gabe 1988; Awiah *et al.* 1990).

In developing truly effective services, two issues stand out: multi-agency co-operation and the adoption of harm reduction strategies as the organizing principle of service delivery. Where multi-agency work is concerned, although there have been significant developments particularly in response to child abuse, there remain many areas of unresolved conflict where agencies are brought into contact within the criminal justice system (Blagg *et al.* 1988; Sampson *et al.* 1988; 1990; Pearson *et al.* 1989). These derive from the different sources of authority of different agencies; struggles over confidentiality and how to devise accountable systems of information exchange; and the fact that different agencies have different routine preoccupations. Differences in management structures and management styles add a further obstacle, and it can also be difficult to establish at what point in an organization's hierarchy it is most appropriate and effective to attempt to establish inter-agency liaison. Silverman (1990) has also identified territorial disputes of a professional nature between health visitors and social workers in relation to HIV counselling.

The desire to devise well-co-ordinated multi-agency responses to drug problems is understandable. However, a frank acknowledgement is equally necessary that multi-agency conflict in the drug field is exacerbated by a number of issues. At a quite fundamental level, there is no necessary agreement between the three constituent elements of drugs policy and practice: law enforcement, health education and prevention, and treatment and rehabilitation. Different agencies also place a varying emphasis on different substances of abuse. For example some interest groups justifiably prioritize alcohol and tobacco, as against minority pursuit drugs such as heroin and cocaine, as the major source of health difficulties; whereas it is not uncommon for street agencies to report that people experiencing difficulties with medically prescribed tranquillizers is the major source of self-referrals. More generally drug issues will also assume a different level of priority within different agencies, as already indicated, and the 'typical' drug user known to each agency can vary to a marked degree. The Hammersmith and Fulham Drug and Alcohol Survey found sharp differences between health visitors and probation officers in this respect (Laister and Pearson 1988: 6–7). The typical drug user known to a health visitor was a young woman with dependent children who was using opiates and living in council property. By contrast, for a probation officer the typical drug user was a single man without dependent children, who was less likely to be using opiates, but more likely to be squatting or of no fixed abode. There is abundant scope for conflict and misunderstanding in circumstances such as these. Indeed as a general rule it is probably better to begin by addressing both the potential and actual sites of conflict between different interests and agencies – and to acknowledge these conflicts as a healthy expression of their different tasks and roles, prior to embarking upon multi-agency initiatives which might otherwise founder because of a naive view of consensus.

The second key area requiring development is that of 'harm reduction'. The principle of harm reduction originated in the context of health education, where two separate strategies can be defined: one intended 'to reduce the recruitment of individuals into patterns of drug involvement', and the other aiming 'to reduce the proportion of those taking drugs . . . who suffer medical or social harm' (ACMD 1984: 40). The second strategy which stresses harm reduction (rather than necessarily requiring drug users to become abstinent) has long been established within British responses to drug misuse, and has been given an added impetus by the emergence of HIV and AIDS. It is undoubtedly the best basis on which effective social work services can be built, and has recently been accepted by the Inner London Probation Service as the organizing principle of its work with drug users (ISDD 1990).

In its most general terms, harm reduction strategies involve identifying intermediate goals (which might fall short of abstinence) and working towards their achievement with the drug-using client. It is a strategy which is particularly helpful with unmotivated drug users who, while they do not define their drug use *per se* as a problem, recognize that they experience other problems. In their research among London street agencies, Dorn and South (1984; 1985) stressed the way in which drug users often face a range of difficulties which are not substantially different from those of other clients of social workers: housing, social security, domestic problems and relationship difficulties. Rather than focusing solely on the client's drug use (as if this were necessarily the source of all his or her other difficulties) it is better to work with the client on those issues which he or she acknowledges as a problem. Work of this nature can also build up trust between worker and client, offering a place where the client can turn for help, if and when he or she does discover the motivation to take action against drug misuse itself.

In the context of HIV and AIDS, the Advisory Council has pushed forward our understanding of the range of possible interventions within a harm reduction strategy, involving a 'hierarchy of goals' whereby it becomes necessary 'to work initially towards whichever goal or goals is most readily achievable'. In other words, the aim would be to work at a pace which is both acceptable to the client and also within his or her reach: 'Once these "intermediate" goals have been achieved efforts can focus on higher goals (ultimately abstinence) but great care must be taken with each individual not to prejudice what has already been achieved' (ACMD 1988: 48). This is, of course, perfectly in tune with the traditions of social work, in that it involves 'starting where the client is'.

In order to maximize its utility, the concept of harm reduction does nevertheless need to be broadened in scope. By virtue of its origins harm reduction has focused almost entirely on the individual and on the potentially

Table 9.1   Different forms of drug-related harm

Type of harm	Impact on individual	Impact on family/ friends	Impact on community
Health	overdose, HIV	HIV (sharing injecting equipment)	potential HIV spread
Social/emotional	loss of friends, self-esteem	family shame, child neglect	fear of crime
Financial	no money	theft from family, reduced family income	burglary and theft to support habit
Legal	arrest and/or imprisonment	stigmatization as 'known associates'	alienation of wider community through 'stop-and-search' tactics

harmful health consequences of drug misuse. However, other forms of harm can result from drug use, including social and emotional harm, financial harm, and legal harm. Equally drug-related harm can affect not only the individual, but also family and friends and ultimately the wider community (Dorn 1990).

If the principle of harm reduction is broadened in this way, it offers a framework within which to conceptualize a number of different categories of harm resulting from drug misuse (see Table 9.1). It is a framework with a variety of possible uses. It can be used by professional workers themselves, for example, as a means of case analysis by which to bring some clarification into their work with drug users: identifying actual and potential sites of harm in any given case, together with targets for intervention. Or it can be used in direct work with drug users, as a means to assist them to identify problem areas, including forms of action and change which seem achievable as against those reserved for longer-term action.

By way of illustration of the possible applications of this framework, we can take a small number of ideal-type cases. In the first, a wealthy middle-class business man consults a drug clinic because of his cocaine use. His pattern of recreational drug use is causing him no problems in the health sphere, he is not in trouble with the law, and he has no social or emotional difficulties. His only problem is that his cocaine use has begun to spiral out of control, leading to a financial outlay which is now becoming unsupportable and threatening to damage his business interests. In this case, the harm currently resulting from his cocaine use is very tightly defined.

In the second case, a probation officer is in contact with a heroin user who has been using illicit street drugs, sharing injecting equipment and supporting her habit by theft and prostitution. She is in poor physical health, as a result of damage to veins in her arms and legs: she has been injecting in the groin and in her neck. Her HIV status is not known. She has now been arrested for shop-lifting, and could face a custodial sentence. Here the immediate targets for intervention might be to devise a community-based programme whereby she is referred to a clinic where she can obtain a prescription for methadone, thus reducing her need to engage in property crime and prostitution, and to make contact with a syringe-exchange facility where she can also receive health care advice.

Finally, we can take a family with dependent children where both parents have a history of opiate use. The family is experiencing severe problems with housing and finances, and there is a risk of child neglect when both parents are absent from the home either in order to score drugs or to hustle for money. The mother has now reduced her drug consumption to an occasional basis, although the father is still a daily user. The couple are on the brink of separating because of domestic rows and financial problems, although in the past they have cared quite well for their children within their means. Here again, a referral of the father to a clinic for a methadone prescription might be considered as an intermediate goal, together with counselling and practical support with childminding facilities.

Above all, this is a harm reduction framework which usefully reminds us that there is no such thing as a single 'drug problem'. Rather, drug problems assume many different dimensions in the form of clusters of a variety of harms resulting from drug misuse. This not only assists with the individuation of drug users, working against stereotyping, but also can illuminate some aspects of inter-agency conflict and miscommunication. Typically for example a priority will be given by social workers with child protection responsibilities to harms falling within the social/emotional sphere as this affects the immediate family: that is potential or actual child neglect. Health workers, on the other hand, will prioritize harms within the health sphere as these affect the individual, whether in the form of general ill-health or needle-sharing practices. Whereas probation officers will tend to focus on potential legal harms such as imprisonment, together with financial harm to the wider community through property crime to support the drug user's habit. One can see at a glance, then, how drug problems make a radically different impact on the routine workloads of different agencies, and how various agencies tend to deal with different kinds of drug-related harms and also possibly different categories of drug users. It can also enable care workers to identify blind-spots in their own practice which result from the priorities defined by their agency's function.

In thinking through a policy agenda, one final and necessary recognition is the limits of social work intervention. The limitations of social work principally derive from three sources: the inability of statutory social services to ameliorate the suspicion of drug users; the limits of conventional social work approaches and the attendant need to develop innovative forms of outreach work; and wider socio-economic policies which threaten not only local authority services, but also those in the voluntary sector, and even the viability of the government's own stated plans for community care and other forms of non-custodial provision.

Statutory social work not only is unlikely to be able to overcome entirely the rational suspicions of drug users, but also is unsuited to the development of services such as a syringe-exchange schemes – and might even frighten away some of those who use these vitally important facilities. Under these circumstances the voluntary sector will remain a central aspect of service provision, and one likely to be particularly relevant to the needs of black and other minority ethnic groups, women drug users, and other groups such as homeless people who are liable to discrimination, stigmatization and marginalization.

The kinds of outreach work which are necessary with high-risk groups such as prostitutes – where the difficulty is compounded by the fact that many will have hostile feelings towards social workers, deriving from unhappy experiences as children in public care – would also be impossible for statutory social work, although there are examples of successful schemes involving street-work (Plant 1990). What is needed here and elsewhere is the style of outreach community work which has never been popular with local authorities and which is poorly developed in Britain. Successful work with prostitutes, for example, must engage with areas of high moral ambiguity and where the involvement of statutory social workers would be quite inappropriate. Other innovations such as the *Smack in the Eye* comic in Manchester, which aims to raise awareness of high-risk behaviours among injecting drug users, fall outside the reach of state social work for similar reasons (Gilman 1988). Quite apart from their necessary engagements with moral ambiguity, these kinds of activities involve styles of work which sit uneasily against social services which are increasingly oriented towards a minimalist provision of statutory requirements and social policing such as child protection and mental health emergencies.

Equally worrying is that constraints on local authority budgets, exacerbated by the poll tax system, mean that the funding of many voluntary initiatives is threatened. Moreover, although the government's stated intention through its community care and non-custodial policies is to encourage the private and voluntary sectors, there are fears in the drugs field that some areas of work could be placed in jeopardy by the new funding arrangements. There are also fears that the essential street-credibility of voluntary agencies might be weakened if they are to be harnessed too closely to the work of the courts and the probation service.

Ultimately, whatever style of social work and community work is adopted, limits are set to its achievable objectives by the wider socio-economic policies adopted by government. In spite of its stated intention to reduce the reliance on imprisonment and to expand community provision, these wider socio-economic policies involve financial penalties against the poor which undermine the ability of many young adult drug users to sustain themselves in the community. The government's hopes and plans might therefore be dashed by successive cuts to benefits, restrictions on benefit entitlement, stubbornly high levels of unemployment, and the failure to provide affordable housing. In this sense drug problems are not merely individual problems, but are truly social and collective difficulties which entail a collective responsibility whereby the possibilities for people to lead meaningful and rewarding lives and to fashion effective identities in the impoverished working-class neighbourhoods of so many of our towns and cities must be rebuilt.

References

ACMD (Advisory Council on the Misuse of Drugs) (1982) *Treatment and Rehabilitation*, London: HMSO.
—— (1984) *Prevention*, London: HMSO.
—— (1988) *AIDS and Drug Misuse, Part I*, London: HMSO.
—— (1989) *AIDS and Drug Misuse, Part II*, London: HMSO.
—— (1990) *Problem Drug Use: A Review of Training*, London: HMSO.
AMA (Association of Metropolitan Authorities) (1989) *Drug Using Parents and their Children*, Second Report of the National Local Authority Forum on Drug Misuse in conjunction with the Standing Conference on Drug Abuse, London: AMA.
Awiah, J., Butt, S. and Dorn, N. (1990) 'Service needs of young South Asian males and African-descent females', *Druglink*, in press.
Berridge, V. and Edwards, G. (1981) *Opium and the People: Opiate Use in Nineteenth Century England*, London: Allen Lane (2nd edn, 1987, New Haven, Conn: Yale University Press).
Blagg, H., Pearson, G., Sampson, A., Smith, D. and Stubbs, P. (1988) 'Inter-agency cooperation: rhetoric and reality', in T. Hope and M. Shaw (eds) *Communities and Crime Reduction*, London: HMSO.
Burr, A. (1987) 'Chasing the dragon: heroin misuse, delinquency and crime in the context of South London culture', *British Journal of Criminology* 27, 4: 333–57.
Carvell, A. L. M. and Hart, G. J. (1990) 'Risk behaviours for HIV infection among drug users in prison', *British Medical Journal* 300, 26: 1,383–4.
Courtwright, D., Joseph, H. and Des Jarlais, D. (1989) *Addicts Who Survived: An Oral History of Narcotic Use in America, 1923–1965*, Knoxville, Tenn: University of Tennessee Press.
Davis, F. and Munoz, L. (1968) 'Heads and freaks: patterns and meanings of drug use among hippies', *Journal of Health and Social Behaviour* 9: 156–64.
DAWN (Drugs Alcohol Women Nationally) (1985) *A Survey of Facilities for Women Using Drugs (including Alcohol) in London*, London: DAWN.
Dorn, N. (1990) 'Drug prevention for health and welfare professionals', in H. Godse and D. Maxwell (eds) *Substance Abuse and Dependence*, London: Macmillan.
Dorn, N. and South, N. (1984) *Drug-Related Social Work in Street Agencies*, Social Work Monograph Series, Norwich: University of East Anglia.
—— (1985) *Helping Drug Users: Social Work, Advice Giving, Referral and Training Services of Three London 'Street Agencies'*, Aldershot: Gower.
—— (eds) (1987) *A Land Fit for Heroin? Drug Policies, Prevention and Practice*, London: Macmillan.
Drug Indicators Project (1989) *Study of Help-Seeking and Service Utilisation by Problem Drug Takers*, London: Institute for the Study of Drug Dependence.
Dubble, C., Dun, E., Aldridge, T. and Kearney, P. (1987) 'Registering concern for children', *Community Care* 651, 12 March: 20–2.
Ettorre, B. (1989) 'Women, substance abuse and self-help', in S. MacGregor (ed.) *Drugs and British Society*, London: Routledge.
Gabe, J. (1988) '"Race" and tranquilliser use', in N. Dorn, L. Lucas and N. South (eds) *Drug Questions: An Annual Research Register*, issue 4, London: Institute for the Study of Drug Dependence.
Gabe, J. and Thorogood, N. (1986) 'Prescribed drug use and the management of everyday life: the experiences of black and white working-class women', *Sociological Review* 34, 4: 737–72.
Giggs, J., Bean, P., Whynes, D. and Wilkinson, C. (1989) 'Class A drug users: prevalence characteristics in Greater Nottingham', *British Journal of Addiction* 84: 1,473–80.
Gilman, M. (1988) 'Comics as a strategy in reducing drug related harm', in N. Dorn,

L. Lucas and N. South (eds) *Drug Questions: An Annual Research Register*, issue 4, London: Institute for the Study of Drug Dependence.

Gilman, M. and Pearson, G. (1990) 'Lifestyle and law enforcement: using criminal justice to help drug users', in P. Bean and D. K. Whynes (eds) *Policing and Prescribing: The British System of Drug Control*, London: Macmillan.

Graham, H. (1976) 'Smoking in pregnancy: the attitudes of expectant mothers', *Social Science and Medicine* 10: 399–405.

—— (1987) 'Women's smoking and family health', *Social Science and Medicine* 25: 47–56.

Home Office (1968) *The Rehabilitation of Drug Addicts: Report of the Advisory Committee on Drug Dependence*, London: HMSO.

—— (1988) *Punishment, Custody and the Community*, Cm 424, London: HMSO.

—— (1990a) *Crime, Justice and Protecting the Public: The Government's Proposals for Legislation*, Cm 965, London: HMSO.

—— (1990b) *Supervision and Punishment in the Community: A Framework for Action*, Cm 966, London: HMSO.

Hough, M. and Mayhew, P. (1985) *Taking Account of Crime: Key Findings from the 1984 British Crime Survey*, Home Office Research Study no. 85, London: HMSO.

ILPS (Inner London Probation Service) (1990) *Drug and Alcohol Misuse: Summary of Demonstration Unit Interviews*, London: ILPS.

ISDD (Institute for the Study of Drug Dependence (1990) 'Probation Service makes harm reduction official policy', *Druglink* 5, 4: 6.

Jamieson, A., Glanz, A. and MacGregor, S. (1984) *Dealing with Drug Misuse: Crisis Intervention in the City*, London: Tavistock.

Johnson, B. D., Goldstein, P. J., Preble, E., Schmeidler, J., Lipton, D. S., Spunt, B. and Miller, T. (1985) *Taking Care of Business: The Economics of Crime by Heroin Abusers*, Lexington, Mass: Lexington Books.

Jones, C. (1989) 'The end of the road? Issues in social work education', in P. Carter, T. Jeffs and M. Smith (eds) *Social Work and Social Welfare Yearbook 1*, Milton Keynes: Open University Press.

Kearney, P. (1987) 'Preparing for birth', *Druglink* 2, 4: 9.

Kearney, P. and Aldridge, T. (1989) 'Drug using parents', in P. Sills (ed.) *Child Protection: Challenges for Policy and Practice*, London: Bruce Reed.

Laister, D. and Pearson, G. (1988) *Hammersmith and Fulham Drug and Alcohol Survey: Final Report*, London: London Borough of Hammersmith and Fulham.

MacGregor, S. (ed.) (1989) *Drugs and British Society: Responses to a Social Problem in the 1980s*, London: Routledge.

McKeganey, N. (1989) 'Drug abuse in the community: needle-sharing and the risks of HIV infection', in S. Cunningham-Birley and N. McKeganey (eds) *Readings in Medical Sociology*, London: Routledge.

Ministry of Health (1926) *Report of the Departmental Committee on Morphine and Heroin Addiction*, Rolleston Report, London: HMSO.

—— (1961) *Drug Addiction: Report of the Interdepartmental Committee*, Brain Report, London: HMSO.

—— (1965) *Drug Addiction: The Second Report of the Interdepartmental Committee*, Brain Report, London: HMSO.

Monitoring Research Group (1988) *Injecting Equipment Exchange Schemes: Final Report*, London: Goldsmiths' College, University of London.

NAPO (National Association of Probation Officers) (1988) *Punishment, Custody and the Community: A Response to the Green Paper by the National Association of Probation Officers*, London: NAPO.

Newcombe, R. (1988) 'Drugs and AIDS: radical proposals shelved', *Mersey Drugs Journal* 1, 6: 10–13.

Parker, H. and Chadwick, C. (1987) *Heroin Use, Mothers and Child Care*, Report of the Misuse of Drugs Research Project, Liverpool: University of Liverpool.

Parker, H. and Newcombe, R. (1987) 'Heroin use and acquisitive crime in an English community', *British Journal of Sociology* 38, 3: 331–50.

Parker, H., Bakx, K. and Newcombe, R. (1988) *Living with Heroin: The Impact of a Drugs 'Epidemic' on an English Community*, Milton Keynes: Open University Press.

Parsloe, P. (1990) 'Future of social work education: Recovering from Care for Tomorrow', in P. Carter, T. Jeffs and M. Smith (eds), *Social Work and Social Welfare Yearbook 2*, Milton Keynes: Open University Press.

Pearson, G. (1987a) *The New Heroin Users*, Oxford: Basil Blackwell.

—— (1987b) 'Social deprivation, unemployment and patterns of heroin use', in N. Dorn and N. South (eds) *A Land Fit for Heroin? Drug Policies, Prevention and Practice*, London: Macmillan.

—— (1990) 'Drug problems and policies in Britain: continuity and change', in M. Tonry and J. Q. Wilson (eds) *Drugs and the Criminal Justice System* Crime and Justice Series vol. 12, Chicago, Ill: University of Chicago Press.

Pearson, G., Gilman, M. and McIver, S. (1985) 'Heroin use in the North of England', *Health Education Journal* 45, 3: 186–9.

—— (1986) *Young People and Heroin: An Examination of Heroin Use in the North of England*, London: Health Education Council (2nd edn, 1987, Aldershot: Gower).

Pearson, G., Sampson, A., Blagg, H., Stubbs, P. and Smith, D. (1989) 'Policing racism', in R. Morgan and D. J. Smith (eds) *Coming to Terms with Policing*, London: Routledge.

Pearson, G., Gilman, M. and Traynor, P. (1990) 'Cyclizine misuse: the limits of intervention', *Druglink* 5, 3: 12–13.

Plant, M. A. (ed.) (1990) *AIDS, Drugs and Prostitution*, London: Routledge.

Power, R. (1989) 'Drugs and the media: prevention campaigns and television', in S. MacGregor (ed.) *Drugs and British Society*, London: Routledge.

Prison Reform Trust (1988) *HIV, AIDS and Prisons*, London: Prison Reform Trust.

Rahman, M. Z., Ditton, J. and Forsyth, A. J. M. (1989) 'Variations in needle sharing practices among intravenous drug users in Possil (Glasgow)', *British Journal of Addiction* 84: 923–7.

Robertson, J. R., Bucknall, A. B. V., Welsby, P. D., Roberts, J. J. K., Inglis, J. M., Peutherer, J. F. and Brettle, R. P. (1986) 'Epidemic of AIDS related virus (HTLV III/LAV) infection among intravenous drug abusers', *British Medical Journal* 292: 527–9.

Rosenbaum, M. (1979) 'Difficulties taking care of business: women addicts as mothers', *American Journal of Drug and Alcohol Abuse* 6: 431–46.

—— (1981) *Women on Heroin*, New Brunswick, NJ: Rutgers University Press.

Sampson, A., Stubbs, P., Smith, D., Pearson, G. and Blagg, H. (1988) 'Crime, localities and the multi-agency approach', *British Journal of Criminology* 28, 4: 478–93.

Sampson, A., Smith, D., Pearson, G., Blagg, H. and Stubbs, P. (1990) 'Gender issues in inter-agency relations: police, probation and social services', in British Sociological Association, *Gender, Sexuality and Power*, London: Macmillan.

Schur, E. M. (1964) 'Drug addiction under British policy', in H. S. Becker (ed.) *The Other Side: Perspectives on Deviance*, New York: Free Press.

SCODA (Standing Conference on Drug Abuse) (1990) *SCODA'S Comments on the White Paper 'Crime, Justice and Protecting the Public'*, London: SCODA.

Scottish Home and Health Department (1988) *Health in Scotland 1987*, Edinburgh: HMSO.

Silverman, D. (1990) 'The social organisation of HIV counselling', in P. Aggleton, P. Davies and G. Hart (eds) *AIDS: Individual, Cultural and Policy Perspectives*, Lewes: Falmer.

Spear, H. B. (1969) 'The growth of heroin addiction in the UK', *British Journal of Addiction* 64: 245–55.

Stimson, G. V. and Oppenheimer, E. (1982) *Heroin Addiction: Treatment and Control in Britain*, London: Tavistock.

10
The last days of
'juvenile' justice?

Mike Nellis

Lest it be forgotten – because it was a long time ago – the Children and Young Persons Act (CYPA) 1969 *intended* that the use of penal custody for juvenile offenders aged 14–16 be phased out. Courts were to lose their power to sentence to attendance centres and detention centres when adequate schemes of intermediate treatment (IT) became available, and to borstal – though this was a little unclear – when adequate secure accommodation had been provided. Echoing the Magistrate's Association, the Conservative party never accepted the idea of replacing custody: when they came to power in 1970 the relevant sections of the 1969 Act were never implemented. In the Criminal Justice Act (CJA) 1982, under another Conservative government, they were repealed. And yet, among social work practitioners in the juvenile justice system, the 1980s ended on a very high note:

> The 1980s have seen a revolution in the way the juvenile justice system operates in England and Wales. There are few areas of criminal justice practice and policy of which we can be proud but this is an exception. While there is no room for complacency there is a core of good practice and inter-agency cooperation which can be built upon in the 1990's. Many notions, which once seemed totally unrealistic, such as the abolition of juvenile imprisonment, are now viewed as achievable.
>
> (D. Jones 1989: i)

Most paradoxical of all, the Conservative government seemed to share some – though significantly not all – of this enthusiasm. The Green Paper *Punishment, Custody and the Community* (Home Office 1988a) had two key objectives. First, to reduce crime – a matter to which we shall return below. Second, to reduce the numbers of young adult offenders (17–20-year-olds) sentenced to custody. In regard to the latter it spoke approvingly of IT, especially of the programmes for more serious offenders that had developed following the LAC (83)3 Initiative (DHSS 1983) – a grant of £15 million to local authorities who wished to develop alternatives to custody and to facilitate inter-agency co-operation, in partnership with the voluntary sector (see Nellis 1989 for a more detailed analysis). The Green Paper explicitly sought to transfer the lessons of this Initiative to the young adult offender field, and the Action Plans which probation services were subsequently asked to draw up were based largely on measures that had been applied in the more 'successful' local juvenile justice systems (Home Office 1988b). 'The policies for juvenile offenders will not be entirely suitable for the older age group, but some features can be the same' (Home Office 1988a: para 2: 18).

Although they still saw 'alternatives' as *options* in a system which retained custody, rather than as *replacements* for custody itself (which is how practitioners saw them), there were a number of factors which had helped move the government towards this position, far removed from the battle-cry with which they had entered the 1979 General Election, touting the 'short, sharp shock' as the panacea for juvenile crime. Not least of these factors was the high cost of imprisonment: the government's determination to cut public expenditure finally clashed with its equal determination to restore 'law and order' by repressive means. Another factor was the European league table of imprisonment rates, which were increasingly becoming a source of political embarrassment, as a Deputy Under-Secretary at the Home Office made clear:

> International comparisons show Britain has a proportionately higher prison population than most other European countries. The position is particularly stark with respect to young offenders. Comparison of ourselves with broadly similar European neighbours – France and Germany – shows that both countries have a young offender custodial population which is only about half the British figure.
>
> (Faulkner 1988: 3)

One major difference in the strategies being proposed for young adults, compared with those that had been 'successful' with juveniles was in philosophy and terminology. The government were insistent that the measures taken to reduce the use of imprisonment for this age group were described as punishment. Despite the brief flirtation with 'justice models' in the early 1980s, that is not by and large how developments in IT had been understood, nor had it been the way in which the LAC (83)3 Initiative had been characterized. In the late 1980s it still did not look as though *punishment* in the community would affect juveniles as such, and optimism prevailed: the elimination of custody for 14–16-year-olds was under serious discussion (Tutt and Giller 1987; Children's Society 1988; NACRO 1989; Doyle 1989). Although the government itself did not share that aim its seal of approval for the LAC (83)3 Initiative seemed to add to its eventual feasibility.

But times have already changed and there are now so many more factors to take account of than when Jones described the 'successful revolution'.

Although its implementation has been delayed, the government's White Paper on community care will substantially change the basis on which local authorities provide social services (Department of Health 1989); it was not directly concerned with juvenile justice but will inevitably affect the organizational climate in which it develops. So too will the Criminal Justice Act 1988 and the Children Act 1989, about whose impact it is still too early to judge. Most significantly, the changes mooted in *Punishment, Custody and the Community* have been developed in a subsequent White Paper (Home Office 1990) and in a Criminal Justice Bill introduced in November 1990. These developments make it clear that punishment is indeed to be the ethos of work with juveniles (at least with 16–17-year-olds), no less than with adults. The Bill is less about *building on* the measures that have been successful with juveniles in the 1980s, and more about *toughening them up*, and among other things it includes provision for electronically monitored curfews for 16–17-year-olds.

The final factor which is reshaping the context of juvenile justice policy and practice has been one of the most neglected. After a period of protracted antagonism towards preventive work of any kind, some practitioners have begun to take note of the Government's massive crime prevention initiative (Hope 1990; Pitts 1990) and to at least consider the possibility that this provides an overall framework for their future work. Juvenile justice in the 1990s is thus developing in what, at the time of an earlier upheaval, was called 'a vortex of changing systems' (Cooper 1983: 96). It is simply not clear what the outcomes will be.

Juvenile justice 1980–90

The broad pattern of developments in juvenile justice social work in the late 1980s are well known, although accounts tend to be partisan and emphases vary considerably (Davies 1986; Pitts 1988; Curtis 1989; Blagg and Smith 1989). Using strategies developed at Lancaster University, the legal framework of the CJA 1982 (which placed statutory restrictions on the use of custody) and the resources of LAC (83)3 Initiative, the emphases shifted away from the so-called 'preventive work' that had constituted IT in the 1970s. It moved towards 'systems management' (monitoring and controlling the way in which young offenders were processed by juvenile justice agencies as a whole, with a particular emphasis on diversion from court) and the provision of alternatives to care and custody (intensive ninety-day programmes for groups or individuals).

The systems management/alternatives to custody approach met with undoubted success in some parts of the country. Juvenile liaison panels flourished and significant increases occurred in the numbers of juveniles cautioned, although massive regional variations were still apparent. Nationally there was a reduction in the overall use of custody, from 7,900 in 1981 to 3,400 in 1988 and in some parts of the country, beginning with Basingstoke but later including the London Borough of Hillingdon, 'custody free zones' were created, jurisdictions where the magistrates were successfully persuaded against the use of custody for a twelve-month period, or more (Rutherford 1986: 136–47). Rutherford (1989: 28) later singled out 'the anti-custodial ethos' of the practitioners as a key factor in these achievements, and on the basis of them Tutt and Giller (1987: 200) had devised a 'policy by stealth', not wholly dissimilar from the notion of 'the unfinished' advocated by Mathiesen (1974) (although it is not usually seen that way) which aimed to eliminate penal custody for all juveniles by 1989.

For the practitioner who subscribed to this approach it was an article of faith that preventive work in SSDs should be jettisoned, first, because it was *apparently* ineffective as a means of reducing crime, and second, because it *apparently* increased the likelihood of youngsters getting more severe sentences if, after a spell of prevention, they still appeared in court (a process dubbed 'uptariffing': see Nellis 1987: 7). For a while diversion from court (not necessarily into any support system) and the targeting of serious offenders at risk of custody seemed to have become the 'new orthodoxy' (R. Jones 1984: 15), but preventive work neither died out in SSDs nor became the exclusive preserve of a grossly underfunded youth service (Jeffs and Smith 1988), although where it occurred in SSDs it tended to be done covertly (as if practitioners were ashamed of it!) and was rarely called IT. The reasons for the survival of preventive work are not difficult to identify (see Bottoms *et al.* 1990) and from the mid-1980s the picture of SSD provision for young people evolved towards broad-based approaches, IT becoming integrated into general child care strategies (Blackmore 1988) and a gradually explicit recognition that the case *for* replacing custody did not rest on a case *against* prevention.

Dissenting voices

It would be wrong to give the impression that there was no sense of difficulty or concern about juvenile justice developments in the late 1980s. Amidst much publicity, disorganization within Brent SSD led to the closure of its IT programme, and the LAC (83)3 project in Hillingdon (where a custody free zone had been created) closed when the local authority refused, on financial grounds, to take it over from the voluntary organization which had set it up (Barker 1989). Rates of custody remained disproportionately high for juveniles in London, but it was not only there that the new strategies had not penetrated, or not worked. Leah and Rawlinson (1989: vi) noted obstinately high levels of custody in the north-west and expressed some cynicism with 'the "systems management" bandwagon'. Curtis (1989) quaintly referred to 'a patchwork quilt of provision' but it was the harder-edged concept of 'justice by geography' (Richardson 1987: 15) which stimulated practitioners to criticize the unevenness and unfairness of provision nationally.

Justice by race and by gender was also put in sharper focus. From the mid-1980s clear evidence began to emerge that black youngsters had not apparently benefited from the successful revolution (Tipler 1989) and would not do so unless an anti-racist perspective was explicitly incorporated (National Intermediate Treatment Federation 1986). It was also noted that while the overall numbers of young female offenders involved in the criminal justice system remained small their needs (in terms of community-based programmes) were different, and their progress through the tariff once in court was more rapid than their male counterparts (Skinner 1988).

Some strongly dissenting voices emerged in the debate, claiming that juvenile justice was not a success at all. For NAPO (1988: 17), with a definite vested interest in the lessons juvenile justice might hold for young adult offenders, the reductions in custody were merely an artefact of demography (the decline in the number of teenagers in the population), and had in any case been bought at too high a price in terms of punitive and controlling methods that betrayed the ideals of social work. Significant voices in the Youth Service also took this latter view (Davies 1986), although it is a questionable one.

Demographic factors are important, but the decline in the use of custody for juveniles cannot be explained in terms of that alone. There was a 50 per cent reduction in the use of custody between 1981 and 1988 – but only a 10 per cent reduction in the population of 10–17-year-olds. Even the government was prepared to admit that the decline in known juvenile offenders from about 174,000 in 1981 to about 119,000 in 1988 was 'a greater reduction than would be expected from the reduction in the number of those in that age group' (Home Office 1990: para. 8.25), suggesting that perhaps policy was having the desired effect.

Against a background of decline in the numbers of young people in the population (although this varies region to region, and some have had increases), some of the alternatives to custody projects began to pay the price of their own success. Decreasing numbers of youngsters going to court and magistrates who had grown to accept the wisdom of keeping youngsters down-tariff, left a number of projects with diminishing numbers of 'customers', and consequent threats to their survival. This provided an incentive for diversification into other fields, which to an extent was beginning to happen anyway. Some moved back into 'middle-range' provision, a step or so below the serious offenders (some had never gone away from it!), others moved into bail support and alternatives to remand (which had been astonishingly neglected for most of IT's history) (Seals and Orders 1989) and some, in the face of much initial criticism, into crime prevention.

Crime prevention had had a life of its own throughout the 1980s, which had not by and large impinged on IT (Bottoms 1989). Like alternatives to custody, it had developed on a multi-agency basis, often involving the voluntary sector and sometimes the private sector. It was the centrepiece of government policy to reduce crime (Faulkner 1988: 3–4), on an area-by-area basis, and is usually characterized as having two distinct but interrelated strands. Situational crime prevention seeks to make crime more difficult to commit by various types of target hardening (more locks, bolts and bars, better street lighting, theft-proof cars, CCTV, neighbourhood watch, Rottweilers) and target removal (switching from coin to token-operated gas meters). Social crime prevention, on the other hand, seeks to reduce the incentive to commit crime, especially among young people, by 'education in citizenship' and/or by reducing their alienation and improving their quality of life in particular neighbourhoods – job creation (where possible), intervening (if necessary) in housing allocation policies, school exclusion policies and policing strategies, and increasing the availability of leisure facilities.

Social crime prevention inevitably touched upon concerns that had once been the preserve of IT, and indeed of the youth service (the two agencies having had a persistently edgy relationship: Skinner 1989), and it was quickly reclaimed by those who had never been fully in sympathy with the perceived narrowness of the Lancaster/AJJ (Association for Juvenile Justice) approach (Paley *et al.* 1986; Pitts 1988; 1990). It did not fit easily with an emphasis on systems management and alternatives to custody; they undoubtedly involved working *in* the community, but social crime prevention involved working *with* the community in ways that had become quite rare in IT (see Thorpe 1972). While recognizing that government initiatives in this area were very half-hearted compared to the equivalent programmes in France, which had at their core a much more elaborate exercise in detached youth work, socialist commentators such as Pitts (1990) have been prepared to exploit them – because they address real fears about crime in inner city neighbourhoods – no less imaginatively than Lancaster had exploited the incipient 'alternatives to custody' climate a decade earlier (Home Office 1980).

The recontextualizing of juvenile justice work in social crime prevention, the expansion of multi-agency approaches in regard to both this and alternatives to custody, and the growth of 'a mixed economy of criminal justice' in which the voluntary sector figures more prominently than hitherto (Mawby 1989: 135) are three developments which one can take for granted in the 1990s. Beyond this, because there are now so many new factors in play, there is a justifiable shying away from prediction. Some of the most recent developments represented the fruition of major campaigns within juvenile justice, for example the tighter restrictions on using custody in the CJA 1988 and the abolition of the Section 7 Care Order in the Children Act 1989 (although how the latter's replacement, residence requirements in supervision orders, works out, remains to be seen). Others flew in the face of its best achievements; educational supervision orders which permit (too?) early intervention in the lives of truants; and making custody available for breach of supervised activity requirements (hitherto only fines and attendance centre had been available).

The abolition of the detention centre order in the Criminal Justice Act 1988 was a victory on the ideological level, but no more than that. It highlighted the bankruptcy of the 'short sharp shock', but it did not end the use of penal custody for juveniles as such. Detention centres and youth custody centres were merged into single 'young offender institutions' catering for the 14–20 age group; short sentences remained (that is from three weeks to four months) but it is not clear what regimes have prevailed in them. Talk about preserving the 'short, sharp shock' within the system may just have been the government's way of saving face; most of those running the institutions had never liked or believed in the tough regimes (they made more work!).

Over and above the shift towards crime prevention – linked to the broader notion of 'youth social work', which has more positive ambitions than mere 'prevention' (Paley *et al.* 1986) – it seems to me that the key changes in juvenile justice, the ones to which all others will be subsidiary, are to be found in the

White Paper *Crime, Justice and Protecting the Public* (Home Office 1990). Only a small part of the White Paper deals with young offenders, and without in any way diminishing the importance of the proposals, at which even the Magistrates' Association appear to have baulked, to foster greater parental control over the under-15s (Home Office 1990: 8,1–8, 13), I shall address only part of that section, concentrating on the creation of a youth court and the significance of including 17-year-olds within its jurisdiction. I will conclude by assessing the prospects for phasing out the use of custody for 14–16-year-olds, a major aspiration of juvenile justice practitioners in the late 1980s, which ought not to be lost despite the valuable shift of attention to social crime prevention.

The youth court and 17-year-olds

The White Paper proposes that the juvenile court will be reconstituted as a youth court and that the upper age limit will be raised to 18, which will bring it in line with the age of majority. The idea of the youth court is not new, although the earlier formulations (Mannheim 1959; Home Office 1965) included the 18–20-year-olds as well (as some present-day European youth courts do), and were set in somewhat different administrative and philosophical contexts. As increasing numbers of under-14s were cautioned, doubts about the viability of juvenile courts had grown throughout the 1980s (Giller 1986), often linked to the long-running campaign for a Family Court.

In demographic and cultural terms the change to a youth court makes sense, although one hopes that it will continue to have regard for the welfare of offenders who appear before it, despite the Children Act 1989 removing 'pure' care cases from its jurisdiction (a split for which the radical justice lobby had also campaigned). In 1988 90 per cent of youngsters appearing in the juvenile court were aged 14–16, and if the new proposals are implemented 75 per cent of its work will come to be focused on 16–17-year-olds. 'Juvenile' is not an appropriate term for them, and although under-16s will continue to appear in the youth court the days of a separate professional sphere called 'juvenile justice', especially given the developments in social crime prevention, would appear to be numbered. (We might note this projection of the youth court's workload implies that the majority of under-14s will continue to be cautioned, and also, presumably, an increase in the cautioning of 17-year-olds). Although the respective responsibilities of the probation service and SSDs for 16–17-year-olds will probably be decided on the basis of local agreement, raising the upper age limit of the youth court could make many more 17-year-olds the responsibility of SSD (or SSD/voluntary sector) programmes. This represents a major challenge to the SSDs, the first opportunity in fact to see whether the lessons of juvenile justice can be transferred to an older age group, both in regard to cautioning and the use of alternatives to custody. In 1988 4,100 young men aged 17 were sentenced to custody – more than the entire number of 14–16-year-olds (3,400) who were similarly sentenced in the same year. That should be more than enough to replenish the alternative to custody centres whose future, in the late 1980s, was imperilled because there were too few referrals in the 14–16 age group, SSD managers who were beginning to worry that their staff–client ratio in IT was becoming top heavy should not take precipitous decisions to cut staff back, despite the recent announcement that custodial sentencing for 14-year-olds is, after all, to be abolished. Indeed the real anxiety is that by the time legislation takes effect the new Griffiths-style SSDs (unless they are in areas benefiting from steep demographic decline in young people) will not have *enough* resources to cope with the influx of 17-year-olds (particularly as even those released from custody will each require at least three months' supervision).

That of course presumes that SSDs will have some success in reducing the use of custody for 17-year-olds, along the lines of the success they have had with 14–16-year-olds. And that a significant proportion of these 'reclaimed' 17-year-olds will be sentenced to IT/supervised activities rather than to the longer Attendance Centre Orders (36 hours) or the longer Community Service Orders (240 hour maximum), which are being transferred down from the adult jurisdiction along with the 17-year-olds themselves. It is at this point that the more negative aspects of including 17-year-olds within the remit of the new court appear, because the measures that applied to them in the adult court are not only being retained, but also being extended to 16-year-olds. This represents a substantial toughening-up process, and it is no surprise that the government now wants the new measures – IT and supervised activities as well – to be characterized as 'punishment in the community', the same as it is (or will be) for the young adults.

This 'transfer down' of adult penalties seems to have been the solution to the 1988 Green Paper proposal for a variable jurisdiction with 16–20-year-olds, the general reaction to which had not been favourable. (It may also have been a solution to the increasing involvement of the Crown Court – deemed to be overburdened – in the sentencing of juveniles). The earlier notion of transferring the less mature 18–19-year-olds down from the adult court to the juvenile/youth court has been dropped completely. The notion of transferring the 'very mature 16 or 17-year-old' up to a higher court (except where the existing arrangements for committal to Crown Court apply) has also – ostensibly – been lost, but in practice the sentencing changes that are now being proposed will (if they are implemented) have a similar effect to that of a 'transfer-up' procedure if it had been pursued.

The White Paper also creates an inordinately complex set of arrangements in regard to supervision and probation orders. Under the proposed legislation the youth court will be able to select either a supervision order with an IT/supervised activities requirement or a probation order with a day centre requirement 'according to the maturity of the offender and the arrangements available locally' (Home Office 1990: para. 8.17). Furthermore, 'both 16 and 17-year-olds will be eligible for the new combined probation and community service order . . . in the same way as those over 17' (Home Office 1990: para. 8.18). IT requirements are already being included in some probation orders (Paul Overton, personal communication), but it remains to be seen what patterns of sentencing might emerge from this, and what multi-agency approaches (combined probation/SSD/voluntary sector day centres?) develop to serve the courts.

Preserving the anti-custody ethos

In the late 1980s many practitioners felt that the elimination of custody for 14–16-year-olds was within their grasp, that the ambitions of the CYPA 1969 could finally be achieved, albeit within a very different ideological framework. Tutt and Giller's (1987) strategy to eliminate the use of custody aimed, by cutting off the supply of youngsters going into custody, to make the custodial system unsustainable, to reduce the numbers in particular institutions so that they would cease to be cost effective. But the 1989 deadline was not met; the Criminal Justice Act 1988 did not incorporate their ideas, not even NACRO's (1989) more minimalist proposal to phase out custody for the 14-year-olds, and demoralization and frustration set in. Beaumont (1989: 36) has pointed out that Tutt and Giller seriously under-estimated the time-scale of change in local authorities: 1989 was far too soon for the great majority, despite good models of practice in some of them. In addition the eliminationist strategy was much more applicable to the age-specific (14–16) detention centres than it was to youth custody centres, which took 15–20-year-olds, and were not dependent for their survival on the younger age groups. The creation of a unified custodial sentence of 'detention in a young offender institution' in 1988 seriously weakened one of the premisses – but not all – on which the eliminationist strategy had been based.

Surprisingly a version of the eliminationist strategy appeared in the 1990 White Paper in its comments on the sentencing of girls and young women aged 15–18 (custody for 14-year-old girls having been abolished in 1967). It pointed out just how low custodial sentencing for such offenders has become (25 15-year-olds, 24 16-year-olds and 109 17-year-olds in 1988) and invited debate on the question of 'whether it is necessary to keep the sentence of detention in a young offender institution for girls under 18' (Home Office 1990: paras 8.26–8.27), mentioning that programmes of intensive supervision in the community already exist in most parts of the country and that detention under Section 53 of the CYPA 1933 will remain available for the minority of female offenders under 18 from whom society still needs protection. While the issue of appropriate supervision in the community for girls and young women is by no means straightforward (Stafford 1989), and the operation of Section 53 requires constant vigilance, the prospect of eliminating custody for this category of offender can only be welcomed, although the difficulty of passing equitable sentences in situations where male and female juveniles are jointly responsible for the same offence may make its survival unlikely.

But what of young men? The number of young men aged 14–17 who are sentenced to custody is nowhere near as low, but a strong case for ending the use of Prison Department custody for this age group has been made on several occasions (see especially Children's Society 1988). Over and above the recognition that custody may itself contribute to crime, by a process of mutual learning among incarcerated offenders and the consequences of stigmatization when they come out – arguments which the government has come to accept – the conventional case against penal custody for juveniles rests on three elements. First, the efficacy and cost-effectiveness of community-based measures for most serious and persistent young offenders – they are certainly no worse than custody in reducing recidivism. Second, the acknowledgement that the 400–600 youngsters who do need to be locked up either to protect society or for their own protection would be better provided for in local authority secure accommodation (of which there is already enough, although its quality needs improving). Third, it is also acknowledged that Section 53 of the CYPA 1933 will have to remain available for serious, persistent and grave offenders, these terms defined with more precision than hitherto, so as to avoid abuse.

It was perhaps too much to hope that the Thatcher government would respond positively to the whole of this strategy, but in the midst of debate on *Crime, Justice and Protecting the Public* it is interesting to note the eventual success of the campaign, started by NACRO and picked up by the Howard League (1990) to abolish the use of custody for 14-year-old boys. The government accepted that there should be provision for this in the Criminal Justice Bill partly because of the small numbers involved, 282 in 1988, and partly because it anticipated defeat in the European Court in a forthcoming test case alleging gender discrimination in the sentencing of juveniles. The same principle would make them vulnerable if custody for young women under 18 were eliminated, which may be one reason why this proposal could be withdrawn (*Guardian* 20 September 1990: 20).

It had long been recognized by practitioners and penal reform groups that the scandal of remanding male juveniles to prison department custody could also be reduced by a combination of community-based measures and more appropriate use of local authority secure accommodation (Rutherford 1983). It none the less took the suicide of a 15-year-old remand prisoner in Swansea Prison – in the context of widespread alarm about a series of prison suicides by young adults – to promise action in the Criminal Justice Bill (*Guardian* 28 July 1990: 2), although the Bill itself makes no reference to it, the Government apparently intend to introduce their own amendment on this. Secure accommodation itself is in fact overused in the remand context; on 31 March 1988 25 per cent of the entire 'secure' population of youngsters were remanded to care awaiting trial or sentence. Lowering this number requires further campaigning for better use of the Bail Act 1976 and an increase in the still rather scarce bail support schemes: a pump-priming initiative from the Department of Health and the Home Office, akin to LAC 83(3), could help to achieve this (AJJ 1990: 30–1).

Positive action still needs to be taken on the issue of black youngsters, both remanded and sentenced, and it is in this area that the different traditions of work with young offenders may fuse most rapidly. In commenting on the failings of the LAC 83(3) Initiative in respect of black offenders, Errol John linked the notion of alternatives to custody to 'working in partnership with the local community' in a way which is still unusual, but hopefully becoming less so:

Juvenile crime is a public issue. The public deserve and have a right, to be given facts and figures, and to be involved in the processes [of decision-making]. . . . It was interesting when the DHSS provided the money for the LAC '83 Initiative that only one black community group participated in any projects at all. . . . Why is this? To what extent is the black community informed and consulted about various equal opportunity policies which are taking place?

(John 1989: 4)

There may be, as Pitts (1988) noticed, the seeds of a new politics of abolition here. It is possible that the sentencing of young black people to custody will become more of a community issue, a more visible sign of injustice – the criminalizing of the poor – than has been the case with the sentencing of marginalized white youngsters. It may be that black communities can be mobilized around the issue of custody more readily than their white counterparts, in which case professionals seeking to phase out custody may have something to gain by allying themselves with them. (Alternatively it may lose them wider political credibility: that is the dilemma.) It may be that as the notion of citizenship acquires greater political potency, as seems likely in the 1990s (Hall and Held 1989), that the denial of dignity which prison all too often entails (over and above the denial of liberty), that an 'anti-custodial ethos' will become the preserve of oppressed communities and not just the juvenile justice professionals who work in or near them. The enhanced safety which local crime prevention initiatives can generate, the confidence they can give communities to cope with trouble, may make this more rather than less likely. The linking – conceptually and practically – of replacements for custody with social crime prevention, through 'rediscovered' community development strategies (Miller 1989), are issues which juvenile justice workers (however termed) might seek to address in the 1990s. Within this area of work there also lies the challenge of working against the racism of white lower-class youth in ways that are consistent with an 'anti-custodial ethos'; it puts the issue of control *within* communities firmly on the social work agenda.

But will Rutherford's (1989: 27) 'anti-custodial ethos', so important to the local successes of juvenile justice in the 1980s, actually survive among the practitioners themselves, in local authorities which have never had a financial incentive to provide alternatives to *custody*, as opposed to residential care, on which they could at least 'make savings'? The only certain effect of introducing 17-year-olds into the erstwhile juvenile justice system will be to increase workloads, but unfortunately it may also make the phasing out of custody for the 14–16-year-olds more difficult. For this reason, declining numbers notwithstanding, work with 17-year-olds will, initially at least, make contact with custody, and people who have been in custody, a far more common and routine occurrence than it is at present. Some of these youngsters, as is already true of some 16-year-olds, will have been brutalized by poverty, abuse and homelessness to the point where they will tax the abilities of even the most experienced workers (Millham 1988: 13). In order to make their work 'manageable, predictable and tolerable' (Satyamurti 1981: 76), particularly at a time of major organizational change and accommodation shortages for this age group (Hester and Welch 1987), workers may find the 'anti-custodial ethos' far too dissonant with their day-to-day experience of both young people and court practice, and simply acquiesce in the existence of custody, accept it as a fact of life, a regrettable but sometimes convenient dumping ground. The influx of 17-year-olds will certainly wipe out 'custody free zones' at a stroke, and make it harder to recreate them. It may normalize custody within the professional culture of youth social work and make the notion of its elimination seem less feasible, that is more difficult to imagine and more difficult to mobilize support for.

So if 'custody free zones' are to be remembered as something more than the urban legends of the 1980s, practitioners should not forget the ideal of abolition, and should seek to push work in and with the community – the tense, fragmented and heterogeneous neighbourhoods of contemporary inner cities, and the agencies which regulate and sustain them – to new limits. As Ball (1989: 16) rightly observes, 'legislative change can most easily be achieved when it is preceded by changes in practice so that it appears that all the legislation is doing is recognising a *fait accompli* and bringing a few "mavericks" into line'. New models of anti-custodial practice are needed, building on the lessons of the last decade, to facilitate legal abolition. Not all the signs are inauspicious. There is European penal practice to embarrass the government, the beckoning candle of citizenship in which to ground new notions of rehabilitation (Mclaren and Spencer 1988), the sophisticated theorizing of Thomas Mathiesen (1990: 161) to provide vision – he seems no longer to see 'alternatives' in quite the negative way he once did (not in all situations) – and above all the recognition that the first seeds of success in the 1980s – such as it was – were sown at a very inauspicious time indeed, when the ideological dominance of the 'short, sharp, shock' was at its zenith.

Acknowledgement

I should like to thank Paul Overton, IT Co-ordinator, Sheffield Family and Community Services, for his comments on an earlier draft of this chapter.

References

AJJ (Association for Juvenile Justice) (1990) 'A response to secure accommodation in community homes', *AJJUST* 22: 26–31.

Ball, C. (1989) 'Major crimes: a need for custodial regimes', in S. Doyle (ed.) *Towards A Custody Free Community*, Peterborough Association for Juvenile Justice.

Barker, J. (1989) 'The greatest crime of all', *AJJUST* 20: 5–7.

Beaumont, K. (1989) 'The manifesto for management', in S. Doyle (ed.) *Towards A Custody Free Community*, Peterborough Association for Juvenile Justice.

Blackmore, J. (1988) 'From IT to ITCASS in Hounslow', *Youth Social Work Mailing* 8: 16–19.

Blagg, H. and Smith, D. (1989) *Crime, Penal Policy and Social Work*, London: Longman.

Bottoms, A. (1989) 'Crime prevention facing the 1990's', James Smart Lecture, Edinburgh: Trustrees of the James Smart Lecture Fund.

Bottoms, A., Brown, P., McWilliams, B., McWilliams, W., Nellis, M. and Pratt, J. (1990) *Intermediate Treatment and Juvenile Justice: Key Findings and Implications of a National Survey of Intermediate Treatment Policy and Practice*, London: HMSO.

Children's Society (1988) *Penal Custody for Juveniles: The Line of Least Resistance*, London: Children's Society.

Cooper, J. (1983) *The Creation of the British Personal Social Services 1962–1974*, London: Heinemann.

Curtis, S. (1989) *Juvenile Offending: Prevention through Intermediate Treatment*, London: Batsford.

Davies, B. (1986) *Threatening Youth: Towards A National Youth Policy*, Milton Keynes: Open University Press.

Department of Health (1989) *Caring for People: Community Care in the Next Decade and Beyond*, Cm 849, London: HMSO.

DHSS (1983) *Local Authority Circular 1983/3 Further Development of Intermediate Treatment*, London: DHSS.

Doyle, S. (ed.) (1989) *Towards A Custody Free Community: A Collection of Papers from Two AJJ Conferences*, Peterborough Association for Juvenile Justice.

Faulker, D. (1988) 'Introduction', in *Round Table Consultation on Strategy for the Reduction in the Use of Custody for Young Adult Offenders (17–20 Year-Olds) 5–8 February 1988*, London: National Children's Homes.

Giller, H. (1986) 'Is there a role for the Juvenile Court?' *Howard Journal* 25, 3: 161–71.

Hall, S. and Held, D. (1989) 'Citizens and citizenship', in S. Hall and M. Jacques (eds) *New Times: The Changing Face of Politics in the 1990s*, London: Lawrence & Wishart.

Hester, R. and Welch, K. (1987) 'Young adult offenders – a problem of housing and custody', *Youth Social Work Mailing* 4: 8–9.

Home Office (1965) *The Child, the Family and the Young Offender*, Cmnd 2742, London: HMSO.

—— (1980) *Young Offenders*, Cmnd 8045, London: HMSO.

—— (1988a) *Punishment, Custody and the Community*, Cm 424, London: HMSO.

—— (1988b) *Tackling Offending: An Action Plan: Letter dated 17 August 1988*, London: Home Office.

—— (1990) *Crime, Justice and Protecting the Public*, Cm 965, London: HMSO.

Hope, B. (1990) 'Youth social work as a response to youth crime', *Youth Social Work Mailing* 12: 7–9.

Howard League (1990) *Ban Prison for Children!*, campaign document dated 14 June, London: Howard League.

Jeffs, T. and Smith, M. (1988) 'The political economy of youth work', in T. Jeffs and M. Smith (eds) *Welfare and Youth Work Practice*, Basingstoke: Macmillan.

John, E. (1989) 'Identifying and eliminating discrimination', in S. Doyle (ed.) *Towards A Custody Free Community*, Peterborough Association for Juvenile Justice.

Jones, D. (1989) 'The successful revolution', *Community Care (Inside Supplement)* 30 March: i–ii.

Jones, R. (1984) 'Questioning the new orthodoxy', *Community Care* 11 October: 15–17.

Leah, B. and Rawlinson, E. (1989) 'Good practice needs good campaigning', *Community Care (Inside Supplement)* 30 March: vi–viii.

Mclaren, V. and Spencer, J. (1988) 'Defining social justice to develop citizenship', *Social Work Today* 6 October: 16–17.

Mannheim, H. (1959) *Courts for Adolescents*, London: Institute for the Study and Treatment of Delinquency.

Mathiesen, T. (1974) *The Politics of Abolition*, London: Martin Robertson.

—— (1990) *Prison on Trial*, London: Sage.

Mawby, R. (1989) 'The voluntary sector's role in a mixed economy of criminal justice', in R. Matthews (ed.) *Privatising Criminal Justice*, London: Sage.

Miller, S. (1989) 'Community development and the underclass', in M. Bulmer, J. Lewis and D. Piachaud (eds) *The Goals of Social Policy*, London: Unwin Hyman.

Millham, S. (1988) 'A researcher's perspective', in *Round Table Consultation on Strategy for the Reduction in the Use of Custody for Young Adult Offenders (17–20 Year-Olds) 5–6 January 1988*, London: National Children's Homes.

NACRO (National Association for the Care and Resettlement of Offenders) (1989) *Phasing Out Prison Department Custody for Juvenile Offenders. Juvenile Crime Committee Policy Paper No 1*, London: NACRO.

NAPO (National Association of Probation Officers) (1988) *Punishment, Custody and the Green Paper: The Response of the National Association of Probation Officers*, London: NAPO.

National Intermediate Treatment Federation (1986) *Anti-Racist Practice for Intermediate Treatment*, Working Party on Racism in the Juvenile Justice System, available from NITFED, c/o Caroline Tote, Leicester C.C. Social Services Dept, Glenfield, Leicester.

Nellis, M. (1987) The myth of uptariffing in IT', *AJJUST* 12: 7–12.

—— (1989) 'Juvenile justice and the voluntary sector', in R. Matthews (ed.) *Privatising Criminal Justice*, London: Sage.

Paley, J., Thomas, J. and Norman, J. (1986) *Rethinking Youth Social Work*, Leicester: National Youth Bureau.

Pitts, J. (1988) *The Politics of Juvenile Crime*, London: Sage.

—— (1990) *Working with Young Offenders*, Basingstoke: Macmillan/British Association of Social Workers.

Richardson, N. (1987) *Justice by Geography?*, Manchester: Social Information Systems.

Rutherford, A. (1983) 'A statute backfires: The escalation of youth incarceration in England during the 1970s' , in J. W. Doig (ed.) *Criminal Corrections: Ideals and Realities*, Lexington, Mass: D. C. Heath.

—— (1986) *Growing Out of Crime*, Harmondsworth: Penguin.

—— (1989) 'The mood and temper of penal policy: curious happenings in England during the 1980s', *Youth and Policy* 27: 27–31.

Satyamurti, C. (1981) *Occupational Survival*, Oxford: Basil Blackwell.

Seals, J. and Orders, N. (1989) 'Alternatives to remands in care and custody', in S. Doyle (ed.) *Towards A Custody Free Community*, Peterborough Association for Juvenile Justice.

Skinner, A. (1988) 'The experience of young women in the welfare and juvenile justice systems: Appendix', in A. Mountain (ed.) *Womanpower: A Handbook for Women Working with Young Women At Risk and in Trouble*, Leicester: National Youth Bureau.

—— (1989) 'IT and the Youth Service', *Youth Social Work Mailing* 10: 1–7, Leicester: National Youth Bureau.

Stafford, D. (1989) 'What about the girls?', in S. Doyle (ed.) *Towards a Custody Free Community*, Peterborough Association for Juvenile Justice.

Thorpe, D. (1972) 'Putting theory into practice at Ryehill', *Social Work Today* 6 April: 23–5.

Tipler, J. (1989) 'Colour-conscious justice', *Community Care (Inside Supplement')* 30 March: v–vi.

Tutt, N. and Giller, H. (1987) 'Manifesto for management: the elimination of custody', *Justice of the Peace* 28 March: 200–2.

11
Care in the community: the social security issues

Geoff Fimister

July 1990 saw the postponement, until April 1993, of the main part of the Government's care in the community proposals. This development, essentially tied up with the politics of the poll tax, has led to much disquiet in social services circles.

'Care in the community' is, in a general sense, a concept with which few would argue. The idea must surely be sound that people who are disabled, frail and elderly, have learning difficulties, are recovering from mental illness or are suffering from some other disadvantage which may lead them into institutional care, should instead be provided with sufficient support to remain in, or return to, the community.

Nevertheless, 'care in the community' can also constitute a flag of convenience for less progressive notions, such as overall service reductions and further impositions on the labour of unpaid carers, usually women. The current planning process which is taking place in the wake of the Griffiths Report (1988) provides the ideal opportunity for care in the community to establish its bona fides, delay notwithstanding. Good quality care in the community will often be cheaper than residential care, but sometimes will not; and should certainly not be regarded as a cheap option overall.

The good faith of the current changes will, then, be proven or otherwise by the priority, and thus the resources, devoted to them. But this should not be construed only in terms of the resources applied to the funding of care services. If we are serious about care in the community, we must consider some fundamental prerequisites of survival in, or rehabilitation into, the 'outside world'. The most important of these are how well people are housed; and whether their incomes are adequate. The White Paper (Department of Health 1989) says virtually nothing about housing, but that is another (if related) story. My brief here is to look at social security. This chapter will assume that the changes now scheduled for April 1993 will be the same as those originally planned for 1991. In reality, much water may, of course, have passed under the bridge by then.

Social security: the background

Disappointingly, official discussion of social security issues has almost entirely focused around residential care and nursing homes. Although a government document (the consultative status of which was unclear) on benefits for disabled people did appear in January 1990 (Department of Social Security 1990a), its proposals were fragmented in themselves (mostly a mixture of cuts and miscellaneous modest improvements) and there was little or no attempt to link it, either conceptually or practically, to the planning process for care in the community.

In October 1989 (the month prior to the publication of the White Paper) the first of a series of meetings took place between central government departments (led by the Department of Health) and the local authority (LA) associations. (I have been involved in these consultations as an adviser to the Association of Metropolitan Authorities: AMA.) The AMA took the view that consideration of social security issues should not be confined to the question of benefits for people in residential care and nursing homes, but should address a number of specific problem areas where people living in the community found that social security rules collided with community care objectives. This was not received with enthusiasm on the central government side, which did not perceive the consultative agenda as embracing these matters at all. The compromise adopted was that bilateral discussions should take place between the LA associations and the Department of Social Security (DSS). As we shall see below, subsequent DSS reaction to the AMA proposals was so comprehensively negative that it was possible to establish a total stalemate by letter, without going to the trouble of having a meeting.

The government's preoccupation with benefits for people in residential care and nursing homes in fact lies at the heart of the proposed changes. Such care is mainly provided by either LA residential care homes or homes in the private or voluntary sector. The benefit arrangements described immediately below are those which apply currently, in the year to April 1991. The benefit formula for LA homes is based on the standard retirement pension. A resident pays over an amount equivalent to 80 per cent of this to the LA social services department (SSD) (in Scotland, social work department: although this chapter is couched in terms of the position in England and Wales, the issues in Scotland are essentially similar). The resident then retains a personal expenses allowance equivalent to 20 per cent. Any income above this level can also be retrieved by the SSD as a contribution towards the cost of the place in the home. Capital is also taken into account. Income support (prior to April 1988, supplementary benefit) need not enter this equation, unless the resident does not receive at least a basic rate of retirement pension.

The benefit arrangements for residents of private and voluntary sector homes are quite different. Here, the DSS (via income support) meets the charge for the place in the home (plus an allowance for any meals not included in the charge), subject to national upper limits ('ceilings') and also pays a small personal expenses allowance (marginally higher than that retained by residents of LA homes). As is usual in income support assessments, other benefits such as retirement pension are taken fully into account in calculating the amount of income support payable. Again, capital is taken into account. This formula is in fact the last surviving relic of the former supplementary benefit 'board and lodging' assessment, abolished in respect of ordinary and supported board and lodgings in April 1989; and in respect of hostels in October 1989.

DSS spending on private and voluntary sector residential care and nursing home charges has escalated in the last decade: the White Paper (Department of Health 1989: para. 8.5) complains that such expenditure 'rose in cash terms from £10m. in December 1979 to over £1,000m. by May 1989'. The desire of the DSS and the Treasury to stem this growth in social security spending is a major motivating force behind the current proposals for community care. Some would say that it is *the* motivating force.

The steep rise in benefit costs in this area initially smiled upon as a spur to private provision, had become a cause of official consternation by the mid-1980s, leading to the installation in 1985 of the system of national ceilings. Herein, though, lay another problem: the more rigid the upper limits, the more claimants would find themselves with charges above the levels which DSS would meet. Social security payments may have some influence on the market, but do not control it to the extent that most proprietors will feel unable to increase charges beyond DSS levels. I shall say more below concerning this 'shortfall' issue.

Government pressure for change has built up over several years, accompanied by the production of three major reports (Firth 1987; NISW 1988; Griffiths 1988). It is no secret that the fact that a White Paper and a Bill took so long to appear after the publication of the Griffiths Report was the result of government attempts to find a way round the central role which Griffiths envisaged for LAs. No such detour could be identified and the government had to reconcile itself to supping with the municipal devil. I am concerned here with the proposed social security arrangements, which I shall describe below. First, though, I should summarize briefly an important subplot, relating to the position of supported lodgings and hostels.

In November 1986 the (then) Department of Health and Social Security (DHSS) informed the LA associations that it proposed to remove the special rules for board and lodgings claims within the supplementary benefit system. From April 1988 (subsequently deferred to April 1989) claimants would need to claim ordinary income support and housing benefit (HB). Limited 'transitional protection' would apply in existing cases. A consultative paper appeared the following month, setting out this approach (DHSS 1986).

The government had found the board and lodging arrangements increasingly controversial, because of deficient upratings, harsh limits on the duration of benefit for young people, and various legal challenges to the regulations. Moreover, this was a system which did not sit well with the new 'simplified' (that is more readily computerized) structure of income support. Thus the desire to get rid of it was unsurprising. LA associations took the view that a measure which would bring a marginal group into the mainstream of benefit provision was welcome in principle, but that there were problems which would have to be solved first. A key difficulty related to the fact that items included within the board and lodging charge which were ineligible for HB – such as meals, fuel, water, 20 per cent of general rates, care costs – would have to be met from ordinary income support (unless LAs stepped in to subsidize placements – see below), leaving little, or even no, remaining disposable income. Especially vulnerable would be people whose income support was particularly low (notably young people) and/or who had to meet charges for items ineligible for HB which were particularly high (notably care costs). Because of this latter factor, the position of supported lodgings, where care is provided as part of the placement, was highly problematic.

Research was commissioned by the DHSS (Young 1988) which served to confirm the fears of LA associations, voluntary organizations and academic commentators: but the change was implemented anyway. It became increasingly clear that, although the DHSS had not originally realized that there was a problem in relation to supported lodgings (which were not even mentioned in the December 1986 consultative paper), once the issue was understood, the assumption grew that SSDs would have to step in (as they already did in a number of cases) to finance the schemes in question. Although the LA role here would be on too modest a scale to activate the above-mentioned official qualms about a key LA responsibility for community care, nevertheless the intended change could not be openly admitted while the government was still considering its response to the Griffiths Report. Eventually, though, a minister let the cat out of the bag. In November 1988 Lord Skelmersdale observed that

> Research shows that just over half of those local authorities which run schemes already fund them in whole or in part. They will continue to be able to fund them after next April. The consideration is entirely as it always has been – in the lap of local authorities.
> (House of Lords *Hansard* 1 November 1988: col. 146)

In the wake of the supported lodgings issue came other changes or proposals for change which raised similar issues. During 1987 the definition of a small unregistered residential home was altered, so as to demote a number of adult fostering-type schemes to the (much lower) board and lodging rates applicable to 'special needs' boarders not living in a home. This time, from the outset, the consequences were intentional on the part of the DHSS. Meanwhile, some schemes sponsored by health authorities were finding that their clients were being designated as hospital patients for benefit purposes, resulting in very low entitlements. It was clear that the DHSS was stepping up its efforts to push the burden of care costs out of the benefit system.

The December 1986 consultative document on board and lodging also announced that the position of hostels was under scrutiny. Research was again commissioned by the DHSS (Berthoud and Casey 1988), to examine the nature and range of hostel provision. Again, inconvenient findings – including the extensive role of care in hostels – were ignored, and changes similar to those in respect of board and lodgings were implemented from October 1989. Substantial protest (including that from within the Conservative party) at the potentially destabilizing effects on the finances of hostels resulted. This led to 'transitional protection' which provided temporary cover not only to existing claimants, but also to hostels themselves, in order to provide a bridge from October 1989 to April 1991, when the resources in question would be transferred to 'traditional funding agencies'. How much this will be, how it will work, how it will interact with the wider funding arrangements for special needs housing and with the community care proposals is currently the subject of further controversy. At the time of writing (September 1990) the government has just informed the LA associations that it expects SSDs to take over the main responsibility for funding care costs in hostels from April 1991. The LA associations have protested at the time-scale and lack of consultation.

Let us return to the benefit arrangements now proposed for residential care and nursing homes from April 1993. I described above the current structure, whereby some claimants receive benefit according to the 'LA homes' formula based on the standard retirement pension figure, while those in private and voluntary sector homes receive benefit on the basis of the old DSS 'board and lodging' assessment. The government's proposals for change are still (at the time of writing) the subject of consultations with LA associations. This is proving a fragmented process, as some aspects are being channelled through discussions with the Department of Health, while others are subject to the established HB consultative machinery with the DSS. Moreover, there have been long delays in securing ministerial decisions on key aspects of the HB proposals. However, the following is an outline of the benefit proposals as they stand in September 1990.

Residents will, from the point of change, fall into three different groups for benefit purposes: new claimants in private and voluntary sector residential care and nursing homes; claimants who were resident in those homes at the point of change; and claimants who are residents of local authority homes.

Claimants who are residents of local authority homes will continue to be assessed on something like the existing basis. Personal expenses allowances, and the rules for assessment of income and capital, will be aligned with those for private and voluntary sector homes; otherwise there will be no change to the general approach of a minimum charge and a personal expenses allowance together equalling the standard rate of retirement pension. As will become apparent below, this means that SSDs will recoup considerably less from residents placed in their own homes than they will from those placed in private and voluntary sector homes. This creates an incentive to use the latter, or a penalty for using the former (depending on which way round one looks at it). This is a quite deliberate policy on the government's part, intended to provide a continuing stimulus to non-LA provision. Many SSDs will, as a consequence, divest themselves of some, or even all, of their own homes – a process which is indeed already well under way.

Claimants who are residents of private or voluntary sector homes at the point of change will continue to be paid on the basis of the old system, complete with ceilings (which has led the DSS to bestow upon them the unfortunate title of the 'preserved group'). This has been a highly controversial feature of the NHS and Community Care Bill as it has wended its way through Parliament during late 1989 and the first half of 1990. The Opposition has sought to amend both this and the then current Social Security Bill with various formulae to protect residents caught by a shortfall between benefit ceilings and charges levied by homes. The government indeed lost one vote in the House of Commons on this issue (see House of Commons *Hansard*, 13 March 1990). For eccentric procedural reasons, this amendment did not stand, but it led to limited concessions. These amounted to modest increases in national ceilings in August 1990, and an undertaking to consider the levels of charges negotiated by LAs in different areas when reviewing ceilings in future – although this will now be affected by the delay. However, the problem remains. There is no precise estimate of the extent of the 'shortfall', but it is clear that, as annual upratings of the ceilings have in many areas increasingly failed to keep pace with charges, it has become widespread and more severe. Evidence produced by agencies such as the National Federation of Housing Associations, the National Association of Citizens' Advice Bureaux and Age Concern has illustrated the consequences (see e.g. Age Concern 1989). Some homes are subsidizing places; some are providing a poorer quality of accommodation (e.g. room-sharing) to residents on income support; many residents are using some or all of their personal expenses allowance to put towards the charge; and many relatives, often themselves elderly and/or on low incomes, are suffering hardship as they top up homes' charges. Nor are SSDs usually able to help, except by fully sponsoring or 're-housing' a resident altogether, for they have no 'top-up' powers unless the resident is under pension age (or was under pension age when the 'top-up' began).

In spite of the concerns expressed by voluntary organizations, LA associations and the House of Commons Social Services Committee (House of Commons Social Services Committee 1990) over the 'shortfall' question, the government has been unable to give any clear assurances. Indeed its brief (five-page) response to the Social Services Committee's representations was both evasive and disconcertingly complacent (Secretary of State for Social Security 1990b). The delay in implementation of the new system will perpetuate and exacerbate this problem. At the time of writing, the government has announced no plans to deal with it.

Claimants who become newly resident in private and voluntary sector homes from April 1993 will fall under a new set of arrangements altogether. Where the SSD decides that the care package should entail a residential care or nursing home, it will normally pay the proprietor the full charge and then recoup as much of the cost as possible from the resident. (There will be slightly different arrangements for housing associations, so as to preserve the 'landlord–tenant' relationship, but the overall sums involved will be unaffected.) The White Paper does suggest that 'if relatives or friends wish, and are able, to make a contribution towards the cost of care, an individual may decide to look for a place in a more expensive home' (Department of Health 1989: para. 3.7.8). Unless a relative or friend makes such a suggestion spontaneously, and can clearly afford the outlay, SSDs should be encouraged to ignore this hint: it could easily deteriorate (especially where care budgets are tight) into an informal system of pressure upon relatives and others.

Residents under the new system will be entitled to claim ordinary income support, including relevant premiums, and will usually be receiving other benefits such as retirement pension also (fully taken into account, of course, in calculating the income support). Most of this will be recovered by the SSD to put towards the cost of the home, leaving the claimant with a small personal expenses allowance (which in real terms will probably be around the level of the corresponding allowance currently paid in private and voluntary sector homes). The formula for charging under this system will be statutorily prescribed, unlike domiciliary and day-care services, where SSDs will have discretion to fix their own charging formulae.

The resident will also be able to claim HB, which will be paid over in full to the SSD (except where the special arrangements for housing associations apply). In order to simplify administration for HB authorities, and financial planning for SSDs, it has been agreed between central government departments and LA associations that a 'notional' standard eligible rent will be fixed for private and voluntary sector residential care and nursing home places in each HB authority area. However, arriving at a formula to determine the *level* of such a standard figure has proved highly contentious. While the matter will be academic for residents who are supported by SSDs (as their disposable income – the personal expenses allowance – will be unaffected) it will be of great importance to those who may be resident in the same home, but without SSD support (for example in projects with very mixed levels of care). Moreover, the higher the HB, the lower the amount transferred to SSDs via the revenue support grant (RSG), and vice versa (see below), so a gap has opened up between those on the local authority side who are prepared to trust the RSG to deliver the goods, and those who are not (essentially the Association of County Councils versus the rest). The lack of unity on the local authority side on this issue is, though, exceeded by that on the central government side, where the tension between the HB proposals for residential and nursing home care on the one hand, and other aspects of funding for special needs housing on the other, has led to a protracted stalemate between departments, the Department of the Environment having a significantly different agenda from the Department of Health, with the DSS caught in the middle (and other departments in supporting roles on either side). Ministers began to consider the options, supposedly urgently, in March 1990, and at the time of writing (September) have not yet announced a decision. Moreover, this has held up consultations on the various administrative issues relating to HB. The shape of the HB arrangements which will result is looking increasingly unpredictable.

We can see from the above how the penalty will operate where SSDs make use of their own care homes, rather than place a client in the private or voluntary sector. Where the resident's income is at the income support level, the SSD will recover in the former case an amount equivalent to (about) four-fifths of the standard retirement pension; whereas in the latter, an amount equivalent to most of the resident's income support 'applicable amount' (needs allowances), plus the whole of his or her HB, will be available.

Most residents will not have enough income to meet the charge made by the home, so SSDs will make up the difference from their 'care budgets'. This additional spending is supposedly to be financed by the transfer to SSDs of the money which the DSS would have spent on claimants in private and voluntary sector homes, had the old system continued. This amount obviously has to be estimated, taking into account demographic and inflationary factors, and there have been detailed consultations to that end. 'Netted off' from the amount to be transferred will be amounts to represent the additional income support paid out by the DSS (as residents will now be claiming on the same basis as others living in the community) and the cost of HB (which, although administered locally, is funded by central government). Also deducted will be the amount of income support which the DSS will continue to pay to the 'preserved group' (about four-fifths of the total in the first year). In theory, SSDs will have the option to use the transferred resources to provide alternatives to residential care where appropriate.

The transferred resources will be allocated to SSDs by means of the RSG system, which is highly controversial. A full discussion of this issue would be beyond the brief of this chapter, but readers will be aware that there are serious criticisms of the fairness and effectiveness of this system, and consequent doubts as to how far resources will arrive where they are needed. Moreover, the DSS will not be transferring an amount to represent the shortfall between homes' charges and current benefit levels, the argument being that, as it is not being spent at the moment, it is not there to be transferred. Any deficiency in SSD resources will have to be met by providing inadequate services or by topping up from the poll tax (if the system of local government finance remains unchanged) which of course presents financial and political problems, especially for LAs which may risk poll tax 'capping'.

In effect, the government is relying on SSDs' 'bulk purchasing' power to keep down homes' charges to the extent that the SSD will be able to pay for the places it needs, while also developing alternatives to residential care. This is, to put it as kindly as possible, a gamble.

Social security in the community

The fact that the focus of attention has been almost exclusively upon social security in relation to residential care and nursing homes is not only ironic, but also highly undesirable in the context of what is supposed to be a 'care in the community' exercise. Let us, then, turn our attention to some of the benefit issues bearing upon people seeking to live in the community rather than in a residential home. How well does the social security system in fact reinforce such efforts?

As I have argued elsewhere (Fimister 1988; see also Betteridge and Davis 1990), there is a general and very real sense in which social security policy militates against care in the community objectives. A major aspect of this is the low level of the benefit rates themselves, resulting from the combination of an overall desire to constrain public spending, with long-established labour market polices which emphasize incentives to take very low-paid employment. Efforts to get by on incomes as low as those provided by our income support system, and by other benefits paid at similar levels, will be difficult even for those with extraordinary budgeting skills. Survival in the community of vulnerable people is scarcely consistent with this set of distributional priorities – an uncomfortable truth which casts a shadow over this entire policy area.

This combination of public spending and employment policies, acting upon social security provision to the detriment of care in the community objectives, is a good example of the way in which different policy areas with different agendas tend to interact and often conflict, frequently to the further disadvantage of those groups and individuals already in an economically weak position. This remains true when we descend from the heights of overall policy objectives and begin to look at specific measures within them. For example on the employment front, benefit penalties for those who are deemed to be pursuing low-paid work with insufficient vigour, or to have left a job without 'just cause', are a particular hazard to those whose hold on the labour market is already tenuous (see e.g. Byrne and Jacobs 1988). This is bad news for those with a background of, say, mental illness or drug abuse, who are seeking to re-establish themselves in the mainstream of community life. Another example lies in the field of local government finance, where conflict between central and local government over spending levels has led the former to cut rate (subsequently poll tax) rebates in an attempt to put financial pressure on claimants in order to encourage them to put electoral pressure on local councillors (Esam *et al.* 1989; Esam and Oppenheim 1989). This has given a further vigorous twist to the spiral of debt which increasingly afflicts some of the most vulnerable people in the community, and left them at the mercy of Draconian poll tax enforcement measures.

The relatively hostile terrain represented by life on benefit in the community creates the ironic effect whereby the greater the progress made by an individual in establishing independence, the greater become the pressures pushing him or her back again. For example somebody who has been unable to work for a long period may be receiving the disability premium as part of his or her income support; but upon reaching the stage when he or she feels ready to register for employment, the premium will be lost, substantially reducing weekly income. Similarly somebody being resettled from a long stay in hospital may obtain a community care grant from the social fund to buy furniture and essential household items; but when these subsequently need replacing, a loan, with heavy repayment commitments, is more likely to be offered.

Has the planning process for the new care in the community arrangements given us an opportunity to identify and iron out, if not the major, then at least some of the more detailed benefit problems? The opportunity has certainly been there, but it has not been taken. I referred above to the proposed bilateral discussions between the LA associations and the DSS. The AMA undertook to draw up proposals, which were set out in a letter to the DSS on

6 December 1989. They concerned a number of issues, including difficulties experienced by hospital patients in retaining accommodation in the community; the non-availability of community care grants to people just above the income support level; and the need to develop a strategy to raise carers' incomes. In its reply of 23 January 1990 the DSS rejected all of the AMA's proposals. The LA associations are continuing to press the government on these issues.

Similarly current consultations around the charging formula for residential care and nursing homes have identified anomalies which would adversely affect the ability of residents to return to the community, or of long-term carers to remain in accommodation vacated by an elderly relative. The Department of Health has proved extremely unwilling to entertain any departure from the rigidity of the income support rules, which it intends to use as a model. One minister, responding to concern about cuts in the earnings which certain younger residents might be allowed to keep, went as far as to say:

> I am afraid the full details of the [earnings] disregard have still to be decided. They will of course be modelled closely on the income support and housing benefit rules, since *our over-riding aim* is to bring the two schemes into line.

> (Lord Henley, House of Lords *Hansard*,
> 14 June 1990, col. 461, emphasis added)

It would seem that this aim overrides community care objectives.

Expectations

I noted above that some commentators believe the government's perspective to be unduly influenced by the desire to remove the growing cost of residential and nursing home care from the social security budget. This would certainly be consistent with the lack of interest in other social security aspects of care in the community policy. This is not to say that a genuine interest in promoting community care does not exist within the Department of Health, but rather that the jettisoning of care costs by the DSS sits comfortably higher on the government's priority list (although not, it seems, as high as pre-election poll tax damage limitation).

Is this unduly pessimistic? Will this agenda dominate? Or will there be opportunities to develop new forms of care, with adequate social security support? At a meeting on 15 June 1990 between the LA associations, the Department of Health and the Department of the Environment (amidst continuing rumours of possible deferment of the changes, to help dampen poll tax increases) civil servants stressed the need to lower expectations, which they said had become too high. This coincided with the appearance of drafts of Department of Health guidance on the new system, one of which observed that:

> Full development of assessment and case management procedures as described in this circular will take time. Priority should be given to having in place by 1 April 1991 arrangements for assessing the needs of people

applying for residential or nursing home care who, but for the benefit changes to be introduced on that date, would have been supported through social security benefits in independent residential care or nursing homes.

(Department of Health 1990: para. 3)

Let us hope that something more adventurous than this can be achieved.

References

Age Concern (1989) *Moving the Goalposts: Changing Policies for Long-Stay Health and Social Care of Elderly People*, briefing, London: Age Concern England.

Berthoud, R. and Casey, B. (1988) *The Cost of Care in Hostels*, London: Policy Studies Institute.

Betteridge, J. and Davis, A. (1990) *Cracking Up: Social Security Benefits and Mental Health Users' Experiences*, London: MIND.

Byrne, D. and Jacobs, J. (1988) *Disqualified from Benefit: The Operation of Benefit Penalties*, London: Low Pay Unit.

DHSS (1986) *Help with Board and Lodging Charges for People on Low Incomes: Proposals for Change*, London: DHSS.

Department of Health (1989) *Caring for People: Community Care in the Next Decade and Beyond*, Cm 849, London: HMSO.

—— (1990) *Caring for People: Community Care in the Next Decade and Beyond – Draft Guidance: Assessment and Case Management*, London: DoH.

Department of Social Security (1990a) *The Way Ahead: Benefits for Disabled People*, Cm 917, London: HMSO.

—— (1990b) *Community Care: Future Funding of Private and Voluntary Residential Care – Response by the Government to the Second Report from the Social Services Committee Session 1989/90*, Cm 1100, London: HMSO.

Esam, P. and Oppenheim, C. (1989) *A Charge on the Community: The Poll Tax, Benefits and the Poor*, London: Child Poverty Action Group/Local Government Information Unit.

Esam, P., Fimister, G. and Oppenheim, C. (1989) *'Ability to Pay'? A Critical Summary of the Government's Proposals for Poll Tax Rebates*, London: Association of Metropolitan Authorities/Child Poverty Action Group/Local Government Information Unit.

Fimister, G. (1988) 'Leaving hospital after a long stay: the role and limitations of social security', in S. Baldwin, G. Parker and R. Walker (eds) *Social Security and Community Care*, Aldershot: Avebury.

Firth, J. (1987) *Public Support for Residential Care: Report of a Joint Central and Local Government Working Party*, London: DHSS.

Griffiths, R. (1988) *Community Care: Agenda for Action*, London: HMSO.

House of Commons Social Services Committee (1990) *Community Care: Future Funding of Private and Voluntary Residential Care*, Session 1989/90: 2nd Report, London: HMSO.

NISW (National Institute of Social Work) (1988) *Residential Care: A Positive Choice – Report of the Independent Review of Residential Care*, Wagner Report, London: NISW/HMSO.

Young, P. (1988) *The Provision of Care in Supported Lodgings and Unregistered Homes*, London: Office of Population Censuses and Surveys.

12
How social fund officers make decisions[1]

Robert Walker, Gill Dix and Meg Huby

The social fund was and continues to be the most controversial of all the social security changes made in April 1988. It replaced single payments as the system for responding to the exceptional financial needs of people which cannot be met by the basic social assistance system (now termed income support). The social fund comprises 'discretionary' and 'non-discretionary' elements, but only the former are discussed in this chapter.

The discretionary elements comprise *community care grants* to help, for example, people re-establish themselves in the community or to avoid institutional care; *budgeting loans* to cover larger items of expenditure for which it may be difficult to budget on income support; and *crisis loans* to tide people over financial crises.

The scheme is administered by staff in 400 or so local offices of the Department of Social Security and each office is allocated an annual fixed budget from which community care grant and loan payments are made. Decisions are taken by social fund officers, graded LO1. They are bound by the Social Security Act and the Secretary of State's directions, and in reaching their decisions officers must consider the Secretary of State's guidance on priorities and the budget and must take account of all the relevant circumstances of each case. In February 1990 the High Court heard three applications for judicial review and found that guidance on budgets was too prescriptive. The guidance was changed to emphasize that the budget was only one of many factors and should not be the overriding determinant of officers' decisions.

However the new Social Security Act passed by parliament in July 1990 allowed the introduction of Directions prohibiting local offices from exceeding their annual budget allocations (SFM, Secretary of State's Directions, 40, 41, 42).

The Social fund has, since its inception, been criticized from many quarters.

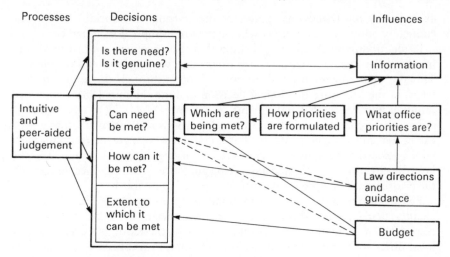

Figure 12.1 Making social fund decisions: a simple model

In its report on the Draft Social Fund Manual the Social Security Advisory Committee highlighted as a main area of concern the discretionary basis on which payments were to be made (SSAC 1987). In their Seventh Report in 1990 they find that 'on the evidence available to date there is no reason to withdraw our fundamental objections' (SSAC 1990). The relative values of entitlement and discretion in the allocation of welfare benefits has long been a subject of debate (Jones *et al.* 1978), but the positive value of discretion depends on its context. 'Discretion is a tool only when properly used' (Davis 1971). Social fund officers make decisions on the basis of individual judgements and in theory have complete discretion in areas not precluded by the Act or directions. In practice they can rarely use 'unfettered discretion.'

This chapter seeks to explore the process of decision-making and use of discretion by social fund officers. It is based on an analysis of interviews with around 200 staff in 39 local offices. The interviews were conducted using a topic guide and took place between 31 January and 3 April 1990, a period which straddles the judicial review judgement in February 1990. Space precludes detailed presentation of the methodology or evidence on which the analysis is based and for this the reader is directed to Walker, Dix and Huby (1991).

Officers have to decide whether or not to make an award, and, if so, what form it should take and how large it should be. The process by which they reach these decisions is correspondingly complex. However, it is necessary here to cut through the complexity by imposing a relatively simple structure on the discussion. From conversations with social fund officers it is apparent that they often make a distinction between decisions relating to the identification and specification of the 'needs' and decisions about 'meeting those needs'. Figure 12.1 makes this distinction clear although in the process of reaching a decision an officer is continually flipping between the one mode of thought and the other. This is most obvious when an officer identifies a 'need' which because excluded by the Directions cannot be met through the social fund; in the context of administration of the scheme the need simply does not exist.

In identifying need, and establishing that it is 'genuine' a word used very frequently by social fund officers, the officer uses various kinds of information. This the officer evaluates and interprets largely through the application of what, in the literature on clinical decision making (Hamm 1988), is termed intuitive and peer-aided judgements (see Figure 12.1). The same forms of judgement are used in the 'discretionary' decisions relating to whether a need can be met and, if so, how and to what extent. However, the set of actions from which a social fund officer can choose is in varying degrees determined by the law, the directions and the accompanying guidance, the local office budget and the priorities which each local office is expected to establish.

Following the model of decision-making (presented in Figure 12.1) this chapter first examines how officers establish need, and second, how they respond to it. A final section examines some of the tensions experienced by local office staff and management in attempting to reconcile discretion with consistency.

Establishing need

Identifying need

The fist task of the social fund officer is to establish the facts of the case and then, on the basis of those facts, to establish whether the need is genuine. The concept of 'genuineness' as employed by SFOs has a number of overlapping meanings. It relates to factual accuracy, and the possibility of 'abuse', but also to whether the need is perceived to cause significant hardship and therefore whether the 'true' situation constitutes grounds for the provision of an award.

An iterative process is usually adopted by social fund officers in which increments of information are evaluated with respect to the questions 'Is there need? and what is its nature, extent and urgency?', 'Is it genuine?' and 'Is it covered by the social fund?' The process stops when the officer decides that his or her mind is unlikely to be changed by any additional information that can be obtained relatively easily. The length of this iterative process will be determined by a number of considerations. Most important are the answers inferred from the information, some of which will provide more or less conclusive reasons for closure, and others which require that a further set of questions be addressed.

However, these inferences are themselves conditioned by other factors which may also act to influence the search for additional information. These include the local office priorities, the state of the office budget and the pressure of work generally. Thus, for example, officers reported that detailed information was less important when budget pressures were not severe and they did not have to discriminate between ostensibly similar cases.

Sources of information

Officers use several sources of information often for different purposes. For a budgeting loan or community care grant the starting-point is the application form. In the case of budgeting loans the forms often fail to elicit sufficient information about the items requested. This is frequently because people ask for a number of items, which may be of different priorities and with different costs, while the form provides space for only one overall cost. Some offices automatically issue a supplementary sheet with the application form in an attempt to overcome this problem.

With community care grants, in particular, staff find that applicants frequently volunteer too little information about their health problems. Officers usually have recourse to the income support case papers to look for evidence of the receipt of health-related benefits or any other indication of health or other needs relevant to the claim.

Officers often write to applicants for further information, telephone them or ask them to telephone the local office. Interviews are relatively rare, except in relation to crisis loan applications. This is primarily the result of resource constraints but also causes less inconvenience to applicants. Home visits are also rare although in some offices they take place quite frequently. In one office, where three or four social fund visits were made each week, officers argued that it was 'very difficult to make judgements from a piece of paper', that income support case-papers contained insufficient information on new applicants, and that a home visit 'helps you to understand how people live and prevents bias'.

As well as care workers, benefit advisers, in some cases were acknowledged as having a significant impact on the outcome of individual applications with the consent of the applicant. Their role may be to provide confirmatory or additional evidence regarding the case, either initiated by themselves, or in response to a query from the social fund officer.

Another source of information used by social fund officers is confirmatory evidence from social workers and others having a professional caring relationship with the applicant. A care worker's input, although only occasionally sought, may well tip the balance of the social fund officer's decision. Contact names may be given on the application form, or may come from the income support case-papers where there has been professional involvement in the past. Very often the social fund officer takes social or health worker involvement with an individual as sufficient grounds for giving an application high priority. On other occasions a telephone call provides enough 'evidence' to ensure an award. As well as providing additional information on a case, their input may be a very practical one, helping an individual overcome the difficulties of presenting his or her case, or simply assisting in completion of the social fund application forms. However, the care worker or benefit adviser must have credibility with the local office and where this is not the case advocacy may work against the interests of the applicant.

Uses of information

Officers use information to build up a rounded picture of each applicant and his or her circumstances. However, in performing their duties as social fund officers they use the information which they collect for different purposes. It is helpful to focus on three of these: 'weeding out', establishing 'genuineness' and interpreting need.

'Weeding out'   'Weeding out' is a term used by some officers for identifying early on those applicants, or potential applicants, who would be unlikely to be granted an award. In most cases these people would belong to groups, or would be requesting items, which are either explicitly excluded by the Directions or which are of very low priority. Examples included requests for work-related expenses, or financial assistance in seeking new employment, both categories excluded by social fund Directions. Other frequent enquiries that could be weeded out were said to be for help with medical appliances, or purchasing school uniforms, which are the responsibility of other statutory bodies. Items and clients of 'low priority' varied considerably from one office to another subject to both the contents of priority lists, and the scope for meeting needs afforded by the fixed budget. Once an application is received it has to be fully processed and it may, therefore, be in the interest of the local office to minimize the number of applications from people unlikely to be given an award.

Reception staff see it as their job to encourage people to make an application to the social fund but they also recognize that they play a filtering role (see Walker, Dix and Huby 1991). Many application forms for budgeting loans and community care grants are collected personally from the local office and receptionists report that often people come to the local office with very unspecific requests for help. Callers may either be encouraged or discouraged to apply.

Filtering is particularly important in the case of crisis loans. This is because of the urgency attached to crisis loans and the requirement for interviews which can place social fund sections under great strain. In some offices reception staff are aided in this task by the provision of a formal check-list of questions. In others, staff have evolved their own set of questions, rely on the social fund information leaflet or the application form itself. Once convinced that the caller is a potential applicant, or that they insist on pursuing an application, the receptionist will contact the social fund section. Typically a social fund officer, or more commonly, a social fund LO2 asks further questions of the potential applicant. Usually this is done through the receptionist, although the LO2 may come to reception to seek further information before deciding to grant an interview. Very often the income support case papers are consulted before an interview is conducted so that the social fund LO2 begins the interview with 'a fair idea' that a crisis loan will be offered.

Applications for budgeting loans and community care grants can be 'weeded out' at two points. First, when an application form is initially requested, and second, when application forms arrive in the office. In the latter case, and in some offices only, applications are looked at briefly, sometimes by an LO2, to see whether the need is urgent. If it is, the application will be dealt with as soon as possible; if not, it will take its turn along with the other applications.

'Identifying genuine need'   A crucial concern for social fund officers is that the need to which they are being asked to respond is 'genuine'. This concern is

heightened by the budget constraint which means that in some circumstances a payment to one person will mean that another has to be turned down.

Additional information is often used to help establish whether or not a case is 'genuine' although, at some point, the social fund officers are forced to make judgements on a balance of probabilities. Often these judgements are made early in the process of assessment. Afterwards attention turns to ways of responding to the need, and to getting a better understanding of its nature and the extent.

Social fund officers are generally sensitive to the possibility of bias entering into their judgements. This is one reason for the frequent discussions which take place between officers. Confirmation from care workers is also a highly valued mechanism for 'sharing responsibility' in decisions about 'genuineness'.

Specifying need   Social fund officers also use information to help locate an applicant's circumstances within the language of the law and guidance: is the applicant or his or her family under 'exceptional pressure', or 'chronically' sick?. This process almost always involves a two-part question. First, 'What do the law, Directions or guidance mean in the context of this applicant's circumstances?' and second, 'Do the applicant's circumstances place them within the meaning of the law, Directions or guidance?'

Officers inevitably find it difficult to interpret terms like 'stress' or 'exceptional pressure' and sound out the opinion of their colleagues in various ways. However, social fund officers as a group often feel themselves ill-equipped to make certain decisions, especially with respect to medical conditions and their effect on applicants' quality of life. In such circumstances, social fund officers come to rely heavily on the judgements of care-workers where these are available.

Where external advice is not available, either because it is difficult to find a named person to refer to, or because pressures of work prevent more thorough investigation, officers tend to rely on rules of thumb. The receipt of attendance allowance or mobility allowance may be taken as an indication of chronic sickness, but this leaves officers in a 'quandary' about conditions such as asthma. To help identify 'stress' in families, officers may look for evidence of sickness, the persistence of adverse circumstances or for an 'effect on family life'.

'In their place'

When attempting to articulate how they reach decisions about need, social fund officers frequently refer to putting themselves in the position of the applicant. This use of empathy is seen as an attempt to overcome the risk of bias entering into their judgements, an attempt to distance themselves from their own values and to discount aspects of the applicant's life-style of which they disapprove. At the same time some officers recognize bias arising from their own personal experience which means that they can put themselves more readily in some people's situation than in other's. This can work in two directions. It is easier to be more sympathetic to people in circumstances which you have experienced. On the other hand, having been in those circumstances one might be better able to detect errors and inconsistencies in the story offered. One might even be less tolerant since, perhaps through one's own efforts, one is no longer in that situation.

Ability to repay

In awarding loans social fund officers have to determine not only whether a person has needs that can be met by the social fund but also whether the applicant has the means to repay. In reaching a decision about ability to repay the officer considers the level of repayment and the period over which the loan will be repaid.

The decision process is necessarily complex and is discussed in detail in Walker *et al.* (1991). Suffice it to say here that the social fund officer's task is to put together the most appropriate package of repayment terms. In deciding what is appropriate, the officer dealing with a first application need not depart from specific guidance which sets out suggested standard deduction rates, unless it is to question the validity of the applicant's statement on other outgoings. When rescheduling existing loans to accommodate repayment of a later one the social fund officer has much more flexibility and, perhaps more so than in the assessment of need, is reliant on intuitive judgement rather than discussion with peers.

Meeting need

Once a need is recognized as 'genuine' the officer has to determine whether it can be met and, if so, how and to what extent. The decisions taken by officers are discretionary but discretion is to a greater or lesser extent influenced, or constrained, by the local office priorities, the Law, Directions and guidance and the budget. Priorities and budgets vary from office to office, so officers differ in the extent to which they have access to 'strong' discretion, where they themselves construct the standards to apply in making a decision, or 'weak' discretion where the standards are effectively determined for them (Dworkin 1977).

Local office priorities

Each local office manager is charged with the responsibility for devising a set of priorities to be taken into account by social fund officers (see Walker *et al.* 1991). In most offices these priorities are central to officer's decisions, especially those concerning budgeting loans and community care grants. However, a few officers make very little use of the office priorities. This sometimes reflects the fact the priorities have been internalized and, in that sense, form a key component of the officer's intuitive judgement. But, in one case, the priorities were not referred to because the office was paying for only the most basic items. There was no need to look beyond a simple decision: 'Was the item allowable or not?' In another case a single social fund officer had few real resource constraints and was paying awards for most items. In her case spending was finely tuned by adjusting the size of payments and, as she said, 'It's really me who sets the priorities'.

The first question asked, often during the process of 'weeding out', is does this person, or the item requested, fall within one of the excluded categories? If not, a decision is taken, in the light of the office priorities, as to whether or not the need can be met.

Three considerations are important: what the priorities are, how they are presented and which kinds of applications are currently being met. The variations between offices, especially with respect to the second two considerations, are substantial. Moreover, they appear to affect the way officers make decisions, and the strength of discretion which is exercised.

The priority lists provide guidance for deciding whether an officer can help an applicant. Some lists reflect the kinds of items and services which officers may consider as a priority for social fund awards. These typically include household furniture, removal and decoration expenses, specified fuel costs and clothing. Other lists specify client groups including elderly people, sick and disabled people, 'families under stress', and ex-offenders. Another alternative is to present the circumstances of the application. Priority may be given to make awards in order to 'avoid risk to health and safety' or to 'prevent hardship'; or more specifically to promote community care (Direction 4, Appendix 1).

Lists differ considerably in their content and specificity. At one extreme items and groups of applicants may be spelled out in detail. At the other, a list may be little more than a restatement of the broad Secretary of State Directions drawn from the Social Fund Manual. On occasion the result is many tens of categories. With very specific lists the officers tend to 'slot people into boxes', applying a set of rules in order to reach a decision in much the same way as an application for income support is processed.

Very often an application does not fit neatly into any category defined by the priority list and the officer determines whether the merits of the case are such as to allow adjusting of the priorities to fit the case. With sufficient 'boxes' (or cells in a notional matrix of priorities) the scope for adjusting priorities, and with it the exercise of a weak order of discretion, may be further minimized. However, in the large majority of offices what officers term as discretion is the ability to move away from the letter of the priority list while paying heed to the spirit. Often this means moving an application up the list, seeking to offer a community care grant where a budgeting loan has been applied for, or perhaps suggesting a crisis loan for someone who is ineligible for a budgeting loan. In operating this limited form of discretion most officers are very sensitive to the possibility that their decisions will be clouded by prejudice and, as when defining need, tend to rely heavily on discussion with peers especially where the case is an unusual one.

When the office priorities are less specific officers are theoretically in a position to take decisions which are more strongly discretionary in that officers have greater scope to determine their own criteria. Not all officers appreciate having to make discretionary decisions. It was clear that some officers rely on their own rules of thumb to help them simplify complex decisions. Many remarked on the satisfaction to be derived from being able to help someone, but equally many disliked 'having to say no'.

In most offices a 'cut-off' line is drawn across the priority list. Although this line is drawn for guidance, all (or at least the vast majority of) applications matching categories below this line are to be rejected. The strength of the discretion available to officers is also affected by the level of these lines. In offices where all kinds of need are being met, and in offices where all but those of the very highest priority are being refused, the discretionary component of decision-making is largely removed. The greatest scope for discretion is in those offices where real choices have to be made between applicants with outwardly similar levels of need.

There is often more scope for discretion in decisions about community care grants than there is for budgeting loans. This is partly because budgeting loan requests are commonly for household items which are specifically mentioned in priority lists. When the priorities for loans take account of client groups as well as items it is often fairly clear whether or not an award should be made. With community care grants, on the other hand, officers have also to think about wider circumstances and very often offices have simply incorporated the appropriate paragraphs from the Social Fund Manual into the office priorities. Certainly many of the reported difficulties of interpretation related to this part of the scheme and caused officers to turn to the guidance manual for help.

The impact of the budget

Cut off lines are added to the priority lists as an explicit reaction to the balance between the demand and the state of the budget and, in most cases, it is these which reflect the budget constraints. Social fund LO1s often play a part in determining where the lines should be drawn, but decisions about individual awards are usually distanced in time and place from decisions about priority lines. Officers typically decide cases with reference to the priority categories and take no direct account of the budget. The daily print-out of the budget from the local office microcomputer is generally of little significance, and entering the state of the budget on every decision form is simply an extra task performed with little, if any, reflection. This situation pertains in many offices even where the budget is under considerable pressure: officers generally turn *individual* applications down because they are of insufficient priority not directly because of the state of the budget.

Nevertheless the budget may, in certain circumstances, have a direct as well as an indirect effect on the outcome of individual decisions and, perhaps especially, on the size of the awards. First, there may be a sense in which the budget is 'always in the back of the mind' when officers take decisions. Certainly requests for very large awards may be set consciously against the size of the budget and officers spoke of the need to spread the available resources as widely as possible.

Second, officers were concerned about the possibility of establishing precedents which it was feared might lead to substantial pressures on the budget. A number referred to their training courses and to the emphasis given to being able to sustain payments throughout the year, while others were mindful of the possible consequences for other types of application if expenditure crept over budget later in the year.

Third, the budget did seem to be accorded special significance in some offices. Why this should have been so is obscure. Sometimes it was related to budgetary pressure, perhaps particularly in offices where the pressure was new and unexpected. Newly appointed officers may pay unusual attention to the budget simply because it is a novelty in social security work. In one office the budget was divided up by social fund officers on a daily basis.

Sensitivity to the state of the budget may be greatest towards the end of each monthly cycle and towards the end of the year. Officers talked of having 'to shuffle and sort claims' as the end of the financial year approached, and it was common practice for the processing of some applications, particularly those of the lower priority, to be held over to the beginning of the next month, although this was seen to have a detrimental effect on clearance times.

The law, Directions and the guidance manual

Social Fund Officers are bound by the Law and the Secretary of State's Directions. In reaching decisions they also take account of the associated guidance assembled in the Social Fund Manual. The extent to which officers rely heavily on the manual is variable and probably affected by a number of considerations. As already noted, in some offices priority lists are very tightly defined and, once officers are experienced in using them, there is little recourse to the manual. Elsewhere, particularly in relation to community care grants, office priorities are no more than a statement of the appropriate Directions. In some offices heavily thumbed copies of the manual are out on all office desks. In other offices copies of the manual are kept in drawers or shelved in fairly pristine condition at one end of the room.

The manual is used in different ways by different officers and sometimes in different ways by the same officer in different circumstances. Perhaps the most common use of the manual is to provide justification for a decision which an officer has provisionally reached. It provides a check that their conclusion is both feasible and justifiable. It sometimes supplies the mechanism for achieving what the officer wants to do. When refusing an application, officers often feel more secure if they can cite 'chapter and verse'. In some offices reference to the manual or legislation is required in writing up decision forms.

Officers tend to consult the manual when an application is borderline in the hope of being able to find a reason to decide one way or another. Similarly some officers faced with a complex decision 'wander through' the manual in a search for inspiration. Other officers tend to refer to the manual only when a decision is challenged. In preparing for a review interview officers will look to the manual to see if they can strengthen the 'legislative basis' of the original decision or find grounds for changing it.

Finally, officers are most likely to use the manual when deciding community care grant cases. This is because the applications tend to be 'one-off' and more complex. Also decisions are driven by the Secretary of State's Direction 4 which defines the basic eligibility criteria for social fund awards but which officers find difficult to interpret (see the Appendix, pp. 164–5). Nevertheless, they have differing opinions on the usefulness of the manual in this regard. Some felt the 1989 rewriting of the guidance surrounding Direction 4, which it was generally agreed had increased the scope for interpretation, had helped. For example additional guidance notes suggested that 'an elderly person's living conditions can be improved to enable them to continue to live independently in the community, or someone can be helped to look after a vulnerable person' (Social Fund Manual, paragraph 6004). Other social fund officers claimed to have ceased to use the guidance manual because the changes had made things 'grey' again.

For the most part, officers do not refer to the manual in each and every case: 'If you kept referring to it you would never get anything done'. The basic elements are generally internalized and used primarily to determine whether an application is excluded. If an application does not fall into an excluded category, the office priority lists are generally applied first and reference made to the manual only when a decision proves to be difficult. In practical day-to-day decision making the manual, like the budget, generally operates through the priorities.

Consistency, consensus and discretion

A distinction has been made between the tasks of identifying and establishing need in the context of the social fund and those of deciding how need should be met. In reality defining and meeting need often come together simultaneously in the social fund officers' mind. Constraints, such as those imposed by the office priorities, which serve to limit the options for meeting need, are equally germane to the definition of need. Filtering mechanisms designed to 'weed out' 'no-hopers' are applied both to excluded categories of need and also to needs which are very low on the priority list of a particular office.

One further important constraint on the application of 'unfettered discretion' is the desire for consistency in decision-making. The existence of local budgets perhaps makes consistency less likely in the social fund than in earlier discretionary schemes. Local office managers face the potential difficulty of reconciling their responsibility for managing the social fund budget with the discretionary decisions of social fund officers.

The consistent application of local priorities is one mechanism for facilitating budgetary control. In many offices, particularly the larger ones, regular meetings of the social fund team take place, chaired by the social fund higher executive officer (HEO), at which the interpretation and implementation of local priorities are frequently discussed.

The agendas at such meetings are informed both by the control checks carried out by the HEO and by difficulties encountered by social fund officers themselves. In the early days of the scheme the discussion at these meetings was heated, and sometimes acrimonious, as officers argued for their interpretations of the priorities and guidance. Among the topics frequently debated were the meaning of 'exceptional' pressure, the definition of 'chronic' sickness, being 'at risk', a 'crisis' and 'stress' and the practical interpretation of the 'prevention of entry into residential care'. Ostensibly less difficult topics also caused dispute. When, if at all, is a refrigerator essential? When is a carpet a luxury and when a necessity? How large should the family be before you countenance the purchase of a washing machine? Is a bed more important than a chair?

In most offices these discussions continue although at a less stressful level. A few offices have achieved consensus within the social fund section; irrespective of individual views officers are expected to follow the majority interpretation. Elsewhere, the officers have refused to have their discretion 'fettered' in this way and the discussions are seen as a means of bringing people broadly into line.

The concern to ensure consistency is not solely a management preoccupation and the push for regular section meetings often comes from the social fund officers themselves. They are frequently concerned that personal bias might enter into their own decisions and are fearful and resentful when they believe other officers are making rogue decisions. Many officers are also aware of the detrimental effects of inconsistency in the interests of applicants.

Team working arises naturally as staff seek to share the burden of difficult decisions through the process of peer-aided judgement. Social fund officers very often feel that they know how their colleagues would react and how their own decisions might differ. Reasonably consistent decisions are frequently seen as a mark of professionalism reinforced, sometimes, by an awareness of the problems which might be generated if consistency was not maintained.

But consistency is not always attainable. It may be introduced when payment lines are altered during the year. Equally importantly, it is recognized in many offices that some staff are more lenient than others and that certain officers will look more favourably on particular kinds of applications. LO2s, working to a number of social fund officers (LO1s), have to take account of this when they, for example, conduct and report on crisis loan interviews. In larger offices staff on one table may work differently from those on another. Sometimes there is little discussion about individual cases and this may partly be an attempt to avoid argument.

Consistency is theoretically incompatible with pure discretion. In the administration of the social fund, management and staff alike generally give priority to trying to ensure consistency.

Conclusions

This chapter has sought to elucidate the way in which social fund officers reach decisions. The social fund devolves responsibility for grappling with some of the most difficult and contentious issues in modern society to officers at relatively low grades in the social security administration. The decisions are often complex and difficult, require patience and experience, and can sometimes be emotionally harrowing.

In presenting the material it has been necessary to underplay the difficulty and complexity of the decisions with which social fund officers grapple. The first section described how officers seek to establish need, the second the way in which officers decide how to respond. In reality officers tend to tackle both problems simultaneously.

Many authors have contrasted the discretionary decisions of social fund officers with the non-discretionary decisions made by staff operating the single payments system which the social fund replaced (Bradshaw 1987; Mullen 1989; Stewart *et al.* 1989; Walker and Lawton 1989). In practice, few social fund officers have 'unfettered discretion'. Rather they operate stronger or weaker forms of discretion reflecting the extent to which their choices, and the standards which they apply in making choices, are constrained by influences such as those indicated in Figure 12.1. Indeed, it may be that 'pure' discretion is no more than an ideal type which, in practice, is unattainable in any system. Certainly a tension exists between pure discretion and consistency of decision making and priority is generally given to consistency in the operation of the social fund. However, complete consistency, like pure discretion, may not be achievable in practice.

Acknowledgements

The authors gratefully acknowledge the invaluable assistance of Anne Corden and Marilyn Thirlway, who helped conduct the interviews, and all the staff in the thirty-nine DSS local offices visited, who responded to our questions with intelligence, generosity and thoughtfulness.

The research was conducted as part of a wide-ranging evaluative study of the social fund commissioned by the Department of Social Security. However, the views expressed are those of the authors alone and do not necessarily reflect those of the department.

Appendix: Directions issued by the Secretary of State for Social Services under Sections 32(2)(b), 33(10) and 34(8)(a) and (b) of the Social Security Act 1986

General

Needs which may be met by social fund payments

1   The needs which may be met by social fund payments awarded under Section 32(2)(b) of the Social Security Act 1986 are those set out in directions 2, 3 and 4 below.
2   A social fund payment may be awarded to assist an eligible person to meet important intermittent expenses (except those excluded by these directions) for which it may be difficult to budget.
3   A social fund payment may be awarded to assist an eligible person to meet expenses (except those excluded by these directions) in an emergency, or as a consequence of a disaster, provided that:
    (a)   the provision of such assistance is the only means by which serious damage or serious risk to the health or safety of that person, or to a member of his family, may be prevented; or

(b) the expenses are rent in advance to a landlord who is not a local authority and a social fund payment is being awarded under Direction 4(a)(i).

4 A social fund payment may be awarded to promote community care:
  (a) by assisting an eligible person with expenses (except those excluded by these directions) where such assistance will
    i help that person, or a member of his family, to re-establish himself in the community following a stay in institutional or residential care; or
    ii help that person, or a member of his family, to remain in the community rather than enter institutional or residential care; or
    iii ease exceptional pressures on that person and his family; or
  (b) by assisting an eligible person, or a member of his family, with expenses of travel within the United Kingdom in order to:
    i visit someone who is ill; or
    ii attend a relative's funeral; or
    iii ease a domestic crisis; or
    iv visit a child who is with the other parent pending a custody decision; or
    v move to a suitable accommodation.

References

Bradshaw, J. (1987) 'The social fund', in M. Brenton and C. Ungerson (eds) *The Year Book of Social Policy 1986/7*, Harlow: Longman.

Davis, K. C. (1971) *Discretionary Justice*, Illinois: University of Illinois.

Dreyfus, H. and Dreyfus, S. (1986) *Mind Over Machine*, New York: The Free Press.

Dworkin, R. (1977) *Taking Rights Seriously*, London: Duckworth.

Hamm, R. (1988) 'Clinical and intuition and clinical analysis: experience and the cognitive continuum', in J. Dowie and A. Elstein (eds) *Professional Judgement*, Cambridge: Cambridge University Press.

Jones, K., Brown, J. and Bradshaw, J. (1978) *Issues in Social Policy*, London: Routledge & Kegan Paul.

Mullen, T. (1989) 'The social fund: cash limiting social security', *Modern Law Review* January: 64–92.

SSAC (Social Security Advisory Committee) (1987) *The Draft Social Security Manual*, Report by SSAC, June, London: SSAC.

—— (1990) *Social Security Advisory Committee: Seventh Report 1990*, London: HMSO.

Stewart, E., Stewart, J. and Walker, C. (1989) *The Social Fund*, London: Association of County Councils.

Walker, R. and Lawton, D. (1989) 'The social fund as an exercise in resource allocation', *Public Administration* 67, 3: 295–317.

Walker, R., Dix, G. and Huby, M. (1991) *Working the Social Fund*, Social Policy Research Unit Paper, London: HMSO.

Note

13
Social work: a force for good or a suitable case for treatment?

Jeremy Walker

Every now and then in the world of social work, an event, report or article pops up into the public domain and, like an intermittent symptom drawing attention to bodily disease, gives us a sensation that there is something strange and puzzling going on. Worried by 'the persisting scapegoating of individual social workers', NALGO commissioned research into conditions in six local authority social services departments and the resulting report, *Social Work in Crisis* (Hayes *et al*. 1989), was published in April 1989. It gives a graphic and moving account of how its respondent social workers saw themselves as 'holding the front line without adequate defences'; patrolling on the cusp between their organizations; overstretched and underfunded; and the random stimuli of 'increased pressure, changing needs and increased social deprivation'. Staff felt they were 'passing through desperate times' and were 'constantly under pressure' from 'uncontrolled demand'. The pervasive mood of anxiety and helplessness was attributed largely to a confederation of external factors such as council policy, the actions of senior managers, legislation and inquiry reports into child care disasters. Military metaphor permeated every corner of the survey and the baton was deftly taken over by the *Guardian* in its account of a working day in an area office in Hammersmith and Fulham, headlined 'Embattled servants of the needy' (*Guardian* 21 March 1990: 21). 'They know the streets', it runs, 'the estates and the families, the impoverished, the drinkers and those with mental health problems'. To an extent articles of this kind present a soft target: they promote a patronizing and sentimental view of users of social work which one can be reasonably certain is completely at variance with the view they have of themselves. It is easy, too, to see the distress of NALGO's respondents, which is endemic in social work as a whole, as part of the fall-out of thwarted omnipotence or unsatisfied reparative urges. As much out of kindness as any ideological malice, some observers, notably David Willetts of the Centre for Policy Studies, have tried to persuade social workers to restrict their all-embracing philanthropic ambitions, to confine themselves to their legal functions as agents of their local authorities (*Social Work Today* 1 February 1990: 14). However, these attempts are almost universally seen by social workers as a ruse of the Right to derail their efforts to reduce disadvantage and deprivation.

There is, however, something rather more complicated going on. People come into social work through a variety of motives, psychological or political, conscious or unconscious, depending on your point of view. Once in, they are expected by society at large to perform a number of functions which are in no way consonant with those original motives. As the radical French psycho-analyst Lacan (1987) put it:

> each of us at any moment and at any level may be traded off – without the notion of exchange we can have no insight into the social structure. . . . it is a well-known fact that politics is a matter of trading wholesale, in lots.
>
> (Lacan 1987: 5)

Thus social workers are traded, in quite large numbers and with not inconsiderable rewards, first to keep unpalatable truths from public conscious-ness in the way that institutions used to before they came to be seen as politically or philosophically undesirable. The fury which greeted earlier child abuse disasters (Beckford, Carlile, and so on) arose in part because social workers, through a toxic blend of naïvety and therapeutic optimism, let the cat out of the bag and they were paid to keep it in. There is no place for the murderous feelings of parents or stepparents towards their children in a world which expects to neutralize or control atavistic impulses such as these. It is interesting that in a more recent case, that of Stephanie Fox, the internal inquiry and the media, with the prompting of NALGO, chose to highlight cuts in services and lack of resources as the primary factors in the child's death (*Guardian* 21 March 1990: 21). They highlighted this rather than lack of vision or wisdom on the part of protecting agencies, or the inevitability that some children will die at the hands of aggressive, inadequate adults, especially if alcohol is involved. A similar reaction emerged from the Association of Directors of Social Services to the NSPCC's estimate that the number of children on child protection registers in England in 1989 had increased to 58,150 (nearly 50 per cent higher than official DSS figures, incidentally). They called for 2,000 more staff even though on closer inspection their statistics revealed that the number of children seriously or fatally injured had fallen by 9 per cent. Moreover 41 per cent of new registrations involved children who had never suffered any actual abuse (*Independent* 20 June 1990: 2).

Social workers are also traded off in the interests of perpetuating and nurturing the cherished illusion that social problems, inequality, deviancy or however you choose to describe the targets of their activities, may be reduced through the periodic application of casework of varying degrees of sophisti-cation, or sheer, honest toil. Indeed it is striking how often outsiders – other professionals it has to be said – believe that the mere allocation of a social worker to a case, like the appointment of a kind of secular guardian angel, can magically produce relief or afford protection. This goes some way towards explaining why 'allocation', which is such a bizarre notion to many ordinary people, who simply expect to be able to go to their GP, solicitor or accountant and get a proper service, has such symbolic importance in some circles. The modern myth of the social worker as potent crusader against contemporary social demons has a certain amount of currency with both Left and Right. The number of social workers employed in local government went up 17 per cent between 1980 and 1987 partly because they are genuinely seen as being able to mitigate the unwanted side-effects of economic growth and turn misfits into compliant and productive citizens.

In their infamous polemic, Brewer and Lait (1980) mercilessly catalogued the ineffectiveness of social work as it is presently organized and practised. Anyone who has worked a decent time in the job will, in moments of quiet contemplation, have become aware of the following principle, lurking and elusive, but adamantine none the less. It is that individuals and families, and certainly communities, are peculiarly resistant to the attempts of outsiders to change the way they do things. This discovery should be reassuring, since the world would be a very unstable and capricious place if people were as easily influenced by the dispensation of casework of various kinds as its practitioners apparently believe. However, its truth for those caught up in the anxiety and utopian fervour of many social services departments leads only to profound disappointment and frustration. Passing insights or academic barracking from the stands will not be enough to convince the crowd as a whole that the therapeutic emperor has few, if any, clothes.

What is happening, of course, is that social workers have found themselves trapped between the ideal and the real; between the illusory hope that bureaucratized altruism can restore individuals and families, and the intractable, intransigent nature of the real world. Gellner, in his book on the psychoanalytic movement, which has much in common with the social work movement, uses the French concept of the *pays légal* and the *pays réel* to illustrate the two spheres between which helpers of this kind operate (Gellner 1985: 16). Social workers are caught between the formal, rather arid territory of legislation, legislative intent and the ideal, and the rich, complex territory of the real world where social problems have ancient, structural roots. This fact of therapeutic life manifests itself in various guises. The Barclay Report into social work talks of social workers operating 'uneasily on the frontier between what appears to be almost limitless needs on the one hand and an inadequate pool of resources to satisfy those needs on the other' (NISW 1982: vii). Similarly Kemmis believes the role of the social worker is 'to manage the gap between identified needs and the resources available' (*Social Work Today* 8 March 1990: 12). Leaving aside for the moment the question of how needs are identified and by whom, those who subscribe to this view, which is widespread in social work, fail to understand that, in the helping business at any rate, needs and resources always operate in tandem. If resources appear to move too close to needs, vested interests become threatened and needs will be redefined and move accordingly. This is currently happening in psychiatry, where now that major tranquillizers are successful in suppressing the symptoms of serious psychotic illness, the hunt is on for so-called hidden morbidity. Consequently the psychiatric goalposts are being widened, in the USA especially, to take in all sorts of less serious conditions.

The seemingly infinite and insatiable nature of needs leads to the feelings of depletion and despair so well documented in NALGO's report and, further, to the belief that things are actually getting worse. The Barclay Report talks of social work having 'to deny increasingly needy people' (NISW 1982). Even an article in *Good Housekeeping* (July 1990: 74–7), which so excoriated social workers that the *Community Care* diarist urged its readers to 'bombard the *Good Housekeeping* office with a mailbag of abuse' (*Community Care* 14 June 1990: 86), also subscribed to this myth: 'their's is a hard-pressed profession deeply stretched by the Catch-22 of resources that dwindle even as caseloads mount' (*Good Housekeeping* July 1990: 74). Szasz (1974) believes that the apparently insatiable demand for help in the second half of the twentieth century has arisen because 'by seeking relief from the burden of his moral responsibilities, man mystifies and technicizes his problems in living' (Szasz 1974: 3). The vacuum left by moral withdrawal has been filled by increasing numbers of professionals, para-professionals and volunteers, who in earlier, less technologically advanced times might have been engaged in productive work or, more likely, converting people to Christianity in a distant corner of the empire.

> This human need and the professional-technical response to it form a self-sustaining cycle, resembling what the nuclear physicist calls a breeder reaction: once initiated and having reached a critical stage, the process feeds on itself, transforming more and more problems and situations into specialized technical 'problems' to be 'solved' by so-called experts.
>
> (Szasz 1974: 3)

Lasch (1988) in a text which should be required reading for every helpless helper, takes up the theme: 'the atrophy of older traditions of self-help has eroded everyday competence in one area after another, and has made the individual dependent on the state, the corporation and other bureaucracies'. The psychological man or woman of the late twentieth century is 'plagued by anxiety, depression, vague discontents, a sense of inner emptiness' but in 'the quest for composure', we have seen 'the reduction of the citizen to a consumer of expertise' (Lasch 1988: 10). In this quest, the citizen trusts that 'the elite of experts can canalize and control' what Berlin (1979) calls 'dark, cosmic forces'. We have seen 'the reduction of all questions and aspirations to dislocation which the expert can set right' (Berlin 1979: 33). The technical and therapeutic have taken over from the creative and the moral, and come together in the hybrid language of 'carespeak'. True caring and moral commitment have ebbed away and been replaced by ersatz care 'packaged' and 'managed' by experts who have mastered the slogans and shibboleths of this brave, new world. Autonomy and control have been ceded to the growing class of experts by ordinary people, seduced by the lure of cure or the prospect of relief from troublesome moral duties to each other – and themselves. Therapy, in all its various forms, not religion, has become the opium of the people.

The USA warns us where this trend is leading. Kramer, an American doctor, is quoted in a *Newsweek* article on the marvellous powers of a new antidepressant, Prozac: 'there may even be a drug ', he enthuses, 'that can change people in ways they want to be changed – not just away from illness but towards some desirable psychological state.' 'Who knows', the article ends, 'maybe wit and insight will eventually come in capsule form' (*Newsweek* 26 March 1990: 41). Who dispenses the capsule and to whom is, of course, not addressed.

It is not enough for social work to try to dissociate itself from other therapeutic activities, medical ones in particular, on the grounds that its model is less contaminated or corrupt than, say, the medical model. Or by claiming that it is founded on the principles of empowerment or self-determination and it therefore liberates where others enslave. In fact, once the rhetoric is peeled away, the central underlying assumption of social work is not very different from that of its therapeutic siblings, medicine, psychiatry, psychotherapy and so on. It may disagree with other professions about the nature of the causes of social problems, mental illness and so forth, but, followers of systems theory apart, there is general agreement about the nature of causality. Factors are seen as acting upon the individual or family to produce certain effects. They may be events, traumas, class or power relationships, unequal distribution of oppor-tunity or wealth, or a combination of some or all of these but essentially the relationship between them and their supposed effects is seen as a linear one. Furthermore, individuals through whom this linear process passes, are seen as merely responding to them, rather than as subjective moral agents, each with a capacity to make choices. People in this twentieth-century scheme of things are responsive rather than responsible.

Freud, of course, with his deterministic, irrationalist view of psychological life, gave a substantial boost to the traditional belief that human beings are the helpless pawns of fate and the gods. He thereby neatly delivered people into the hands of the pastoral or therapeutic guru or expert, without whose inter-vention no semblance of free will or freedom of choice or action is possible. Many social workers today would deny any allegiance to Freud but in fact all they have done is to develop his sleight of hand a bit further with the currently popular notion of empowerment. This is often actually a sophisticated therapeutic double-bind: 'I empower you (but in my terms, in my language and so on)'.

Out of self-interest, social work colludes with the disowning of responsi-bility by people for themselves and each other. It colludes, it should be said, with a culture which depends on self-centredness, geographical mobility and the splintering of family and social relationships which inevitably follows. Providing examples is almost superfluous so watertight and widespread is the view that individuals and families should not be held accountable or responsible because they are seen as chaff on the politically or psychologically determined wind. In fact virtually all those who use social work services do so because they have been abandoned or failed at some time by those close to them. This is, perhaps, particularly true of children who are abused and, topically, of homeless people whether mentally ill or not. To her credit,

Elizabeth Howlett, chair of Wandsworth's Social Services Committee, reminded people that it was Stephanie Fox's father who was responsible for her death after a night's drinking rather than Tory heartlessness or a shortage of resources (Radio 4 interview 21 June 1990). Where legislation allows for families to be involved in making decisions and retaining responsibility for their members, this is often circumvented on the spurious grounds that these duties are too onerous for families or they can't be trusted with them. The Mental Health Act 1983 gives the nearest relative, in addition to an approved social worker, the power to apply for the compulsory admission of a patient to hospital. However, this rarely happens and is often discouraged on the grounds that a social worker is in a better position to make a sound decision, or that it might contaminate or sour family relationships. The tendency to use compulsion in the form of proceedings to bring children into care, rather than come to voluntary agreements with parents, which leaves their rights and status intact, has been well documented during the past decade (Packman *et al.* 1986). Once in care, children are often effectively colonized by staff who take to their quasi-parental role with gusto, rather than encourage or oblige parents to remain in the forefront of their children's lives.

We are, it hardly need be said, in rather difficult philosophical waters here. The extent to which people are free to make choices, or should be held accountable or responsible, and to which the state, or local state, rather than families or neighbourhoods, should provide for the casualties of what passes for progress, are taxing moral questions. Generally the suppliers of services see no difficulty in dismissing the view that there should be a retrieval of moral responsibility at best as sentimental, impractical and reactionary and at worst as a conspiracy to deny those in need access to the comforts and expertise they are eager to dispense. They would go along with Marcuse when he talks of 'the myth of autonomous man' (1987: 252) and see the Szaszian view as a precursor of the Thatcherite ethic of individualism and anti-statism. However, responsibility, like free will, may be a fiction but it is a necessary one for the simple practical reason that institutionalized altruism and therapeutic expansionism, which conspire to intervene in everyday life and to assume responsibility for those that are vulnerable, have been shown time and again to fail. Quite simply, children are killed or injured by their parents or guardians, and people become homeless or disconnected from the mainstream of society, if there aren't people close to them who care about them and claim them. While it is usually possible for organizations and those who work in them to care for the vulnerable and rejected, it is rarely possible for them to care about them in a way that is committed, connected and, above all, sustained. The proceduralized protection of logging and monitoring children at risk of abuse is no substitute for the instinctive protectiveness that should be available to children and vulnerable adults from kith and kin. It is also simply emotionally not possible, even though they may earnestly desire it, for individuals who work in the system to provide it by proxy since the number of people that any of us can truly care about, either privately or publicly, is extremely small.

Now we come to the crux of the matter, or the point of no return. The belief, so widespread among the social workers interviewed for NALGO's report, that in spite of their dedication things are getting worse and people are not getting better, and their feelings of beleaguerment and threat, can lead in one of two directions. On the one hand, these experiences, genuinely felt, can lead to the straightforward and seemingly logical conclusion that what is needed is more staff, more resources and more money to do more of the same thing in the same way. This, as we have seen, was the reaction to an apparent increase in the incidence of child abuse and is also the favoured response to perceived or real increases in homelessness, delinquency among teenagers, alienation and loneliness among old people and so on. There are, however, other directions in which these puzzling experiences can lead, less attractive to vested interests perhaps, and certainly more disturbing.

First of all, the more investigators, methods of investigation, and systems for reporting and collation there are in any field, the more discoveries will be made and the greater the tendency for facts to be redefined as problems fit for intervention. What is being discovered, of course, is real life with its habit of being nasty and brutish, if not short. However, the more discoveries are made, the more investigations are called for – and it should be remembered that the targets of these investigations are often working-class families of a particular vulnerable and isolated kind, because stronger, more resilient families are less prepared to tolerate state intervention and surveillance. More important, however, is that what appears to be going on outside social work, and other agencies which provide their mixture of therapy and control, is actually the echo of a misconceived philosophy and misdirected effort: the greater the effort, the louder the echo. A movement which says that it has answers to the troublesome facts of human existence or that it can keep them from public view; that people should hand over responsibility for themselves and others to its adherents or practitioners; and which, perhaps above all, promises so much more than it delivers, has been hoist with its own petard. The application of more resources, far from bringing relief, will only increase disappointment both inside and outside. Illich (1985), writing of physical health and well-being and the growth of iatrogenic ill-health, states that 'man-made misery is the by-product of enterprises that were supposed to protect ordinary people. . . . Healthy people need minimal bureaucratic interference to mate, share the human condition and die'. When they become dependent on the management of their intimacy, as he puts it, their autonomy and health, physical, spiritual and emotional 'must decline'. This decline is 'the negative feedback of social organizations that set out to improve and equalize the opportunity for each man to cope in autonomy and ended by destroying it' (Illich 1985: 263). This, too, is the age of therapeutogenic distress in which appetites for help are stimulated, then disappointed. In misreading the signals of increased social anxiety and anomie as an indication that reinforcements are needed rather than a planned retreat which hands territory back to ordinary people, social work has become the disorder it purports to remedy.

Social work is not dead, as one director of social services was reported as being tempted to say (*Community Care*, 12 July 1990: 4). Nor is deconstruction to the point of non-existence possible, even if it were desirable. It has become part of an age which is intolerant of the real and it has overreached itself. It first of all has to recognize its tendency to overestimate the good it can do and underestimate the harm it can do. The injunction in the Hippocratic oath – '*primum non nocere*' ('first of all do no harm') – should be adopted as a motto for all social services departments. Second, it should ruthlessly identify and define those basic, inescapable duties and functions which society, through legislation, has handed over to it and then gracefully withdraw to carry them out while all the time reminding others of their non-legal, moral duties. All societies going back to classical Greek and Roman times have thought fit to delegate some functions, usually protective or policing ones, to officials of the local state or parish. These, essentially quite modest, functions tend to be rather despised by social workers on the grounds that they are repressive. Often they are simply overlooked because of a preference for coming in at the wrong end of Maslow's (1954) hierarchy of needs; concentrating on 'self-actualization' and personal growth, rather than basic, practical human needs. The *locus classicus* of this is the Jasmine Beckford case, where energy and attention were directed at repairing the relationship of Jasmine's stepfather and mother rather than ensuring her safety. In fact during the 1970s and 1980s other groups have gradually taken over many of these functions and carried them out rather well. The police are now much more involved in child abuse work because of the lack of rigour on the part of social workers. They are also, along with social security officials, community psychiatric nurses (CPNs), psychiatrists and GPs, seen as more helpful and supportive than social workers by sufferers of schizophrenia and their carers (Took and Evans 1990). CPNs, especially, have taken on much of the practical, supportive work with mentally ill people. Welfare tasks are increasingly carried out by prison staff while the probation service prefers to attend to more rarified, therapeutic activities.

One of the reasons for this trend is the predeliction social work has for false dichotomies. Social workers tend to distinguish between 'statutory work' and 'therapy', the former being somehow tainted and the latter being rather more pure. They fail to understand that statutory intervention can be therapeutic, rather than anti-therapeutic, and that 'therapy', far from always being liberating, has a strong element of control. Another erroneous distinction which gets them into trouble is the one between 'statutory' and 'non-statutory' work. Any work carried out by social workers as employees of a local authority has to be statutory otherwise it would be unlawful or involve a misapplication of local authority funds. But many social workers have not grasped this and the distinction they make is symptomatic of the common tendency they have to see themselves as freelance free spirits doing what is attractive and congenial rather than as agents of their employing authority, carrying out its policies and duties. This is not to say that there is no place anywhere for counselling or individual and family therapy, which is what many social workers prefer to be doing. However, it is very difficult to construe any current legislation involving local authorities as validating the amount of what could loosely be called psychotherapy that goes on with all client groups. In the whole of the Barclay Report into the roles and tasks of social workers, only very cursory attention is given to the very legislation which determines these, and the relevant acts are simply listed at the end. One of the main reasons for the disappointment and frustration that social workers feel, and the accusations of ineffectiveness and negligence that they often have to field from the public, is that they are wanting to be round, therapeutic pegs in square, bureaucratic, legally determined holes.

As well as legal and practical reasons for social work largely disentangling itself from therapeutic activities, there are actually therapeutic ones. Psychotherapy is arguably something that should take place between consenting adults, or if children are concerned, with the informed consent of a responsible adult, and the parties should share linguistic, cognitive and intellectual common ground. Whether or not psychotherapy is effective is the subject of endless debate (Brown and Pedder 1979: 193; Gellner 1985: 157; Masson 1988: 225), but serious practitioners do insist that possible recipients are rigorously assessed for their suitability, and that providers of the service are prepared to open themselves up to therapy and supervision. This rarely happens in local authority social work where therapeutic efforts are often brought to bear on those who have not given informed consent because that common ground does not exist or who may not even be aware of what is going on in the transaction at all. Perhaps the giving of insight against a person's will should be included in the Mental Health Act along with medication, ECT and psychosurgery.

Rather than confining themselves to relatively straightforward and achievable tasks, social workers, even though feeling under pressure, often paradoxically and rather perversely tend to indulge in a kind of back-door expansionism. This often takes the relatively harmless form of groupwork in which a social worker decides that work with a group of people with a common disability or problem might, for a variety of reasons, be beneficial or attractive. The net is then cast around for possible members who may or may not already be clients. This activity is almost always supply-led rather than demand-led. It is in part generated by the fear which providers of helping services share with the private, commercial sector, which is that standing still or contracting will lead to extinction. Expansion and the carving out of markets and territories, though sometimes traumatic and leading to increased pressure, is felt to be necessary. With the invention of post-traumatic stress disorder, social work has discovered fertile territory in the aftermath of disaster for extending its activities, although on occasions it has bumped into competitors on a similar mission.

In a rather interesting article about services provided after the Towyn floods in North Wales, the principal social worker involved, Mike Mason, writes: 'after an initial trawl of 1,500 households, about 220 referrals were logged', and the rate 'appears to be increasing as people become aware that we are a significant resource established in the community'. Like a salesman on the scent of a deal, he goes on: 'we're helping people with consequent social difficulties and the exacerbation of pre-existing family discord' and 'we are now detecting a significant number of relationship problems coming in the mask of practical need '(*Community Care* 7 June 1990: 16). In this little vignette we can see how the capitalism of care operates. A potential market is detected, a product is devised and advertised, a demand for it is generated and the customer is in the bag. Of course, the customer may come wanting one particular product (practical help) but the salesman might have a stronger, more effective product under the counter (therapeutic help). It needs to be said again that, as with conventional advertising and marketing, potential middle-class consumers are far less susceptible to these kinds of manoeuvres than a particular kind of working-class consumer.

Social work, of course, is being jostled in the market-place by an increasing number of rivals, who use similar techniques, which adds to its sense of insecurity. A huge range of voluntary organizations, pressure groups and lobbyists seek also to convert people into customers. The Carers' National Association marked its first birthday in 1989 by launching a national campaign to find Britain's 'hidden carers'. So far their target is merely the '6 million unpaid carers' looking after elderly, ill or disabled people, who as Baroness Seear put it, 'may be unaware even that they are carers' (*Community Care*, 25 May 1989: 4). There is no logical reason why they should not go on to include, say, ordinary men and women burdened with the very difficult job of looking after small or teenage children. In this new feudalism we are all potential vassals, and should be grateful for the opportunity.

Social work needs, above all perhaps, to acquire a little of the insight it is so keen to impart to others, and to understand the disabling effects of many of its activities. Its practitioners need to develop a sense of history. This is the best antidote to the omnipotence which you will usually find if you scratch the surface of most dedicated helpers. This is the origin of that peculiar, lurking, but sometimes exhilarating, feeling that most of us who have practised social work at some time will recognize when we are in close contact with an individual or family in distress. It seems to convince us that we are pioneers in virgin territory, up against it but with a unique ability to put things right and make people whole. That, rather than paid officials, with limited powers, pitched in to deal with phenomena – madness, cruelty or mere unhappiness – that have been around for thousands of years. Those who ignore history are not so much doomed to repeat its mistakes as wear themselves out in pursuit of the impossible. Although there would be no progress without a certain amount of idealism, rampant idealism exhausts the idealist and enslaves ordinary people.

Once reined in, social work needs to devote itself to the gaining of wisdom, a concept which is rarely mentioned in social work circles and which, though difficult to define, is recognized by almost everyone once it appears. There are some reasonably simple practical steps that can be taken. First of all, when there are failures, as there must be, we should embrace them and learn the correct lessons from them, rather than collude to pretend they haven't happened. Child abuse inquiry reports, which tend to be seen by social workers as rather persecutory, as NALGO's report revealed, are a rich source of help and information. They are' helpful, not so much for the rather terse recommendations which tend to be listed at the end and to provoke anxiety and a certain amount of procedural reform, but because, if read in full, they reveal that serious child abuse is generally something that builds up over time. That it is identifiable, perhaps preventable if people are not blinded by therapeutic optimism or ideological zeal, is probably quite rare.

Unfortunately the indications are that the average social work practitioner, or manager, avoids reading these reports in full, or at all. In Re E (a minor), a case heard in the High Court about allegations by three children of sexual abuse, the judge stated: 'it was disappointing that, despite the passage of time since the Cleveland Report, several witnesses had either not read it or ignored its conclusions in many respects' (*Independent* 13 April 1990: 18). What tends to happen is that precisely the wrong conclusions are drawn from what should be very helpful material. In the three years after the death of Tyra Henry, the number of children on the Lambeth child protection register increased by 63 per cent (Bebbington and Miles 1989: 349). A total of 22,000 children were added to child protection registers in the year up to March 1989 and, of course, a huge number were also removed from registers. The Association of Directors of Social Services referred to a 'substantial turnover' and said that for every child placed on a register, five were assessed but not registered (*Community Care*: 31 March 1990: 6). This tremendous amount of bureaucratic activity is both consequence and cause of the anxiety that feeds, and chokes, the system, leaving less energy available to concentrate on the serious, preventable cases of child abuse in which society as a whole demands intervention. If the right lessons were learned, the spectres of children killed or seriously injured by their carers would not haunt, as they undoubtedly do, the routine investigation into parental failure and inability to cope which makes up the bulk of local authority child care work. Most important of all, it is the failure to make a rigorous and substantive distinction between cases which merit firm, formal state surveillance and intervention, and those which need an entirely different approach, that jeopardizes the rights of children to protection from abuse by adults. It also jeopardizes the rights of parents to struggle along with the very difficult job of bringing up children in the late twentieth century, with minimal intervention from outside agencies.

The second modest step that social work should take is to identify defensive mechanisms which are net consumers of energy that should be devoted to the objective task, or which restrict experience and prevent staff developing mastery and confidence. Many case conferences, panels and meetings which create an illusion of purposeful activity, but whose main function is often a social one, providing support for the system's disaffected workers, frequently absorb time and energy unnecessarily. They reduce the opportunity for extensive, direct work from which increased competence will flow. The introduction of reduced caseloads was in part a response to stress and anxiety but caseloads are not exempt from Parkinson's Law. Work, often in the form of unnecessarily detailed or inappropriately analytic written records, merely expanded to fill the time available. Student social workers, especially, tend to have very small caseloads at a time when, with plenty of supervision at hand, they should be encouraged to have as many experiences of social work in practice as possible. Workload management schemes are another, relatively new, mechanism devised with the intention of containing stress and anxiety. Yet they are highly subjective, open to collusive manipulation, and superfluous if there is a supervisory relationship which is open, honest and concerned with managing anxiety by setting modest goals and reducing expectations. Rigid vertical hierarchies which are often favoured by social services departments and which have grown up for the purpose of diffusing responsibility, tend to infantilize especially those working at lower levels. They tend to stifle initiative and appropriate risk-taking, and the maturation that flows from this. Finally, the habitual, cyclical reorganization of social services departments is rarely, if ever, a healthy adaptation to changing external circumstances but a diversion away from internal discomfort and a missing sense of achievement and purpose. Invariably in these upheavals energy is devoted to means at the expense of proper discussion about ends.

All professions, as George Bernard Shaw put it, are a conspiracy against the laity and most professions, social work being no exception, feel at times that the laity are conspiring against them. This kind of incipient paranoia is characterized, in the case of social work, by feelings of unease, a difficulty in learning from experience or the legitimate views of others, defensiveness and, above all, a sense that what lies on the outside is hostile to its aims and endeavours or potentially overwhelming. Paranoia, even in its early stages, is notoriously difficult to shift. However, remission, or even complete recovery, can happen if we accept that peace of mind and greater effectiveness, which are mutually dependent, will come only from healthy self-criticism, modesty and reduced ambition. Social work needs to abandon its affair with the ideal and learn the art of the possible.

References

Bebbington, A. and Miles, J. (1989) 'Children who enter local authority care', *British Journal of Social Work* 19: 349.
Berlin, I. (1979) *Four Essays on Liberty*, Oxford: Oxford University Press.
Brewer, C. and Lait, J. (1980) *Can Social Work Survive?*, London: Temple Smith.
Brown, D. and Pedder, J. (1985) *Introduction to Psychotherapy*, London: Tavistock.
Gellner, E. (1985) *The Psychoanalytic Movement*, London: Paladin.
Hayes, P., Glastonbury, B., Marks, E., Stein, M. and Frost, N. (1989) *Social Work in Crisis*, Southampton: NALGO.
Illich, I. (1985) *Limits to Medicine*, London: Pelican.
Lacan, J. (1987) *The Four Fundamentals of Psychoanalysis*, Harmondsworth: Peregrine.
Lasch, C. (1988) *The Culture of Narcissm*, London: Abacus.
Marcuse, H. (1987) *Eros and Civilization*, London: ARK.
Maslow, A. H. (1954) *Motivation and Personality*, New York: Harper and Row.
Masson, J. (1990) *Against Therapy*, London: Fontana.
NISW (National Institute of Social Work) (1982) *Social Workers: Their Roles and Tasks*, Barclay Report, London: Bedford Square Press.
Packman, J., Randall, J. and Jacques, N. (1986) *Who Needs Care? Social Work Decisions about Children*, Oxford: Basil Blackwell.
Szasz, T. (1974) *Ideology and Insanity*, Harmondsworth: Penguin.
Took, M. and Evans, T. (1990) *Provision of Community Services for Mentally Ill People and their Carers*, Surbiton: National Schizophrenic Fellowship.

14
The 'new' managerialism in the social services[1]

Aidan Kelly

Politics in Britain during the 1980s was dominated by successive Conservative governments committed to radical restructuring of the rôle of the state and the creation of an enterprise culture (Burrows 1990). There were a series of government initiatives to 'roll back the state' in welfare provision and reduce the 'burden' of state welfare expenditure; expenditure which was thought to be squeezing out private sector investment and undermining through the taxation system entrepreneurial and managerial incentives. Of equal importance was the government's promotion and support of the values of entrepreneurialism and methods of business management. Local authorities and their social services departments (SSDs) have been subject to a resources squeeze and put under considerable pressure to become more 'business-like', more concerned with value for money, and more performance oriented.

In attempting to reshape the social services, governments have to work through the organizational structures and processes that have traditionally provided some considerable autonomy for local authority policy makers. Unlike district health authorities, SSDs are not agencies of central government and their managers can be only indirectly influenced. Governments can, of course, act on their ideas and beliefs by introducing legislation that force action on those local authorities who might choose to do otherwise: the introduction of compulsory competitive tendering is one example of this approach. This legislative procedure, does have its limitations for the changes which, if they are to be implemented, require considerable formal and informal support from those who work in the state agencies concerned. It is no doubt in recognition of these constraints that previous governments had tended to emphasize indirect, normative means of achieving change in social services departments (Webb and Wistow 1982).

In the 1980s there were two aspects of this normative strategy: the use of expenditure restraint and the promotion of a new managerialism. The government budgeted, for most of the 1980s, for a 2 per cent growth in social services expenditure. This is clearly insufficient for the maintenance of a constant level of outputs (Webb and Wistow 1983). At the same time, the government has attempted to develop and promote a new management culture that would thrive under conditions of resource pressure.

The government introduced legislation such as the Local Government Planning and Land Act 1982 to control local government spending, to penalize over-spending authorities and finally, to cap the 'high' spending councils. At the same time, the government gave only the most general guidance to local authorities on how to cope with the consequences on expenditure restraint. In abandoning circulars and guidelines as means of producing change, the government visibly handed over responsibility for the determination of local policies to local authorities and SSDs; the 'detailed planning and management of resources . . . to those on the spot who know local needs and priorities' (Patrick Jenkin, quoted in Webb and Wistow 1982: 31). Instead the government set up an 'independent' agency, the Audit Commission for England and Wales, with a brief that would offer local authorities and their SSDs a means of coping with expenditure restraint.

The Audit Commission and the social services

The role of the auditor in the public sector has been enhanced considerably during the 1980s. In1983 the National Audit Office was established to report to Parliament on the efficiency and effectiveness of central government departments and a range of other bodies including the National Health Service. In April of the same year the Audit Commission was established, under the terms of the Local Government Finance Act 1982. It replaced the former Audit Inspectorate of the Department of Environment (to whom it reports), and took over the District Auditing Service. The former District Audit Service was responsible for ensuring the probity of local authority accounts: that government and rate-payers' money was spent honestly and within the legal framework.

As part of the enhancement of the auditing process the Audit Commission became responsible for ensuring that local authorities made proper arrangements for securing economy, efficiency and effectiveness in their use of resources. By economy is meant the acquisition of the appropriate quality and quantity of resources at the lowest cost; by efficiency obtaining the maximum output for a given set of resource inputs acquired; and by effectiveness the degree to which established goals are achieved.

In performing this function, the Audit Commission has played an important part in promoting the kind of changes in the management of local authority departments that the government was hoping for. While central government applied the resources brake, the Audit Commission stepped on the managerial accelerator. The Audit Commission has established premises that would shape responses to expenditure restraint and over the decade has constructed and published an agenda for change

The world of local authority auditing was, no doubt, enlivened by this wider, more speculative, brief and the higher profile given to audit reports. The Audit Commission has actively promoted its ideas by means of the publication of major reports documenting management weaknesses. McSweeney (1988: 40) argues that publicity is an important part the Commission's strategy, a strategy reflecting the received wisdom on how to achieve successful organizational change. This strategy involves supporting agency leaders in exploiting environmental disturbances (that it declining resources and increased demand) to intensify the belief or awareness of crisis. Notions of crisis, implying the need for action, determine an agenda for change and wrong foot the forces of stability in organizations.

The Commission exposed the management of social services to close external scrutiny and evaluation, defining both 'crisis' and 'response' in management terms. The Commission has asserted that there are substantial opportunities for saving money in local government and that these savings would not substantially affect services (Audit Commission 1984: 2). For example the 1985 study, *Managing Social Services for the Elderly More Effectively*, examines services in seven SSDs. The following management weaknesses were identified:

1 in three authorities about half the residents in care might have been able to be supported in the community
2 in four SSDs half of the expenditure on community services was allocated to those who do not obviously need it
3 these community services, especially the home help service, suffer from unclear objectives, lack of policy and guidelines, lack of systems for controlling their use.

The report also indicated many other areas of waste and inefficiency (Audit Commission 1985: 2).

According to the Commission, SSDs face more management challenges than most other local authority departments (Audit Commission 1986a: 6). Amongst these challenges the need for greater economy and efficiency are paramount, but the Commission has called for the clarification of policy objectives, and for improved organizational arrangements for effective delivery of services.

In addition, the Commission is very concerned about the low level of strategic rationality in SSDs. The wide variation in level and balances of services between SSDs imply variation in strategy, but the Audit Commission study teams question whether these variations reflect deliberate choices made by politicians and senior officers or are the result of 'happenstance'. They have found, for instance, that decisions on levels of service for elderly people are often based either on past practice or on value judgements rather than on strategy reflecting the 'facts' (Audit Commission 1985: 39). In the study of services for elderly people, none of the authorities appeared to have clear agreed statements of objectives concerning the provision of day care services; and the meals on wheels services had multiple and unclear objectives.

To remedy this state of affairs, the Audit Commission has encouraged SSDs to clarify and make explicit their policies and to justify these on the basis of improved information about the local situation. Management information systems are under-developed in the social services and the Commission emphasizes their important role in monitoring the impact of policy change in order that measurable progress will be revealed and fed back into the policy-making process. The Commission has promoted these ideas by producing a Performance Review manual for SSDs and by sending to each local authority an annual 'profile'. This describes the authority's performance across the range of services compared with a 'family' of similar authorities. Despite the widespread cynicism about the data on which these performance profiles are based (Miller 1986: 16), they have stimulated the Social Services Research groups to work on their own indicators, and predated the Social Services Inspectorates Key Indicators (Department of Health 1987; Warburton 1989). However, performance indicators in some form are probably here to stay, and whatever their limitations they are effective in creating a climate of performance that questions current policy and practice, and encourages the search for performance-improving innovations (Flynn 1986: 402).

The Commission aims to reorient the organizational culture of SSDs from professional to managerial themes. I has identified management culture as a key source of 'failure', for example the inability to respond appropriately to expenditure restraint in a period of increasing demand (McSweeney 1988: 39). The Audit Commission guidance encourages SSDs to accept expenditure restraint and to manage in a context of scarcity and shrinkage. Effective management in these circumstances might gain a wider legitimacy for management and the management process in the social services where there has been a reluctance to accept hierarchy and formal managerial styles (Palfrey 1981: 126–8).

The Audit Commission's emphasis on the specification and achievement of measurable objectives complements the trend towards performance related pay (PRP) for senior managers in the public sector. Although 'PRP' is currently 'conspicuous by its absence' (Audit Commission 1984: 52), individuals and groups can be managed by an annual performance review, referring to these objectives and the degree of progress made towards achieving them. As is the case in the National Health Service, promotion and performance related pay can be the reward for the ownership of identifiable achievements.

Models of 'administrative management' are widely criticized by professional practitioners as 'bureaucratic', yet ironically they tend to be more respectful of claims to professional autonomy. With the move towards the new managerialism, management practices reflect the greater emphasis placed on determining priorities, rationing resources. This will necessarily mean greater management involvement in 'shaping' professional decisions tasks in order to achieve managerial resource and service objectives, and greater professional involvement in delegated managerial tasks.

Table 14.1 presents the contrasts between the 'old' administrative management and the 'new' managerialism. Elements of both will no doubt coexist for some time, but the figure offers a check-list of the changes and pressures for change to be found in the social services.

Table 14.1   Changing management styles in the public sector

	Administrative management	The 'new' managerialism
Management goals	system maintenance and stability	system performance and change
Resource strategy	reliance on state resources	proactive search for non-state resources
Resource allocation	by rules of eligibility and professional needs judgements	by target 'norms' and charges
Financial management objectives	to ensure probity	to inform management decision-making
Cost reduction pressures	internal search cost efficiency	external search for 'opportunities'
Incentives	rewards for conformity	rewards for innovation
Supervision style	rule/procedure based	review-based achievement
Employment relationship	long career hierarchy	short-term contracts
Orientation to consumers	defensive paternalistic	receptive responsive

This emergent 'new' mangerialism has implications for organization structure which largely reflects the more formalistic approaches dominant in the early 1970s (Whittington and Bellaby 1979). In the early 1980s management problems in SSDs often focused on the potential clash between bureaucratic management and professional social work values (Palfrey 1981) and the solutions offered by the less formal, less hierarchical organic model of organization structure (Burns and Stalker 1961). Professions often express sympathy with the organic model structure emphasizing as it does processes such as project groups, colleagueship and lateral communication. However, the debate between organic and mechanistic approaches to the structuring of social services has been superseded by more recent approaches to the public sector management. Table 14.1 attempts to summarize the changes which are likely to take place.

Pollitt (1986) had provided an excellent summary of the new emergent form of state organization which is worth quoting at length:

the department of the future will have a clear set of strategic objectives. Within it each division and section will have its own objectives . . . directly related to the overall strategy. Each individual manager will work to an annually renegotiated set of personal targets, performance against which will figure as an important factor in his/her superiors' decisions about merit pay increases, promotion and training. [Management] staff . . . will be employed on short term contracts. . . . Specialist skills in particular will be brought in for specific projects. A sophisticated system of activity costing will encourage a keen awareness of resource use at all levels of the hierarchy. . . . Cost centres will be widely used, with senior management more concerned with maintaining and developing control systems rather than with approving specific decisions. . . . Personnel management responsibility will . . . be decentralized and line management will be expected to seek those combinations of all resources which yield the best value for the taxpayer's money. All this would be underpinned by computerized information systems.

(Pollitt 1986: 155)

This new organizational form reflects the major reorientation in the management literature from structure to process. Approaches to formal organizational analysis have tended to take goals for granted, or not as important contingencies compared with size, for instance, in shaping structures (Child 1972). An exception is Perrow (1970), who ascribes great importance to goals (defined in terms of technologies) in shaping the structure of 'people processing' organizations such as SSDs. By focusing on the decision-making process itself and the process of achieving organizational objectives, this approach builds flexibility into the management of complex organizations. There is less interest in specifying how to perform, more emphasis on the outcome of performance.

The Audit Commission has identified the perverse incentives for SSDs that flow from defects in government policies. The block grant system, for instance, does not encourage and reward local authorities who attempt to manage their resources more effectively. SSDs who spend more in order to implement community care will be penalized for doing so. The planned switching of resources involved is also undermined by the high level of uncertainty generated by the grant allocation procedures. The grant system thus works against sound business management principles such as the need to have clear incentives related to objectives, and to formulate long-term expenditure plans to meet those objectives (Audit Commission 1984).

Another well-known example concerns social security payment for residential care in the independent sector. These payments have encouraged the private and voluntary sectors to become the largest provider of long-term care for elderly people (Day and Klein 1987; Baldwin *et al.* 1988). Since social security was funding this care, SSDs were subject to a perverse incentive not to increase their use of the independent sector services (Audit Commission 1986b).

A further example serves to illustrate how the Audit Commission locates the policy response to social problems in the management of public agencies. *The Management of London's Authorities: Preventing a Breakdown of Services* (1987b) is of particular relevance to social services in that it focuses attention on inner city poverty and deprivation. The Audit Commission describes a vicious circle of social and economic decline that operates in the poorest urban areas. The focus of the report is not on social and economic decline so much as on the quality of management within the local authorities. In comparing some London SSDs with others with similar levels of deprivation, the Commission suggests that poor performance is reflected in high unit costs, high staff turnover, political interference in the management process, and poor financial management. The Commission's comments on local political processes are not flattering, and it clearly commits itself to a dismantling of current political management arrangements and to more corporate, Cabinet-style ones for the running of local government, arguing that there are far too many councillors and, in London, too much management by members (1987b: 12–13).

The Commission has been a major source of policy guidance in state welfare and has been set up by government with a clear intention to change the role and philosophy of management and the managerial tools used. The Audit Commission's change strategy is centred on the notion of crisis. It seeks to use this crisis to develop a stronger management culture within SSDs and thereby promote the emergent form of state organization. These activities may also be seen as preparing the ground both in terms of ideology and practice for the major transformation of local social services provision outlined in the White Paper *Caring for People* (Department of Health 1989b) and becoming law as the 1990 National Health Service and Community Care Act.

The National Health Service and Community Care Act 1990

So far in this chapter we have been solely concerned with government and Audit Commission attempts to shape the management culture of social services departments. We have not dealt to any large extent with the government's preferred solution to the problem of welfare provision, namely privatization. The 1990 Act does, however, make significant strides in this direction.

As Figure 14.1 illustrates, privatization involves three kinds of shift away from the welfare state model. The 1980s did not witness any major shift from an all-public to an all-private model of funding and provision. Privatization policies were limited to contracting out, competitive tendering, and the public purchase of social care from the private and voluntary sectors. It has witnessed increased contributions by users, particularly for home help services; increases in its funding of provision in the private sector, especially residential care; and continued support for the voluntary sector.

What these marginal changes signify is the government's preference for non-statutory provision, and are part of a general strategy of talking up the quality of independent sector provision to the detriment of state provision. The movement towards privatization along all three fronts is significant in its implications for the management of state provision (Kelly 1990).

It was the rapid expansion of the private sector provision for elderly people that prompted the Griffiths Report (Griffiths 1988) and subsequently the White Paper *Caring for People*. Social security support for people in independent residential care and nursing homes rose from £10 million in 1979 to over £1,000 million in 1989 (Department of Health 1989b: 3) and thus became a major cause of concern for the government. Although there was some reluctance to see an expanded role for local authorities, the government did finally agree to the transfer of responsibility for this expenditure to SSDs. Subsequently there has been some backtracking on the timetable for this transfer.

Funding

		Public	Private
Service provision	Public	The welfare state model	Charges
	Private	Purchasing care Contracting out	Insurance schemes Private practice Businesses

Figure 14.1   Models of welfare provision and funding

Source: Adapted from Klein 1984

Caring for People describes a future in which much state provision will be 'off-loaded' by the creation of self-managed units for residential and domiciliary care. Authorities are to be encouraged to set up autonomous state provider agencies: residential care, day care centres and domiciliary care teams being 'floated off' and then contracted to provide services. One of the key objectives of the 1990 Act is to develop a flourishing independent sector alongside good quality public services. In 'the enabling authority' (Brooke 1989) maximum use will be made of voluntary and private sector providers and it will take all reasonable steps to ensure that there is a diversity of provision, especially in the domiciliary care sector where there is far less choice at present. Where the independent sector is languishing, SSDs will be required to stimulate its growth. SSDs must change from being monopolistic providers to being orchestrators and purchasers: their own providers being just one of a range of contractors that the SSD as purchasing agency might draw up a contract with.

> The government envisages . . . that the statutory sector will continue to play an important role in *backing up*, developing and monitoring private and voluntary care facilities, and providing services *where this remains the best way* of meeting care needs.
>
> (Department of Health 1989b: 22 my emphasis)

The 1990 Act withdraws from a complete commitment to marketization in two ways: it retains state provision for core services and it places SSDs in the crucial role of planning to meet need and to ration demand by need assessment. The market is not allowed to allocate resources, providers will compete, but users will not. Whether a user gets a service will be determined by regulated need assessment by a case-manager. The case-manager's budget will be determined by a more global analysis of likely demands based on both demographic and service usage data.

As things stand, local social services will continue to be funded by taxation and community charge payments; SSDs will be performing the functions of purchasing, planning and quality control, and managing and providing core services that cannot be contracted out. These will be services for people with high levels of dependency, particularly long-term care and those with challenging behaviour. In what follows I want to focus on the structures and procedures outlined in the Act.

Initially it was thought that priority would be given to the establishment of a purchasing function, especially for private residential and nursing home care (the former social security funded element). This was the most significant proposal in the 1990 Act and it aimed to break down the alliance between managers and providers. Instead of welfare managers having responsibility for professional staff *and* the local community, those who manage purchasing would be fundamentally concerned with the needs of the community. Once purchasing and provision of welfare are separated, those responsible for meeting needs, it was argued, would be able to make choices as to the most appropriate form and balance of services to provide with less concern for any loyalty to providers.

In this scenario, improved management information systems will be necessary to monitor more closely the flow of resources and services provided. Budgetary planning would be introduced for the new case management system and the new purchasing function. Such financial planning will require data on the batches of services provided for each user and their costs. Enhanced financial planning would be linked to objectives over a three year period, and further planning activities relating to meeting needs and developing relationships with the independent sector. It is envisaged that plans will be monitored by Department of Health review processes and the inspectorate and there will be intervention to stimulate improvements.

Providers in the core welfare and self-managed state units will compete with those in the independent sector. As a result they will have to be more concerned with the costs and will require information about these and workload, especially in the self-managed units. There is also to be a greater emphasis on resource management with budgets delegated to case-managers. The decentralization of budgeting should make front-line social services providers in the state sector more sensitive to the resource implications of their decisions. With the greater specification of contracts involved in the establishment of a purchasing function, and in providing through self-managed state units, the private and independent sector contractors will be able to tender more effectively and for a much wider range of services than has hitherto been possible.

Caring for People aims to improve arrangements for consumer complaints in the social services, but it is generally assumed that consumer interests will be promoted by competition for contracts, and the creation of arms-length inspection units within SSDs. It is expected that the presentation and packaging of services will be of higher standard and, a higher proportion of the total costs, when consumers and their agents can choose between alternative sources of provision. The slowdown in the implementation of the scheme announced in July 1990 was excused by the Department of Health on the grounds that SSDs are ill-prepared for their new purchasing role. This was something that was recognized in *Caring for People* and that the strengthened management function in SSDs must be more 'vigorous' in its approach. This new managerialism, as we have seen is less concerned with the control of internal processes, rather than with the development of links with other organizations and with the co-ordination of agencies operating in the organization's environment (Stoker 1988: 258). The latest reforms add entrepreneurialism to the list of desirable qualities for the SSD manager.

Entrepreneurialism means searching for opportunities rather than being concerned with day-to-day provision; it means being innovative, taking risks with new ideas, but being flexible in implementing them. It looks outward for resources in the community and builds links with organizations, or creates new organizational forms, that bring the state and external bodies together in joint ventures. It relaxes the traditional bureaucratic controls which can prevent the above (Stewart 1986: 43–4). Klein and O'Higgins (1985: 229) call for a 'purposive opportunism' whereby welfare managers are encouraged to plan to meet objectives in a variety of possible ways and to design in flexibility in order to respond to opportunities as they arise. The creation of purchasing agencies fits this dynamic vision of a new entrepreneurial welfare management in the 1990s.

Will it be that straightforward? When assembled, the new managerial elite in SSDs will be confronted with questions that, at present, remain unanswered. It is to these that we now turn our attention.

Unanswered questions for the management of welfare

The new performance management presumes that SSDs can develop a set of integrated, explicit and specific policies. These objectives are communicated, co-ordinated and implemented through a hierarchy of management and increasingly specific goals and attached guidelines that legitimize the activity at all levels in the organization. This contrasts sharply with the more typical view that social services are no more than a collection of services that at various times be assigned vaguely defined goals. The programmes of service production do not give expression to coherent and explicit policies because the social problems SSDs confront are both vaguely defined and little understood. Policies may be vague because they result from competing and conflicting objectives (for example care and control; quality and efficiency), or because there is no certain relationship between intervention and outcome.

Difficulties also arise with the concept and methodology of needs assessment. The Audit Commission avoids this issue by taking a comparative approach. For the Commission an appropriate level of service output is that provided by the average of a 'family' of SSDs facing similar socio-economic conditions. The annual dissemination to each SSD of comparative statistics on performance and balance of provision (Audit Commission 1987a) may eventually even out the large disparities in the level of service provision (Audit Commission 1986b). In practice, one suspects that these norms of service provision will be used to justify service reductions in those SSDs currently providing above the norm. The Commission is still working on its methodology of comparisons, but thus far it has contributed little to our understanding of the factors producing variations in level of provision.

Considerable managerial planning expertise is required to define needs, to draw up contracts and to plan for future provision and expenditure with a wide variety of agencies who are themselves subject to change and development contingencies outside the direct control of SSDs. SSDs are not well placed, in this respect, they are considerably smaller than health authorities who have established financial, planning and information units that have taken on these tasks. A high level of analytical capacity and management skill, and some considerable investment in new technology and training, is necessary to perform the complex purchasing and planning tasks of the new social services departments. There is comparatively little time to define these tasks and to marshal the appropriate managerial resources, the recruitment rush has already begun but there must be doubts about the availability of talent and SSDs' ability to recruit it (Jefferies 1989).

Earlier it was suggested that the government has refrained from the legislative approach to change in local social services management and provision. The 1990 Act presumes that sufficient normative control has been exercised and there is some enthusiasm for the new tasks, as indeed there is in many SSDs (Warner 1990). The government has taken on powers to review plans for extending the private sector and must be hoping that SSDs will co-operate in this respect. It would be an unprecedented action to force these developments on SSDs, even for a government intent on challenging the traditional order in local government. It seems therefore that the government must be either confident, or willing to accept a variable implementation of is community care scheme or it hopes that SSDs will embrace the structures when their community charge level comes under local electoral or central government pressure.

There is still much uncertainty as to the funding arrangements. Standard spending assessments which determine how much an authority should spend on its social services, and it formula for children and elderly people appears to have changed very little. These assessments are also used to determine which local authorities have their community charge capped. Further uncertainty concerns the sums to be transferred from social security when and if the community care scheme is finally implemented. There was strong pressure for the creation of a community care budget, to stop the former social security element leaking in child care or other provision, but the government successfully resisted this. If such a budget was identified at this early stage, it would have to have some relation to current 'high' levels of non-assessed social security spending. Once such a sum is made visible it can be easily monitored for decline in real terms. One suspects this will happen, but that the government wants to hide it in the general grant to local authorities.

What role for the state in the future of welfare?

Conservative governments during the 1980s have defined and pursued policy objectives based on a belief in the superiority of the private sector. It is a great irony that some of the more lasting effects might be in clarifying the role of the state. The future of the state might be limited in terms of direct service provision, but occupying a central position in the management of welfare.

The Audit Commission has clearly demonstrated the potential role of an independent monitoring body for local government. Auditing is occupying a central place now, and, given its wider brief, its potential as a stimulus for change is unlikely to go unrecognized in the future. Its narrow disciplinary basis has tended to restrict its recommendations to ways of not spending money. If, as Garrett (1986) suggests, it would acknowledge more than it does the contribution of the social sciences then this would broaden the scope and increase the depth of its analysis to include gaps in provision and non-managerial sources of inter-authority differences. For example Knapp has criticized the Commission's disarmingly simple approach to the assessment of efficiency in service delivery and its failure to make reference to studies of the impact of care (1984: 16).

An independent body will be important in monitoring the impact of the 1990 Act. It is crucial that the quality of data is maintained and enhanced, since private and voluntary sector organizations have less incentive to produce it. A future government committed to more egalitarian objectives may well decide to keep an organization committed to efficiency *and* equity. This would require a commitment to 'territorial justice' with the monitoring body being responsible for identifying the way in which the grosser inequalities in provision could be remedied. It is apparent that, despite its current limitations, it is useful to have an independent monitoring organization, such as the Audit Commission.

The performance management approach may be less than perfectly applicable to all or some aspects of the social services, yet one could argue that its implementation will identify these areas, and others where performance management is more appropriate. Performance management allows some central direction of professional activities without overly structuring professional work or subjecting it to close supervision: these options being just as difficult and probably more expensive in terms of management overheads. Performance management might enable professionals to be made more accountable to directorates, politicians and the community and it might be a way of reconciling professional autonomy and job satisfaction with this accountability.

The 1990 Act, if fully implemented, will strengthen the managerial function within SSDs by removing global resource decisions from front-line providers, and making those providers more responsive to the needs of the community as defined and articulated by SSD management. Constructing a divide between producer and purchaser, and introducing competition between provider units, will undermine professional power and professional resistance to change in SSDs.

The government, in attempting to marketize the provision of local social services has in fact strengthened the planning function in SSDs. SSDs are now recruiting planning and research staff to manage the process of collecting more systematic data relating to the needs of their populations. The 1990 Act has called for independent needs assessment by the purchasing agencies. Provided that these sections of the Act are fully implemented, the distribution of resources is less likely to follow individual, unscrutinized provider judgements, and more likely to reflect needs determined by demographic and client usage data. There is also a potential force for shifting resources into preventive measures designed to keep spending down. These and other processes of policy analysis, resource allocation and review are likely to be crucial in any future state initiative to promote social justice in welfare provision.

Conclusion

During the 1980s governments have attempted to reshape SSDs: changing definitions of problems; shifting perceptions of appropriate solutions; and changing expectations regarding the resource base and the role of the independent sector (Webb and Wistow 1986: 92–3). The Audit Commission is one agency that has played a major role in advocating change and a new managerialism in local government and the social services.

Many aspects of this new managerialism are a necessary precondition for the implementation of the proposals contained in the National Health Service and Community Care Act 1990. The new managerialism was promoted when local government was 'under siege' and in preparation for the implementation of post-1987 programme for local government reform (H. Davies 1988). The changes before and after 1987 will have a lasting impact on state management of welfare. The government has made a strong case for a central 'quango' to monitor changing patterns of provision in local authority social services; it has separated the purchasing of services from their provision; and it has enhanced the role of needs assessment, planning, quality control in welfare (see Figure 14.2). These three reforms recognize a central role for the state in the management of welfare provision and if sustained, appear to mark something of a return to non-market solutions to the problem of resource allocation in welfare. This is one reason why the alterations in the time-scale for the implementation of the 1990 Act are significant.

The two-year delay in the implementation of the Act announced in July 1990 was justified in terms of the lack of preparedness of social services departments. It might also be the case that the government, which has always been reluctant to increase the responsibilities of local authorities, wishes to rethink the purchasing role for local authorities and attempt a more full-blown market solution. The delay will also allow more radical proposals to be developed and avoid adding to the destabilizing potential of the implementation of internal markets in the National Health Service. The government would also be sensitive to the implications of implementation for the community. Postponement of implementation in addition ensures some degree of 'steady state' in the management of welfare during the run up to the next General Election.

The revitalization of the state's management of local welfare provision will no doubt outlast Thatcherism itself and be taken up by a government more committed to social justice in welfare provision. If this happens, then those dependent on state welfare or at risk of being dependent, may have good

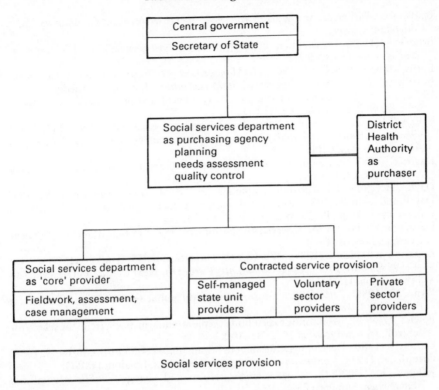

Figure 14.2 The 'new' model of social services provision

reason to be grateful for the new managerialist challenge to traditional bureaucratic and professional organizational forms in the social services.

Note

1 I have refrained from detailing the previous incarnations of the 'new' managerialism. What I am referring to in this chapter is a 'new' managerialism that was in part newly developed or in part given renewed emphasis in the 1980s.

References

Audit Commission (1984) *The Impact on Local Authorities' Economy, Efficiency and Effectiveness of the Block Grant Distribution System*, London: HMSO.
—— (1985) *Managing Social Services for the Elderly More Effectively*, London: HMSO.
—— (1986a) *Performance Review in Local Government: A Handbook for Auditors and Local Government*, London: HMSO.
—— (1986b) *Making a Reality of Community Care*, London: HMSO.
—— (1987a) *Local Authority Profiles*, London: Audit Commission.
—— (1987b) *The Management of London's Authorities: Preventing a Breakdown of Services*, Audit Commission Occasional Papers no. 2, London: HMSO.
—— (1988) *The Competitive Council*, London: HMSO.

Baldwin, S., Parker, G. and Walker, R. (1988) *Social Security and Community Care*, Aldershot: Gower.

Brooke, R. (1989) 'The enabling authority: practical consequences', *Local Government Studies* September/October: 55–63.

Burns, T. and Stalker, G. M. (1961) *The Management of Innovation*, London: Tavistock.

Burrows, R. (ed.) (1990) *Deciphering Enterprise Culture*, London: Routledge.

Child, J. (1972) 'Organisation structure, environment and performance: the role of strategic choice', *Sociology* 6, 1: 1–22.

CIPFA (Chartered Institute of Public Finance and Accountancy) (1979; 1983; 1986) *Chartered Institute of Public Finance and Accountancy: Personal Social Services Actuals*, London: CIPFA.

Davies, B. (1987) 'Review article: making a reality of community care', *British Journal of Social Work* 18: 173–87.

Davies, H. (1988) 'Local government under siege', *Public Administration* 66: 91–101.

Day, P. and Klein, R. (1987) 'Residential care for the elderly: a billion-pound experiment in policy-making', *Public Money* March: 19–24.

Department of Health Social Services Inspectorate (1987) *Key Indicators Development Exercise*, London, DoH.

Department of Health (1989a) *Working for Patients*, Cm 555, London: HMSO.

—— (1989b) *Caring for People: Community Care in the Next Decade and Beyond*, Cm 849, London: HMSO.

Flynn, N. (1986) 'Performance measurement in the public sector services', *Policy and Politics* 14, 3: 389–404.

Fowles, A. (1990) 'Monitoring expenditure on the criminal justice system: the search for control', *Howard Journal* 29, 2: 82–100.

Garrett, J. (1986) 'Developing state audit in Britain' *Public Administration* 64: 421–33.

Griffiths, R. (1988) *Community Care: Agenda for Action*, London: HMSO.

Jefferies, R. (1989) 'Local government reform and change', *Public Money and Management* Summer: 23–8.

Jenkins, L., Bardsley, M., Coles, J., Wickings, I. and Leow, H. (1988) *How Did We Do? The Use of Performance Indicators in the National Health Service*, CASPE Research, 14 Palace Court, London W2 4HT.

Kelly, A. (1990) 'Enterprise culture and the Welfare State', in R. Burrows (ed.) *Deciphering Enterprise Culture*, London: Routledge.

Klein, R. (1984) 'Privatization and the Welfare State', *Lloyds Bank Review* January: 12–29.

Klein, R. and O'Higgins, M. (1985) 'Social Policy after incrementalism', in R. Klein and M. O'Higgins (eds) *The Future of Welfare*, Oxford: Basil Blackwell.

Knapp, M. (1984) 'The three "E"'s', *Community Care* 20 September: 14–16.

McSweeney, B. (1988) 'Accounting for the Audit Commission', *Political Quarterly* 59, 1: 28–43.

Miller, N. (1986) 'Management information and performance measurement in the personal social services', *Social Services Research* 4/5: 7–55.

Palfrey, C. F. (1981) 'Management training needs in Social Services Departments', *British Journal of Social Work* 15, 2: 125–35.

Perrow (1970) *Organisational Analysis: A Sociological View*, London: Tavistock.

Pollitt, C. (1986) 'Beyond the managerial model: the case for broadening performance assessment in government and the public services', *Financial Accountability and Management* 2, 3: 155–70.

Stewart, J. (1986) *The New Management of Local Government*, London: Allen & Unwin.

Stoker, G. (1988) *The Politics of Local Government*, London: Macmillan.

Warburton, W. (1989) 'Outlying principles' *Insight* 5 July: 22–3.

Warner, N. (1990) 'Kent hops to it', *Insight* 31 January: 22–4.

Webb, A. and Wistow, G. (1982) *Whither State Welfare? Policy Implementation in the Personal Social Services, 1979–80*, London: Royal Institute of Public Administration.
—— (1983) 'Public expenditure and policy implementation: the case of community care', *Public Administration* 61: 21–41.
—— (1986) *Social Work Social Care and Social Planning: The Personal Social Services since Seebohm*, London: Longman.
Whittington, C. and Bellaby, P. (1979) 'The reasons for hierarchy in social services departments: a critique of Elliot Jacques and his associates', *Sociological Review* 27, 3: 513–39.

15
Residential care after Wagner: developments in policy and training

Ian Sinclair and John Brown

When the White Paper *Caring for People* (Department of Health 1989a) was published at the end of 1989 it brought to a head months, perhaps years of speculation and rumour about the future direction and shape of community care. Yet while the main thrust of the report had been widely predicted – that social services were to have lead responsibility for purchasing and co-ordinating services across all sectors of provision – publication did little to quell discussion and comment. In part this was because of the volume of related policy changes that has taken place.

The closing years of the 1980s have seen, among other policy developments, *Working for Patients* (Department of Health 1989b) the Children Act 1989, *Caring for People*, and the introduction of the community charge. The purpose of this paper is to examine the likely effect on residential care of just two recent developments – the White Paper *Caring for People* (Department of Health 1989a) and the changes proposed for professional and para-professional training. In this way we shall cast light on whether the White Paper and the policies associated with it are likely to further the aims set out by the Wagner Report (NISW 1988), namely that residential care should be accepted as a positive choice rather than a last resort.

In pursuing this question we shall consider the resources likely to be available for residential care and three different ways through which the White Paper might improve its quality and scope: competition; regulation and training. We argue that within the framework of the White Paper all three methods of improving quality are essential but that as things stand at present their combined effect is likely to be weak. This means that even if the White Paper's proposals are fully implemented, more will need to be done if the Wagner Committee's (NISW 1988) vision of a new start for residential care is to be achieved.

Impact of the White Paper on residential care

The future impact of changes in policy and legislation is almost always hard to predict and particularly so in the case of the *Caring for People*. At the time of writing the first draft of this chapter the Thatcher government had just been defeated in the House of Lords on an amendment to the Bill so that even the final shape of the legislation is uncertain. At the time of revising the chapter, the government's apprehension about the impact of the White Paper on public expenditure had thrown the whole timing of its implementation of the White Paper into doubt. Moreover at its most definite the White Paper is a motorist's rather than a walker's map, describing the outline of the territory it wishes to see rather than filling in the details. Major issues are left for future decisions, of which perhaps the most crucial has concerned the overall size of the budget to be made available to local authorities for their new responsibilities. The authorities have waited uneasily for government guidance and circulars on a rumoured thirty or forty separate issues, only to find that the implementation of most parts of the White Paper have been put off.

Despite these difficulties the White Paper sets out the main lines of government thinking on residential care and it is possible to begin to make an assessment, if not of its outcome, at least of the elements in it which will have an important effect on the outcome. Roughly these elements can be grouped into three main areas:

1 values and assumptions
2 financial arrangements
3 organization and practice arrangements.

Despite the delay in implementing the White Paper it is worth examining the likely impact of these different aspects. Some of the regulations notably, those on arm's length inspection units, are to be implemented. The anticipation of other regulations, notably those concerned with finances, have already begun to affect behaviour, whereas other of the White Paper ideas (for example in care management) are becoming accepted as relevant to good practice. It seems an appropriate moment to take stock. If we do not entirely like what we see there may still be time to press for changes or, at least, further delay.

Values and assumptions

To deal first with the values and assumptions of the White Paper these are on the face of it impeccable. Community care is recommended primarily as a humane rather than an economical policy. Choice (and hence flexibility and consumer rights) is to be encouraged; carers are to be supported; efficiency, accountability and good management are to flourish within a clear framework; collaboration between service providers will grow. More controversially the mixed economy of welfare is to take over from the state welfare system we have learned to know, if not love. But then, so we are told, this mixed system is the necessary condition for the greater degree of choice and efficiency, which we all desire.

In practice, and inevitably, the glossy covers of the White Paper contain contradictions as well as eternal truths. On its own each clarion call arouses enthusiasm for the symphony to come, but together they give forth an uncertain sound: there are questions over whether the orchestra will be hired, the players on speaking terms and the score harmonious. Is it possible to support carers without a massive increase in expenditure, which the White Paper does not envisage and which indeed the current government seem to have ruled out? How is the choice for consumer and provider implicit in the private system to be married with the need to conserve public funds through assessment, and to ensure that resources are distributed according to need? Whose choice is to be encouraged, that of the carer, the dependant or the case-manager struggling to stay within a tight budget?

The insistence of such awkward questions makes it hard to decide which of the competing values in the White Paper will on balance prevail and hence what the overall effect on residential care will be. Nevertheless the language of the Paper and hence implicitly some of it ideology is entering the jargon of social services professionals who in the recent past would have shuddered at the use of such phrases as 'bottom line'. One effect is likely to be a greater consciousness of the importance of 'the consumer' in residential care. Something to which the statutory sector has always paid lip-service, but in respect of which its practice has been somewhat lacking – witness the number of elderly people still sharing rooms in Part III homes. A less benign consequence could be an emphasis on economy rather than effectiveness in residential care. For in assessing the relationship of value and money, the latter often has the greater power to concentrate the mind.

Financial arrangements

More educated guesses about the likely effect of implementing the White Paper are made possible by consideration of the financial arrangements it proposes. Under its proposals local authorities would have to take these arrangements into account, however variously they might respond to them. The most important proposal obviously concerns the distinction between 'care costs' and 'maintenance costs' such as lodging and food. As is well known, where people needed care and maintenance and were unable to pay for these themselves, the local authority would in general be expected to meet the care costs, while the income support and housing benefit systems would meet the maintenance costs. Local authorities would therefore be able to pay for the care of an old person in a private home or in the community. In order to enable them to do this, the government would transfer to them the funds which it estimated had been spent on care through the social security system. In this way the government would remove the perverse incentive provided by the ability of the social security system to pay for care in residential but not community care.

At the time of writing a great deal about these proposed arrangements remained unclear. The arrangements themselves would be phased in so that those currently supported on income support or attendance allowance in residential care would continue to be supported in the same way with a corresponding reduction in the funds handed over to local authorities. It is not, however, clear, at least to us, how the government would distribute the money. Would authorities which had large quantities of private residential care eventually receive correspondingly large grants, thus continuing the inequitable government subsidy to the better-off authorities in which the private sector tends to be strong? Or would they not, thus reducing the flow of public money to private homes in those areas and perhaps inducing homes to close down? More importantly still, how would the government calculate the amount of money which has been spent on care through the social security system and which would therefore be made available to the local authority?

Irrespective of how these questions are answered, the new arrangements would be likely to reduce the money available for residential care in the local authority sector and thus affect its quality or quantity or both. The arrangements would stem the leakage of funds from the social security system to the system for providing care, while local authorities were struggling to contain the level of the community charge. Health authorities equally pressed for finance might welcome the clarification that their responsibilities are more clearly for 'cure' rather than 'care', and become increasingly eager to shift the costs for such things as respite care on to local authorities. The additional costs of the proposed new system in terms of inspection, planning, monitoring, contracting, assessing individuals and complaints procedures would be far from negligible. In short public money for residential care would be unlikely to increase in line with costs.

One area in which local authorities are seeking economies is their own provision of residential care. The White Paper provides a direct incentive for them to do this. The hotel costs of residents supported by the state in private or voluntary sector residential care would be borne by the social security system. The same costs in local authority care would fall on the authority itself. In addition local authorities would be able to rely on attendance allowance to finance some care in the community but this would not be possible in residential care. In response to these pressures local authorities may seek to privatize their own residential care, to seize the opportunity to close out-of-date homes (an approach suggested by the 'even-handed' inspection discussed below) or to switch homes from providing long-term care to providing respite care (a form of provision for which the government would, in some as yet undetermined way, provide funds). Whatever combination of approaches an authority used the result would be likely to be a further increase in the degree to which residential provision, at least for elderly people, is dominated by the private sector.

For its part the private sector on which so much of residential care will depend is not in as strong a financial position as once it was. In the future, it is proposed, social security will not be available to fund new growth in residential care on the same basis as in the past. Local authority case-managers, some perhaps ideologically opposed to private provision, will scrutinize those potential residents who will need to rely on state funds with a view to keeping them out of residential care altogether. Old people who might have been able to afford to pay for their own care through the sale of their house are finding that houses are difficult to sell. Costs are rising: many proprietors have seen the interest rates on their houses double while contemplating uneasily the implications of the community charge and business rate. Moreover the proprietor can no longer be so confident that whatever their day-to-day profit or loss, the capital tied up in the bricks-and-mortar of their establishment is accumulating a satisfactory nest egg for their old age.

Some of the consequences of these financial pressures are already apparent. Many have raised their charges above the levels payable by income support with the resulting pressures on relatives to 'top up', others require old people to devote the whole of their income support to paying the fee, and some proprietors now hand on clothes from deceased residents to current ones in straitened circumstances (Baldwin and Corden 1987; Corden 1990). News of these pressures reached the House of Lords, which voted to raise the level of income support available to residents in private homes. At the same time two 'levels' of provision have appeared in private care so that some old people in single rooms and on income support have had to move to shared rooms, while at least in some parts of the country new residents on income support are virtually unable to get a single room at all (Baldwin and Corden 1987; Corden 1990). Choice and hence, presumably, quality in residential care is thus reduced, at least for that majority of elderly people whose income is no more than 40 per cent above the level of income support.

Organization and practice arrangements

These financial pressures on both the public and private sectors of residential care provide an unpropitious climate for the introduction of the other organizational and practice changes proposed by the White Paper. Taken together these proposals are intended to ensure that an overall community care plan is created and co-ordinated; that proper contracts are made with bodies in the independent sector to ensure that they carry out their part in the plan; that case-managers ensure that services from this mosaic of provision are appropriately tied together for individuals; and that there are control mechanisms under complaints procedures for ensuring that the system operates to a high standard.

The logic of these proposals is impressive but the practical difficulties of carrying them through are formidable. In the first place community care plans will not be easy to create or to police. Difficulties in the joint planning of health and social services are well documented (e.g. Audit Commission 1986). In particular problems have arisen over differences in professional attitudes, in objectives, in the geographical areas of responsibility and budget cycles of health districts and local authorities and in the political affiliations of some of those involved. The new proposals contain some incentives to collaboration, notably in the field of mental health, but overall collaboration is unlikely to be easier in the new world where hospitals can 'opt out'; GPs have an incentive not to take on time-consuming patients; and the differing responsibilities of health and social services have been more clearly spelt out. Nor is it likely to be easier for local authorities to co-ordinate plans with housing and social security than it has been in the past.

The difficulties of local authority planners will be particularly acute in relation to the private and voluntary sectors. These sectors are highly diverse and are not themselves co-ordinated. For example private proprietors have a number of different associations to which they can belong but many belong to none of them. Traditionally providers in these sectors have 'done their own thing', providing the type of service they think is most profitable or which most appeals to them in the places where they wish to provide it. The private sector has responded massively to the incentives to provide residential care for elderly people whereas the voluntary sector has not. Both sectors are far stronger in some parts of the country than others and within the same local authority they may be virtually non-existent in some districts and massively evident in others. So in Torbay or Harrogate, it may seem as if there is a residential home on every corner, whereas one may walk all day through the housing estates of Barnsley without finding a single private home. Local authorities required to ensure that at least a minimal standard of service is available in all the areas they cover will therefore have to rely on their own services or on 'preferred suppliers' and 'block contracts' to ensure that residential care is available throughout the authority.

The difficulties of implementing the White Paper effectively will be equally great at the individual levels of assessment, case-management and inspection. Case-managers will, like the social work assistants and social workers of the present, have difficulty in ensuring that their clients have access to services such as community nursing which their own authority does not directly control. As resources are likely to remain equally short they will face the choice between providing an adequate package of services to a few or a sparse level of service to many. Except in such favoured areas as Harrogate they will have little by way of choice in terms of residential care. At present it seems that few elderly residents feel that they have had much choice over which establishment they enter or indeed over whether they enter residential care at all (Sinclair 1988). It is hard to believe that in the future they will feel that they have a much greater degree of choice.

The quality of residential care, under threat from lack of resources and lack of effective competition, is unlikely to be greatly improved by inspection or indeed by complaints procedures. Inspectors will find it is hard to determine the quality of residential care (as opposed to the size of the bedrooms), harder still to provide the evidence that a home should be de-registered, and daunting to contemplate the prospect of closing anything other than a tiny minority of establishments. One only has to consider how much time would be spent on the procedure of doing so and what would happen to the residents in the mean time to recognize major constraints on local authorities regarding closure. Complaints procedures are associated with similar difficulties. In the field of residential care complaints will often be made to the local authority which will not have direct control over the establishment concerned and may be reluctant to take any decisive action.

In short, the case for making training, as opposed to inspection or competition, the key plank in improving the quality of residential provision is a strong one. Traditionally residential homes have had very few trained staff. In addition demands on residential homes to provide regimes emphasizing choice will require more skilful staff while the new roles required by the White Paper (planners, case-managers, middle managers versed in both finance and care) imply the need for staff trained to perform them. Also competition is unlikely to be a sufficient condition for high quality residential care (in most parts of the country it will be weak), and the conclusions of inspection will be hard to enforce. What then are the prospects for the effective regulation of care through training?

Training: the changing policy scenario

Residential care has traditionally been provided by untrained staff, a situation which the shift towards a greater reliance on private sector would seem unlikely to change. Private old people's homes, the main suppliers of residential care in this sector, are generally small (typically they have fewer then twenty beds for residents) and rely heavily on part-time staff. Employers have little incentive to train these staff, when their staff complement is not such as easily to allow staff to go on training; there is no evidence that the training will increase the marketability of their establishment, and the main beneficiaries may be the staff themselves, who may use their new expertise to get better jobs or demand higher wages.

There are two more general logistic difficulties. First, the 'demographic down-turn' which is of so much concern to the health and education services, will equally reduce the pool of staff available to residential care. Second, the shrinking of the local authority sector of residential care means that local authorities cannot play the role of supplier of trained labour to the private sector which the National Health Service has so far played for the private sector in the field of health. The consequences could be that little or no training is done in residential care which remains as in the past dependent on recruiting some trained nurses from the health service.

In practice the training which has relevance to residential care is in a state of flux. Training programmes for social workers and for nurses, the two main professions represented in the residential sectors, are being radically restructured across the range from pre-qualifying through to post-qualifying courses. The White Paper emphasizes the need for inter-disciplinary training. It also envisages training initiatives for community care which apply to managers as well as to direct-care/hands-on staff, and which use top-sliced monies distributed by the Social Services Inspectorate. These developments are taking place at a time when the government has challenged, in an unprecedented manner, the work of all professions so that not even long-established occupations such as medicine and law are exempt from scrutiny.

A notable feature of this government activity has been the establishment of a National Council of Vocational Qualification (NCVQ). Introduced in the latter half of the 1980s NCVQ has begun the task of classifying all vocational activities in terms of the competences required to carry them out (DoE/DES

1986). This exercise includes the work of the caring professions and has, so far, been concentrated upon 'levels of competences' that could loosely be described as falling within the pre-qualifying arena. The immediate impact has been to encourage the introduction of a new range of courses, for example BTEC Caring Services, that complement the more familiar professional qualifications in social work, nursing and education. With the long-recognized problem of how best to recruit and deploy scarce professional skills such a development at the pre-qualifying level clearly has particular relevance to residential care where the majority of staff have traditionally been unqualified (CCETSW 1987a).

It is too soon to begin to discern the full import of NCVQ upon training in residential care. What is clear is that NCVQ indicates a trend towards employer-led training rather than profession-led education. The model of training has changed as has the language used with talk of 'Industry Lead Bodies', 'competence' and 'outcome'. It is a language that has its parallels in the White Paper. The introduction of managerialism in the health service, and its adoption of an industrial perspective, has now spread to community care and training. Training is increasingly carried out in the workplace and based on an identified set of skills which an employer is likely to require.

The way the professions have responded to this challenge has varied. Social work has at least partially embraced the new perspective. The new Diploma in Social Work, for example, can be achieved through 'work-based routes', is designed around a set of 'competences', and can be obtained only on programmes associated with a consortium including both educational and social work agencies. Nursing, on the other hand, has traditionally been taught in the workplace but still has to get to grips with elements of the new scenario. To date only one of its specialist areas of training, mental handicap, has adopted a competence model within the proposals for a new nurse training, Project 2000 (UKCC 1986).

A similar hesitancy has marked the response to the call in the White Paper for joint training. In the past the relationship between social work and nursing has too often been characterized by antipathy and conflict. In relation to residential care the general public and private proprietors – the latter generally trained, if trained at all, in nursing – are unlikely to agree on the kind of training required with local authority managers imbued with the ethos of social work. Nevertheless, in the field of mental handicap/learning difficulties, where debate has often been most heated, a start has been made on introducing joint training, validated by the social work and nursing bodies, at the qualifying and post-qualifying levels (Walton 1989). This has required an open approach to problems of administrative responsibilities, organizational structures and training programmes that contains lessons for preparing staff to work with other client groups. Not least it is apparent that in overcoming professional prejudices and stereotypes clear direction and positive support is required at the national level. Regrettably this is not apparent in the White Paper.

Despite this hesitancy there is no doubt about the possibilities offered by NCVQ and much will depend on whether these are taken up by the private sector. Since its establishment NCVQ has begun to establish a substantial infrastructure. In job training, for example, initiatives for Technical and Vocational Education Initiative for school children through to Employment Training for adults are incorporated within its framework. The proliferation of new pre-qualifying level courses that this has encouraged in social care could be taken by managers from all sectors – statutory, voluntary and private – not just as complementing professional training programmes but as alternatives to them. This is encouraged by two factors.

First, the new patterns of training have encouraged a proliferation in the market of open/distance learning packages whose immediate appeal to those with hard-pressed budgets is their relative cheapness and apparent adaptability. Second, it is not generally believed that residential care requires much professional input when most of the activities it involves are apparently simple. In this context forms of training and assessment that focus on the tasks to be done and can be carried out in the workplace have an obvious attraction.

As far as we know, the advantages and disadvantages of the competence approach have not been the subject of research. Nevertheless the advantages seem clear enough. Training is likely to be practical and linked to the roles people actually perform and the organizational goals they have to pursue. The disadvantages are a matter for speculation. It may be, however, that training becomes too imbued with the values of organizations and employers so that a concentration on technical procedures leads trainees to lose sight of the clients with whom they deal. The danger is that with very few trained staff on the ground, any opportunity for training is grasped. Employer-based NCVQ courses provide one possibility to fill the long-standing void with their use justified as compatible with the ideology and language of the White Paper. Managers and proprietors, however, could use such courses in ways where they are an end in themselves rather than a means to an end (Brown and Shaw 1989). Without careful monitoring the contribution to quality could be tenuous.

Conclusion: strategies for residential care

In this chapter we have looked at how the recent White Paper on community care and recent developments in training might enable a new start for residential care to be achieved. Crudely our conclusion is that they will not be of much help. Except perhaps in a few favoured areas such Harrogate competition will not be sufficient to encourage excellent residential homes – indeed greater profits may well be made by homes which fall somewhat short of excellence. Regulation in the form of inspection, complaints procedures, and performance indicators is unlikely to have a major impact. Highly trained staff, other than nurses, in the residential sector are likely to remain few and their influence correspondingly dilute. The effectiveness of NCVQ is for the moment unproven, and the new forms of training may well have more impact on the technical competence of staff than on the spirit in which they do their work.

Within this context it is nevertheless important to look at the following.

1 *Competition*   ensuring that where possible case-managers are aware of the qualities of residential homes in their areas, that inspection reports are

published so that relatives and old people have access to information on potential homes, and that as far as possible (perhaps not very far) local monopolies are avoided.

2 *Regulation* ensuring, for example, that clear standards are developed, that residents, staff and relatives are all aware of what these standards are, and that they know how to make a complaint if the standards are breached.

3 *Training* ensuring that schemes of training are developed which are linked to quality assurance, that public funds are available for training staff likely to work in the private sector, that nurses, likely to form the bulk of trained staff in residential care, are offered appropriate 'top-up' training and that requirements related to training are built into contracts.

Despite the financial incentives to local authorities to divest themselves of residential care, we hope they do not entirely do so. If they do, they will be unable to ensure that residential care is reliably available to those who need it most in all parts of their authority or that local monopolies in residential care do not spring up. They will be at the mercy of a private sector, which is itself vulnerable to changes in interest rates and in the housing market.

Above all it is important to recognize the vital importance of staff. Small residential establishments depend on those who run them. They must also have an adequate number of staff deployed at appropriate times to meet the physical needs of residents without being rushed off their feet. It follows that personnel policies are the key to residential care: good heads of homes must be recruited, trained, supported, and if necessary removed, if residential care is to function effectively. By splitting the monitoring and providing functions of local authorities the White Paper's proposals will make it difficult for the authorities to ensure that such policies are in place.

Some way has to be found whereby heads of establishments are vigorously screened before being allowed to run homes, and that unsatisfactory heads are offered support and training but are, if ultimately necessary, removed.

References

Audit Commission (1986) *Making a Reality of Community Care*, London: HMSO.

Baldwin, S. and Corden, A. (1987), 'Public money and private care: paradoxes and problems', in S. Di Gregorio (ed.) *Social Gerontology: New Directions*, Beckenham: Croom Helm.

Brown, J. and Shaw, I. (1989) 'A foundation for the future: the concept and implementation of joint training', *Journal of Social Work Practice* 4, 1: 66–76.

CCETSW (Central Council for Education and Training in Social Work) (1987a) *Care for Tomorrow: The Case for Reform of Education and Training for Social Workers and Other Core Staff*, London: CCETSW.

—— (1987b) *Workforce Planning and Training Needs in the Personal Social Services*, Report of a Working Group (Chair, A. Webb), London: CCETSW.

Corden, A. (1990) 'Choice and self-determination: an aspect of quality of life in private sector homes', in S. Baldwin, C. Godfrey and C. Propper (eds) *Quality of Life: Perspectives and Policies*, London: Routledge.

DoE/DES (1986) *Working Together: Education and Training*, Cmnd 9283, London: HMSO.

Department of Health (1989a) *Caring for People: Community Care in the Next Decade and Beyond,* Cm 849, London: HMSO.
—— (1989b) *Working for Patients,* Cm 555, London: HMSO.
Griffiths, R. (1988) *Community Care: Agenda for Action,* London: HMSO.
Sinclair, I.A.C. (1988) 'Residential care for elderly people', in I.A.C. Sinclair (ed.) *Residential Care: The Research Reviewed,* London: HMSO.
UKCC (United Kingdom Central Council for Nursing, Midwifery and Health Visiting) (1986) *Project 2000: A New Preparation for Practice,* London: UKCC.
NISW (National Institute of Social Work) (1988) *Residential Care: A Positive Choice – Report of the Independent Review of Residential Care,* Wagner Report, London: NISW/HMSO.
Walton, I. (1989) *Workforce Needs and Training Resources,* London: CCETSW/ENB.

16
A new diploma for social work or Dunkirk as total victory

Noel Timms

> My mother explained to me how Dunkirk was a great victory
> really, because of the little ships sailing to the rescue. . . . But I
> was only just nine and asked some naive questions. A moral
> victory, my mother insisted. I asked what that meant. Then
> my father took me aside and told me it was a terrible defeat,
> but not to let my mother know.
> (Peter Levi, *The Flutes of Autumn*, 1983, pp. 29–30)

This chapter is in three parts: an introduction which sketches relevant aspects
of my present situation and of the recent work of the Central Council for
Education and Training in Social Work (CCETSW); a consideration of the
Council's new regulations concerning what is described as the knowledge base
of social work; and a more extensive discussion of CCETSW's handling of the
venerable but vexed topic of social work values. The work of critical inquiry
moves from areas of possible confusion in the Council's intentions (exempli-
fied in treatment of the knowledge base) to topics in which over-ambition is
more evident than ambiguity (the treatment of social work values). The overall
objective of the essay is to begin an overdue consideration of recent
developments in what we are persuaded is still education for social work and in
particular to question the results of what CCETSW (1988) describes as 'a
remarkable consensus'.

Introduction: personal and more general background

What follows runs the risk of dismissal on at least two grounds. The arguments
could be explained away as products of a gloomy mood on the part of a
professor in early retirement, a kind of demob *'après moi le deluge'*. Or the
essay could be treated as a symptom of an over-anxious concern with the
precision or lack of precision in the usage of certain, admittedly key, words in
some recent CCETSW documents.

The first objection refers indirectly to a serious hindrance to the possibility of present controversy concerning social work education. Those with responsibility for training courses have become circumspect in the face of a freshly proactive Council attentive to the interests of employers and the wishes of government. How else can we explain the absence of a lively and sustained criticism of the Council's conduct over the last few years? Moreover, the Council's responses in the face of various pressure groups have helped to create a climate unfriendly to open and rational discussion.

The second objection – that the essay is just about words and precision in their usage – derives from a misunderstanding of conceptual analysis in the critical reading of a text. Some years ago (Timms 1968) I attempted to argue the special relevance of the analysis of concepts for a profession in which language played such a crucial role in relation both to what constitutes social work and to descriptions of the external goods social workers attempt to deliver. The language of social work is to be found in the practice of social work, and a critical reading of the working texts of the profession (such as the documents of the Central Council) will illuminate the work to which key concepts are put. The objective is not to hammer out a set of precise definitions. Nor should it be expected that the effort to achieve understanding of the way concepts are used will, as it were, achieve every conceivable worthwhile objective. If the method of the close, critical reading of texts had no limitations it could not sensibly be called a method. Yet if it is to achieve anything worthwhile it must be seen as more lively than abstract logic chopping and something other than a tiresome fretting about 'being nicely precise'. (I once sought clarification of the phrase 'the illumination of practice by theory' which was used by the Council in connection with an earlier set of regulations, whose content but not their over-ambitious scope has been modified for the new Diploma. My request was not understood, and the Council official referred me, with bemused exasperation, to a dictionary. This would have given me a listing, of course, of dictionary definitions, but would not have told me, for example, of the ways in which this 'illumination of practice' differed from other uses of a phrase that had a history in the language of social work. I wanted to see the work demanded of 'illumination' on this occasion. I was interested in use or function and not in mere usage.)

In terms of more general background, it was perhaps unwise of CCETSW in 1981 to choose a process of general reform as the best way of resolving its own bureaucratic bewilderment. Muddle had arisen as a result of the decision in 1975 to create the Certificate in Social Service as an additional Council award in the field of social work which did not carry a qualification for the practice of social work. The reform process once initiated was not well managed and was poorly grounded politically and intellectually. It has reached culmination in the publication of regulations for the new Diploma in Social Work. It is sad, after so much travail, to be forced to the conclusion that the Diploma and the attendant regulations signal no victory for social work and social work education but rather, as my subtitle suggests, a significant defeat.

I have two main reasons for reaching this negative conclusion. First, and substantively, in order to preserve an impression of successful outcome the Diploma now has to deliver in two years all that was expected of the ill-considered three year programme, and in a context constituted in part by such unstable notions as 'joint programme provision' and such implausibilities as an enhanced role for the Council in the 'ownership' (to use a favourite Council term) of the new qualification. Second, the whole conduct of the process of change and the various positions advanced by the Council lead to the conclusion that the initials by which it is known should be reinterpreted. I recall that when the Council's title was originally considered, several social work educators expressed satisfaction that education as well as training finally described the Council's function. After almost a decade of attempted reform the Central Council appears as one concerned only with the Establishing of Training in Social Work.

This change was not accomplished in any particular year nor are particular officials or members to blame. The Council owes its origin and early years of life to an encounter between public inattention and a professional social work establishment struggling to distinguish its literature from its journalism. As such, it was unlikely to develop a useful power base, but such positions as it has sought to advance have been undermined by failure in argument and proposal stemming from avoidance of the work of establishing theoretical foundations: the traditions of the social practice called social work have been truncated when they called for elaboration.

The story of CCETSW is comparatively long and social work has much to learn from the telling. That story does not constitute my present topic, but the polemical position already emerging requires that I at least illustrate from previous years my view that as an engine of social improvement the Central Council was deprived of sufficiently rich intellectual fuel.

Consultative Document 3 (CCETSW 1977), which anticipated something of the shape of things to come, was criticized at the time for a certain anti-intellectual attitude towards the contribution of the social sciences to social work education. More serious is the failure to appreciate that the tradition of the social science contribution stretches back to the origins of social work, that it encourages the careful use of research findings and alerts us to the differential use of concepts. So, in Document 3, 'support' as a concept of significance in and for social work is treated in a list of words and outside any consideration of the riches and possible difficulties in the use of the idea. 'Support' to be understood requires consideration at four levels. We should consider the possibility of a differential impact from the elements that constitute support (for instance aid, affirmation and liking); the theoretical and practical implications of 'negative support' or support that does more harm than good; the different ways in which support might be accomplished; and relevant theoretical controversies, such as the extent to which lack of support acts as a direct psychological stressor.

Those who have followed the chances and changes of the reforming of social work education will have noted both shifts and difficulties in the arguments advanced. The Report on Responses stated that 'on the basis of the comments received, we do not believe that the Council has evidence that it should institute immediate and radical changes in any particular direction' (CCETSW 1983: 29). This proved a misleading prelude to what followed. The Council came to support radical changes but on the basis of notions used only at the level of rhetoric. So, 'narrowness of the definition of social work', widespread employer dissatisfaction, the proclaimed unsatisfactory state of social work education as a whole – that education, be it noted, that had been developed under CCETSW auspices – were all used as simple tokens in a currency whose exchange rate no one troubled to establish. Similarly the case for lengthening training by a whole year was scarcely taken beyond the conventional wisdom that few people had ever proposed to shorten anything – at least since Delilah.

I now wish, having sketched aspects of the background of this essay, to offer more detailed arguments concerning important and unrecognized difficulties in the new order of the social work training recently confirmed by CCETSW.

The Diploma in Social Work: the knowledge base

In a previous work (Timms and Timms 1977), my co-author and I summarized the different kinds of knowledge that social workers have claimed to use and indeed to help to create as follows: know-how, know-that, and knowledge by acquaintance. The basic problem for an epistemology for social work is to give each kind of knowledge its due. The construction of such a knowledge base requires hard work and close analysis of the historic texts of the profession, and there are those outside the profession who would support the primacy of one form of knowledge. So Dilman (1987) in a recent philosophical study of love – a notion with a lengthy connection with social work – is 'almost inclined to say that one cannot aim at coming to know another person, as one can aim at finding something out and pursuing this aim by conducting an inquiry' (1987: 12). The Council, however, appears to have opted for the primacy of know-how.

At face value this criticism may appear unfair. The regulations make clear that all students will be expected to study 'as a key area' the applied social sciences (knowledge that). However, this knowledge will be assessed in the mode of know-how. 'Students will be assessed for their understanding of relevant knowledge and theory in the context of its application to social work practice and their ability to apply it' (CCETSW 1989: 7). A similar concern for know-how can be found in the requirement that 'Qualifying social workers must demonstrate their competence in practice to transfer their knowledge and skills to new situations' (CCETSW 1989: 13). Incidentally this requirement creates some unease at the sureness of the Council's grasp of its own epistemology. If new (that is fresh) situations could in no way be accommodated, one could not easily speak of knowledge or skill at all, but neither knowledge nor skill can cope with the (radically) new by simple transfer.

It is possible, however, that the Council did intend to encompass (personal) knowledge by acquaintance within its new requirements. A thematic refrain in the regulations takes the form of 'knowledge and understanding'. Social workers, in order to qualify, must show that they know and understand 'change theory', 'social welfare', 'individual liberty', 'the range of human needs, especially those of vulnerable, disadvantaged, and stigmatized groups', and so on. Unfortunately no indication is given of how the complex and contested notion of 'understanding' is to be used. 'Knowledge and understanding' could simply be an equivalent for 'know thoroughly' or it could be a short-hand reference to that understanding that comes from personal knowledge. Some idea of the implication of taking such a knowledge base more seriously can be gained from the work of Polanyi (1958), who has examined in detail the possibility and scope of personal knowledge.

> The arts of doing and knowing, the valuation and the understanding of meanings, are thus seen to be only different aspects of the act of extending our person into the subsidiary awareness of particulars which compose a whole.
>
> (Polanyi 1958: 65)

The Council's concern with discrete competencies of knowledge leaves no place for the holism that has figured in social work since its beginnings in the Idealism of the nineteenth century, nor apparently for that personal knowledge which has been from time to time explicitly valued in social work.

The Diploma in Social Work: the values of social work

There can be little doubt concerning the Council's treatment of the values of social work nor the ambitious nature of its intention to establish 'values' in the list of requirements for qualification in social work. So the first formulation (CCETSW 1986) stated that holders of the new award should be able to

> Articulate a coherent value system governing his/her actions and attitudes as a professional social worker, and as an employee, and to demonstrate:
>
> ● an understanding of the origins of such a value system;
> ● a recognition of value systems other than his/her own, which may be held by others with equal sincerity;
> ● a beginning recognition of the role and responsibilities of an employee in public or voluntary services, and a capacity to identify the potential for conflict between agency policy and professional values;
> ● a commitment to upholding the individuality and dignity of people and to challenging, within his/her professional/employee role, racism, sexism, ageism and other institutionalized and oppressive attitudes which affect the delivery of service to the clients of his/her employing agency.
>
> (CCETSW 1986: 8–9)

These requirements raise a number of questions which I outlined in an inaugural lecture at Leicester University (Timms 1986). I suggested that the emphasis on coherence failed to address the problem of conflict between 'goods'; that too much was expected of 'articulation'; and that if we understood better a social practice we would see more readily that the rules by which practitioners make judgements about what is right and good, about commendations, prescriptions and evaluations 'belong together in a tradition or traditions and articulating a tradition is altogether different from articulating a system'. In general, it seemed that CCETSW was following the advice of one omnibus passenger to another: 'Be philosophical, dear. Don't think about it'.

Subsequent formulations have changed somewhat in scale, but the Statement of Minimum Requirements refers to undifferentiated 'professional, ethical and moral issues' (CCETSW 1988: 8) and considers that qualifying students should demonstrate 'the capacity to apply a system of professional values' (1988: 15). If values can indeed be said to be applied, it is clear that in reaching particular decisions it is not a whole system that is applied: a whole system could not be so used. Even the idea of a systematic application of values faces questioning when considered in the light of the real world. An incident in a Jane Bowles novel suggests some of the difficulties. In *Two Serious Ladies*, Arnold invites Miss Goering to spend the night at his house in the spare bedroom.

> 'I probably shall', said Miss Goering, 'although it is against my entire code, but then, I have never even begun to use my code, although I judge everything by it'.
>
> (Bowles 1979: 19)

The present and binding requirements in relation to the values of social work are the following:

> Competence in social work requires the understanding and integration of the values of social work. This set of values can essentially be expressed as a commitment to social justice and social welfare, to enhancing the quality of life of individuals, families and groups within communities, and to a repudiation of all forms of negative discrimination.
>
> (CCETSW 1989: 10)

My comments on this are partly logical and partly substantive.

It is the clear intention of the Council to associate values and competence requirements, but the form chosen is not without difficulty, even ambiguity. Espousal of values may be considered insufficient but it should not have been expected that values and behaviour could be linked by the pantomime horse of integration totally exhausted by ineffectual attempts in the history of social work to connect 'theory' with 'practice'. Does the opening sentence in the paragraph quoted mean that those with defective understanding and incomplete integration are as a matter of fact incompetent in the practice of social work or are not to be licensed because they have failed a logically necessary requirement? Would a more clear statement of a distinction between the values constituting a practice and the values to be achieved by a practice have helped social workers to understand 'the set of values' they are expected to express? Certainly understanding, now required by the Council, is a complex and demanding accomplishment. Barnsley (1972), in a thorough discussion of the materials for a sociology of ethics, correctly observes that 'values always imply certain beliefs, and part of the task of understanding any set of values is to understand the beliefs which lie behind them and give them meaning' (Barnsley 1972: 23). We may say that different people (families, social workers, community activists) share the same values, but 'the sameness' may dissolve as the beliefs which inform the values are appreciated. For example Hindu people and those holding no religious beliefs, may appear to uphold the common value of toleration, but the value for the first group stems from a conviction that life consists of many different ways to God. Obviously the second group cannot make their value intelligible in the same way. So, we may go on to ask, what are the beliefs to which qualifying social workers should give assent and expression?

The new regulations indicate that these beliefs centre on the two ideas of social justice and social welfare, but these constitute no clear direction: the two notions are clearly within the category of essentially contested or contestable concepts (Timms 1983: 149). Unsurprisingly the literature on social justice and on social welfare is considerable, and within the confines of this chapter I can refer only briefly to some of the problems, concentrating on the meaning and function of the ideas. The point is not that CCETSW should have provided or commissioned learned treatises on social justice and social welfare, but that the simple statements provided offer students and educators no means by which to navigate deep and troubled waters.

For some, the notion of social justice operates as no sign at all. Hayek (1978), for example, states firmly that it is 'nothing more than an empty formula, conventionally used to assert that a particular claim is justified without giving any reason'. He believes that

> the complete emptiness of the phrase . . . shows itself in the fact that no agreement exists about what social justice requires in particular instances; also that there is no known test by which to decide who is right if people differ.
>
> (Hayek 1978: 57–8)

Others believe that progress can be made if distinctions are made between kinds of justice. Stevenson (1973), for instance, uses Tillich's differentiation between creative and proportional justice to illuminate certain problems in social security. Others would lead us to question reliance on social justice as a means of securing such historic social work objectives as responding to unmet need. Campbell (1974), for instance, has argued that because of a close logical association between the concepts of justice and of desert or merit, the idea of distribution according to need is more securely based on the common humanitarian obligation to relieve human suffering than on a principle of social justice. Miller (1976) believes that this issue has important consequences for the forms of social provision prescribed, the moral importance attached to such provision and the ways in which we understand the relationship between service providers and service users.

A consideration of 'social welfare' suggests at least two problems: the force of 'social' and whether welfare or well-being can function as a primary value at all. The first problem emerges from the attempt to connect the essential commitment to social welfare (and social justice) with the particular commitments which qualifying social workers are required to incorporate. If social welfare is to be treated as some kind of sum of individual utilities, how does that idea support the commitment of the social worker to the 'strengths and skills embodied in local communities'? Social workers are also required to incorporate a commitment to 'the right of individuals and families to choose' *tout court*, but surely a welfare that is social (and a justice similarly described) must qualify such a right rather than summarize or re-express it. The second problem emerges from a recent wide-ranging inquiry into the concept of well-being which concludes that

> Well-being is not to be seen as the single overriding value, in fact not as a substantive value at all, but instead as a formal analysis of what it is for something to be prudentially valuable. . . . Well-being, therefore, is not what it is about objects that makes them desirable. What makes us desire the things we desire is something about them – their features or qualities.
> (Griffin 1986: 235)

The Council's requirements in relation to values stake out a new territory, compared to earlier attempts at mapping, in a clear call for the 'repudiation of all forms of negative discrimination' (CCETSW 1989: 15). However, operationalizing this presents problems of fairness, of description, and of relationship with other commonly asserted social work values. The question of fairness arises from a difference between the anti-oppressive requirements in relation to gender and to race. These are separated from other sources of discrimination, such as poverty, age, etc., but in relation to the former, students are required 'to develop an understanding of gender issues and to demonstrate anti-sexism in social work practice (CCETSW 1989: 16), while in relation to race, students must demonstrate 'awareness of both individual and institutional racism and ways to combat both through anti-racist practice' (CCETSW 1989: 16). What a fair treatment of all groups liable to stigma and discrimination requires are reasons that justify what appears to be differential treatment, but perhaps the Council's discrimination was purely verbal.

In relation to prejudice and negatively discriminative behaviour, a particular range of responses is now required. References are made to counteraction, to challenge and to combat, but these all suggest incomplete directions. To be told 'to challenge', 'to combat', and so on is not intelligible unless we are also given some description under which the behaviour is to be challenged – as irrational, as moral evil, as false consciousness – and some indication of the appropriate response to other forms of irrationality or moral evil, or false consciousness. If the prejudices of white clients and male clients are to be challenged, confronted and so on, social work educators and students also need to consider the consequences of this stance in relation to such commonly asserted values as acceptance, client self-determination, ethical restrictions on the uses to which information gained in the course of client contact may be put. To raise such questions is not to cast any doubt on the ultimate possibility of answers, but to point to the work of reasoning required. This applies also to all the questions raised in this essay. It is a measure of a wasted decade in social work education that so much of the work remains to be done. The trenchant character of this essay is a measure of depth of concern that the decade has seen little justice done to the social practice we call social work.

Conclusion

The fact that academics could be considered to have a vested interest in conceptual analysis serves as a reminder that such analysis cannot, as it were, stand complete on its own. As Warnock (1971) has observed:

> the concepts people use are not timelessly, independently, part of the furniture of the universe; they emerge and evolve, change and sometimes decay, in human thought and speech and action, and cannot but be intimately related to what people find occasion to say and do, and to what in general they think about.
>
> (Warnock 1971: 5)

So, in considering the concepts used in CCETSW documents, we should also consider the interests served thereby. These concepts are useful in the maintenance of reputations of different kinds, in bolstering the certainties attached to earlier 'generic' forms of professional training, in the pursuit of a social work with a new and distinctive character attractive to employers and to government. This character has finally become clear. Social work is now to be considered as a collection of assessable competencies from which social work emerges fundamentally as a matter of management: the selves of social workers and clients are to be managed as are time, objectives, limited contacts, packages and resources. In terms of the traditionally formulated twin objectives of social work (cause and function, the expressive and the instrumental), the new Diploma represents the triumph of function and of an instrumental orientation. Above all, the Diploma represents a significant increase in the Council's control of the profession rather than in its concern that social work should flourish.

> The flourishing of any form of practice requires a shared vision of the goods internal to that practice, shared beliefs about the procedures necessary to achieve these goods and about the allocation of roles and rights within that practice necessary to sustain procedures and achieve goods, and shared acceptance of the constraints necessary if the practice is not to be subvented by the pull of those external goods which often derive from successful practice – power, money, fame.
>
> (Macintyre 1977: 201–2)

Vision, genuine sharing of belief, a distinction between the goods achievable by a practice and the goods that constitute a practice, constraints and so on, are scarcely visible in the newly packaged social work required by CCETSW. Larger forces may have defeated traditional social work, but it would be more honest – to refer to a value used in social work practice though it does not appear in the usual lists (Ashford and Timms 1990) – not to try to pass off the defeat as a total victory.

References

Ashford, S. and Timms, N. (1990) 'Values in social work: investigations of the practice of family placement', *British Journal of Social Work* 20, 1: 1–20.

Barnsley, J. H. (1972) *The Social Reality of Ethics*, London: Routledge & Kegan Paul.

Bowles, J. (1979) *Two Serious Ladies*, London: Virago.

Campbell, T. (1974) 'Humanity before justice', *British Journal of Political Science* 4: 1–16.

CCETSW (Central Council for Education and Training in Social Work) (1977) *Expectations of the Teaching of Social Work*, Consultative Document 3 (author R. Wright), London: CCETSW.

—— (1983) *Review of Qualifying Training Policies*, Paper 20 London: CCETSW.

—— (1986) *Three Years and Different Routes*, Paper 20.6, London: CCETSW.

—— (1988) *Statement of Minimum Requirements of the Social Worker at the Point of Qualification*, Paper 20.9, London: CCETSW.

—— (1989) *Requirements and Regulations for the Diploma in Social Work*, Paper 30, London: CCETSW.

Dilman, I. (1987) *Love and Human Separateness*, Oxford: Basil Blackwell.

Griffin, J. (1986) *Well-Being*, Oxford: Clarendon Press.

Hayek, F. A. (1978) *New Studies in Philosophy: Politics, Economics and the History of Ideas*, London: Routledge & Kegan Paul.

Macintyre, A. (1977) 'Patients as agents', in S. F. Spicker and H. T. Engelhardt, jnr (eds) *Philosophical Medical Ethics: Its Nature and Significance*, Dordrecht and Boston: D. Reidel.

Miller, D. (1976) *Social Justice*, Oxford: Clarendon Press.

Polanyi, M. (1958) *Personal Knowledge*, London: Routledge & Kegan Paul.

Stevenson, O. (1973) *Claimant or Client*, London: Allen & Unwin.

Timms, N. (1968) *The Language of Social Casework*, London: Routledge & Kegan Paul.

—— (1983) *Social Work Values: An Enquiry*, London: Routledge & Kegan Paul.

—— (1986) 'Taking care: the value and values of social work', inaugural lecture, University of Leicester.

Timms, N. and Timms, R. (1977) *Perspectives in Social Work*, London: Routledge & Kegan Paul.

Warnock, G. J. (1971) *The Object of Morality*, London: Methuen.